Supply Chain Security

Contemporary supply chains operate under the pressure of customer requirements, increasing price competition, sudden increases or decreases in demand, unforeseen obstacles and new threats. The right way to improve the functioning of the flow of material and accompanying information is not only the continuous collection of data but also their collection, analysis, inference and decision making with the use of decision support systems, expert systems and artificial intelligence. Such procedures make it easier for logisticians not only to forecast processes but also to predict (forecast) and identify potential problems and facilitate the implementation of optimal modern solutions, paying attention to current trends in the supply chain market.

An important issue that affects the quality, efficiency and availability (continuity) of the processes implemented within the supply chain is security. This is an area that is not clearly defined. This book uses theoretical and practical knowledge to define security in the supply chain as a state that gives a sense of certainty and guarantees the flow of material goods and services (in accordance with the 7w rule) as well as a smooth flow of information for the planning and management of logistics processes. Tools and instruments used to ensure the security of the supply chain contribute to the protection and survival in times of dangerous situations (threats) and adaptation to new conditions (susceptibility to unplanned situations).

When analyzing the needs and structure of the 21st century supply chains, in the context of their security, it is impossible to ignore the problem of their digitization, which enables the determination of optimal routes and the anticipation of possible threats (crisis situations). Automatic data exchange between various departments of the company along the upper and lower part of the supply chain improves the functioning of the warehouse management through, among others, automation, robotization and pro-activity. It also contributes to efficient, good communication and market globalization. Automation also brings new, extremely attractive business models with regard to occupational safety, ergonomics and environmental protection. To meet the needs of creating modern supply chains, the book analyzes and presents current and future solutions that affect security and the continuity of supply chains.

Supply Chain Security

How to Support Safety and Reduce Risk in Your Supply Chain Process

Andrzej Szymonik and Robert Stanisławski

Routledge
Taylor & Francis Group

A PRODUCTIVITY PRESS BOOK

First published 2023
by Routledge
605 Third Avenue, New York, NY 10158

and by Routledge
4 Park Square, Milton Park, Abingdon, Oxon, OX14 4RN

Routledge is an imprint of the Taylor & Francis Group, an informa business

ISBN: 9781032260181 (hbk)
ISBN: 9781032260174 (pbk)
ISBN: 9781003286110 (ebk)

DOI: 10.4324/9781003286110

Typeset in Garamond
by Deanta Global Publishing Services, Chennai, India

Contents

Authors

Andrzej Szymonik (PhD, Professor) is a graduate of the Military
Communications Academy (currently known as CSŁiI) in Zegrze, Poland
and the Military Communications Academy in Saint Petersburg, Russia.
In 2001, he defended his doctoral dissertation at the Technical University
of Czestochowa. In 2008, the Faculty of Management of the University of
Warsaw granted him the degree of a Postdoctoral Research Associate (dr
hab.) in the field of Management Science. In 2018, he received the title of
Professor in the field of social sciences at the University of Natural Sciences
and Humanities in Siedlce.

During the years 1972–2010, he served in the army and reached the rank
of general of the brigade; he was the commander of the Command Support
Brigade and the Head of the Science and Military Education Department
in the Polish Ministry of National Defence. Currently, he works as a professor at the Lodz University of Technology, Faculty of Organization and
Management.

His achievements include 19 original monographs (www.gen-prof.pl), 31
original scientific publications in national and international journals, 85 co-
authored scientific publications and participation in collective studies.

He is interested in: security of logistics systems, use of the tools of the
fourth industrial revolution in modern logistics, developing models to
increase the efficiency and effectiveness of logistics processes in a changing
environment and growing customer needs, design for logistics in Industry
4.0 and comprehensive logistics management (Total Logistics Management).

Robert Stanisławski is a graduate of the University of Lodz. In 1999,
he defended his doctoral dissertation in the field of logistics. He obtained
the degree of a Postdoctoral Research Associate (dr hab.) in the field of
Management Science in 2018.

Robert Stanisławski has been a professor (PhD) at the Department of Supply Chain Management (Institute of Management) in the Faculty of Organization and Management at the Technical University of Lodz since 2004.

His scientific publications include over 150 articles (authorship and co-authorship) in national and international editions and many monographs which were edited by him in Polish as well as the English versions.

His research interests are related to innovation and the implementation of new solutions under "open innovation" by enterprises of all sizes. In addition, he is interested in issues related to logistics and the new technological solutions used within it (Logistics 4.0 and 5.0). The main areas of his research include: innovation, innovativeness and open innovation among economic organizations of all sizes, logistics, eurologistics and ecologistics at various stages of application in relation to economic organizations – modern systems in logistics and production (Internet of Things, big data, cloud computing, SCADA etc.), use of RPA (Robotic Process Automation), the development of centers of competence and excellence (CoE) among various organizations (economic and public) and organizations' management on the international market – instruments in international exchange.

Introduction

Contemporary supply chains operate under the pressure of customer expectations, growing price competition, sudden increases or decreases in demand, unforeseen obstacles and new threats. Therefore, proper planning is required to deliver goods of the right quality, in the right place and time and at a relatively low price acceptable to the end recipients of the goods (Mangan & Lalwani, 2016). This is related to the continuous process of improving efficiency and optimizing costs in the supply chain (Shivajee et al., 2019). The right way to improve the functioning of the material stream is digitization, which means not only the continuous collection of data but also their analysis, exchange, inference and decision making with the use of decision support systems, expert systems and artificial intelligence (Li et al., 2015). Such a procedure makes it easier for logisticians to forecast processes and helps to predict (forecast) and identify potential problems. It also facilitates the implementation of optimal modern solutions, paying attention to the supply chain market trends in the third decade of the 21st century, especially Logistics 4.0 (Culot et al., 2020).

In addition, digitization enables the logistic analysis of the company, determining optimal routes, designing logistics systems, optimizing processes, optimizing storage costs and predicting possible threats (crises) and their effects (losses). IT support and automatic data exchange between various company departments along the upper and lower part of the supply chain improve the functioning of the warehouse management through automation, robotization, pro-activity and digitization of documents, among others. They also contribute to efficient, good communication and market globalization. Automation also brings new, extremely attractive business models, including improved working conditions, ergonomics and environmental protection. The concept of security is related to the development of digitization and automation.

Security is not clearly defined. Based on theoretical and practical knowledge, it is often defined in the supply chain as a state that gives a sense of certainty and guarantees the flow of material goods and services and a smooth flow of information for planning and managing logistics processes. It is related to introducing specific tools and instruments (rules, procedures and technologies) to protect supply chain resources against theft, destruction or terrorism (Closs & McGarrell, 2004). Their choice and proper use in managing the security of the supply chain minimize the risk and contribute to the protection and survival during dangerous situations (threats) and adapting to new conditions, bearing in mind the susceptibility to unplanned situations.

Apart from its positive aspects, digitization brings a number of challenges. One of them is undoubtedly the need to ensure digital security (Greer et al., 2019). This is related to the concept of risk management in supply chains. As a result of the development of new technologies (drones, robots) and digital solutions, cyber risks have emerged in cyberspace (Cheung & Bell, 2019). The manifestations of these risks include hacker attacks (cyberattacks – viruses, worms and Trojan horses), which contribute to the loss of millions of dollars for logistics companies worldwide. Moreover, these risks have proved the high susceptibility of these entities to external attacks, hence the need to increase digital security through a set of tools, policies, security concepts, safety measures, guidelines, risk management methods, activities, training, best practices and technologies, both in relation to organizations and individual users of the logistics sector (Brookson et al., 2016).

In order to meet the needs of creating modern supply chains, the authors have written a monograph in which they analyze and present current and future solutions that affect security and the continuity of supply chains. It is also a signpost for building optimal logistics processes and accompanying information, which should be organized and implemented according to the plan, even in emergencies (threats). The proposed proprietary security management model of logistics processes is helpful for creating and supporting security and reducing risk in the supply chain process.

This book consists of eight main chapters. **Chapter 1** defines the essence of security for the needs of the supply chain, paying special attention to threats that may arise and affect the course (efficiency) of logistics processes. This chapter is particularly useful because it describes threats in detail and divides (classifies) them according to their place, duration, physical properties and range. The illustrated approach also contributes to the risk evaluation in the context of the likelihood of risk occurrence, the value of possible losses, the extent to which the supply chain is vulnerable to threats and the level of potential effects: the exposure factors determining the supply chain importance from the point of view of the risk. The last section of the chapter presents the standards and legal regulations contributing to the continuity of the supply chain operation, considering the flow of material stream and information.

Chapter 2 indicates current conditions for the functioning of supply chains. It focuses on selected tools that shape and support the image of the existing, innovative supply chains and impact their security. These include seven areas: the Internet of Things, cloud computing, big data, 5G, smart factories, automation and robotization, and blockchains that support security and reduce the risk of failure in logistics activities in supply chains. Problems such as management strategies and factors integrating enterprises in the supply chain, which affect the security of logistics processes and reaction to unplanned situations, have also been detailed.

Chapter 3 presents important issues related to supply chain security management, which was defined as a set of coordinated actions taken when threats (disruptions) occur. Such actions are directed at logistic resources to achieve a goal such as the certainty of supplies, reduction of threats, meeting the agreed conditions set by the cargo owner or protection of the market position and brand. Helpful measures in achieving the desired security of the flow of the material stream and accompanying information include crisis management stages, progressive management, conservative management and management through reference models. Much space is also devoted to risk management in the supply chain, focusing on implementing effective, proven rules that ensure value creation while delivering products and services to end consumers.

Chapter 4 contains five sub-chapters that concern the operation of selected links in the supply chain and are closely related to security and risk management tools. The first three contain selected information on road, rail, sea, inland and air transport in the context of such issues as human safety, environmental and social safety, traffic congestion and costs. Many measures and indicators related to the safety of transport in Poland in comparison with other countries have been presented. Much space has been devoted to intelligent transport systems, including a wide range of technological solutions aimed at improving transport performance by increasing mobility and safety in passenger and freight traffic and protecting natural resources. The penultimate section deals with the safety of warehouses. The areas determining warehouse safety are presented, including technical factors (warehouse equipment and infrastructure), legal and organizational factors (documentation and its implementation as well as procedures minimizing the risk of an accident or material loss) and personnel (competences, qualifications and experience, professional development). Figures on health and safety in Poland are shown, indicating that we have a lot to do in this area to avoid human and material losses. The last section deals with food security, which covers supplier selection and monitoring – tracking, hazard analysis, food defense, external control and biological hazards.

Chapter 5 concerns technologies supporting the safety and risk management of logistics processes in the supply chain in unplanned situations (emergencies). Selected IT systems that facilitate planning, implementation, control and monitoring of logistics processes are described. These include the following: effective consumer service, customer relationship management, supply chain management, warehouse management, transport management, logistics needs planning, fixed assets management and returnable packaging management. In addition, tools such as automatic identification, electronic data exchange and traceability are described, which contribute to the effective monitoring and tracking of the flow of the material stream, which positively impacts the safety assessment of logistics processes. The last section presents innovative technologies for the needs of supply chains in Industry 4.0. They include innovative methods of picking goods, robotization – automation – IoT, augmented and virtual reality, artificial intelligence and machine vision.

Chapter 6 deals with ecology, which gains significant importance due to global concern for the natural environment, which in many cases is degraded by economic activities, exhaustive non-renewable resources, development of production technology, ecological and reusable goods and customer requirements. For safe functioning of the processes in reverse logistics, along the waste supply chains, an ecological model (network) has been presented, which allows activities in retrogistics to be identified and promotes the safety of processes such as selective collection, storage, transport, recovery, sale, recycling, processing, incineration and disposal. In this chapter, a lot of space is devoted to issues such as circular economy, cleaner production and minimization of waste. Understanding these issues allows safe waste stream flows to be created along the supply chain and reduces the risk of non-compliance when hazards arise.

Chapter 7 deals with information flow security in supply chains. It should be remembered that logistics is not only the flow of physical things or services but also the accompanying information flow. Coordination and cooperation between the links in the supply chain depend not only on good communication but also on information security (more often called cybersecurity) to prevent destruction, loss, copying and modification of data content.

Threats that improve in terms of quantity and quality, such as stalkerware, living-off-the-land (LotL) or ransomware, are presented. Also noteworthy is a set of methods such as social engineering, helping cybercriminals obtain classified information. Hackers often use the ignorance or credulity of IT system users (more and more often mobile ones) to defeat security measures that are resistant to all forms of attack and disrupt the flow of information along the entire supply chain.

Chapter 8 concerns the proposed supply chain security management model based on the research carried out using the indirect and direct method, including a questionnaire, which contained 18 items, including 16 closed- and 2 open-ended questions. The questionnaires were sent to 168 different companies, of which 92 responded, including 4 micro-companies, 24 small, 29 medium and 35 large companies. Additionally, five interviews were conducted with experts, i.e. logisticians from large private and state-owned companies, based on the materials collected in the questionnaire, to verify the research results. The purpose of the questions was to obtain answers concerning problems related to the legal, organizational and technical bases, and the procedures, monitoring and management systems in situations of threat that may arise in the supply chain. Using the research results, an illustration of the most important features of the developed system, its environment and the security of the supply chain was prepared using a special graphical notation. The identified research areas discussed and analyzed in supply chain security management include supply chain structure (participants), threats (intentional and unintentional human activity, the influence of the environment – climate) in the links of the supply chain, computer-aided decision making, requirements of national and international standards in the security of the supply chain, information technologies supporting the flow of information, safety in transport and warehouse management, and new techniques and technologies (automation, robotization, augmented reality, virtual reality, drones, autonomous means of transport etc.).

This book is intended primarily for students in fields of study such as logistics, transport, management, production and logistics management, economics, security, as well as managers and directors managing logistics divisions in production and service enterprises.

It is a useful tool for individuals who want to understand the principles of supply chain functioning, risk evaluation in the environment of a highly innovative and demanding Industry 4.0., threats to the flow of the material stream and accompanying information. This book is also a map for creating a modern supply chain security management model. It is certainly a one-of-a-kind guide that introduces in a simple way the principles of the functioning of the supply chain in a turbulent environment and risk management in unplanned situations.

The authors would like to emphasize that their works related to logistics do very well on the market. About 14,000 copies have been sold in the last ten years. Their books are very popular among ResearchGate users.

Chapter 1

Safety Determinants for the Needs of the Delivery Chain

1.1 Genesis and Essence of Supply Chain Security

In contemporary views, "security" is more and more often defined in the categories of threats to protected values (i.e. the way of defining the goal) and countermeasures aimed at reducing threats or limiting the effects of their destructive impacts (i.e. appropriate actions and expenditures ensuring the desired state). Hence, it can be said that threats are an integral part of both negative and positive interpretations of security. A threat most often results from the lack of predictability of the occurrence of certain phenomena, and it has a random nature.

Dictionaries define "security" as "the state of being safe and protected from danger or harm" (Oxford Advanced Learner's Dictionary, 2021) and a set of threats as being dangerous for someone or something (Oxford Advanced Learner's Dictionary, 2021). This approach to security highlights two main aspects of its perception[1] (A Dictionary of the Social Sciences, 1964):

- absence of risk;
- feeling confident or protected against risk.

For a full understanding and in-depth analysis of the essence of security, it is advisable to add adjectives to both categories, which makes them more specific and narrower by indicating who or what they refer to (indicating

DOI: 10.4324/9781003286110-1

the object or subject of considerations). For example, in the first case, one can distinguish such aspects as personal security, enterprise security, supply chain security and environmental security. When referring to security in the subjective approach, one should mention, for example, technical security, logistic security and similar factors. It is also obvious that security can be substantiated by threats (the subject of impact and the characteristics of the sources of threats) (Sienkiewicz, 2015a). As a result, several new (detailed) classes (categories, topologies) of security are created.

The understanding of security also changes depending on the nature of science that determines the research perspectives. The most useful, from the point of view of the problems discussed in the paper, are the views that perceive security through the prism of an area of knowledge:

- social sciences – security is treated as a commodity of fundamental importance for people and their community;
- exact sciences – they allow the precise definition, description and conduction of scientific experiments and simulations, and model security-related phenomena (statistics, probability theory and IT are mainly used for this purpose);
- natural sciences – in the perception of safety, they emphasize the issues of adaptation of organisms to changing conditions and a change in the form of existence, i.e. qualitative leaps that allow the obtaining of a different, better form of existence (safety) or the gaining of an advantage over others in the environment (Świniarski, 1997);
- technical sciences – they investigate phenomena and determine regularities that take place in the world of products and processes resulting from technical human activity (in the perception of security, emphasis is placed on the issues of system reliability and redundancy of security structures) (Jaźwiński & Ważyńskia-Fiok, 1993).

It should be remembered that the supply chain is also a contemporary organization that operates in a turbulent environment that is difficult to predict. These conditions inextricably link the structure, competences, management etc. and make the supply chain dependent on contemporary security paradigms, which include (Gryz, 2013):

- challenges (problem situations generating decision dilemmas faced by the entity in resolving security matters);
- threats (direct or indirect destructive impact on the entity);

- opportunities (circumstances independent of the will of the entity favoring the realization of the interests and the achievement of the entity's security goals);
- risk (the possibility of the occurrence of negative consequences of the entity's own actions in the sphere of its security).

It should be considered that in systemic terms, supply chain security is associated with hazards, reliability and risk. To assess these values, quantitative or qualitative measures are used in conjunction with a uniform approach for a specific logistic system.

Numerous original articles and monographs (Szymonik, 2010, 2011, 2015a, 2016b, 2016c; Szymonik & Bielecki, 2015) discussing security in the supply chain lead to the following conclusions:

- security, regardless of its place of functioning, should be treated as a system of action, which should be recognized in specific categories and systemic-holistic dependencies. The supply chain should operate in accordance with its organizational and functional principles. The main task of logistics subsystems in the supply chain is to satisfy the needs of its participants so that they can pursue their vital interests (concerning its existence) and requirements (e.g. related to the quality of existence, duration and reliability).
- the following subsystems are important elements influencing security in supply chains: management, material, transport, infrastructure and warehouse subsystems.
- relationships between the links in a specific supply chain result from official and functional subordination. Moreover, there are cooperation and information processes that result from the need to communicate.
- security in the supply chain can also be treated as a set of management and executive bodies interconnected by information and supply relations, designed to maintain the continuity of logistics processes on a local and global scale.

The state of security is not stable – it is not a resource given to the economic system once and for all. There are constant threats in the real world, both caused by natural forces and by unintended or deliberate human activities (Jörn-Henrik et al., 5511–5525).

Each supply chain must therefore make efforts to ensure stable conditions of security; it should develop in its activities the ability to quickly respond to any changes in the internal and external environment, including the possibility of cooperation within the security system with other entities. This statement is nothing new, as already in the middle of the last century, the father of modern management, P. Drucker, proposing the criteria for selecting and designing an organization, stated that an enterprise (which is an important link in the supply chain) should have the final durability to survive in the period of turmoil (crisis) and the ability to adapt to new conditions.

The adopted strategy for the functioning of the supply chain should not only be focused on the implementation of the logistic processes in it and reducing costs but it should also take into account the issues of contemporary threats. The security system in the supply chain should be adapted to its potential threats (crisis situations) and the desired level of security that must be provided to it (Aqlan & Lam, 2016). Thus, the quantity and quality of resources necessary to ensure the desired level of security in operations, within the supply chain, their organization and the manner of conducting activities (or more precisely, processes) after the occurrence of a threat (occurrence of an event or a crisis) depend on its type and scale and forecasts of the possible occurrence of other types of threats.

Security in the supply chain is a state that gives a sense of certainty and guarantees:

■ the flow of material goods and services, and consequently meeting the material needs of participants in the supply chain in accordance with 7 Rs;
■ information flow for the planning and management of logistics processes;
■ protection and survival in the time of dangerous situations (threats, crisis situations);
■ adapting to new conditions (vulnerability to emergency situations).

The security level of the supply chain depends on the supply chain itself and on its micro- (e.g. direct suppliers and recipients) as well as its macro-environment, which is determined by resistance to disruptions of cooperating participants of economic networks in the local and global dimension. The security of the supply chain is related to:

■ the level of preparation – and resilience – of the system to counteract emergency situations (the main focus is on recognizing, monitoring and analyzing data, and making accurate decisions in the area of logistic activities);

■ quality of the created and functioning safety system – understood as a set of forces and means ensuring a safety level acceptable to the logistic system.

A certain level of security in the supply chain can be achieved in many ways – not only by ensuring a particular level of effectiveness of direct prevention of incidents. In this case, controllable values are parameters characterized by factors influencing the level of security of the supply chain, that is, parameters related to (Kołodziński, 2021): preventing possible security threats; preparing the supply chain in case of activation of these threats; resources to counter these threats; and removing the consequences of a given event.

1.2 Threats to Processes Carried Out within the Supply Chain

Ensuring the security of the supply chain is not possible without the need to use human, material and financial resources. The potential and amount of resources allocated to the security of the supply chain depend on:

■ external threats coming from the supply chain itself;
■ internal threats that are "cumulated" within itself;
■ resilience to threats of the supply chain (its reliability);
■ the available management, executive, information and decision-making potential.

It should be emphasized that, as a whole, the security of the supply chain is related to risk, threats and reliability. Risk in supply chains is defined as "the likelihood of an adverse and unexpected event that can occur, and either directly or indirectly result in a supply chain disruption" (Myles et al., 2015, 618–627). For its evaluation, quantitative or qualitative measures are used, bearing in mind the need for a uniform approach to a specific logistics system. All activities in the supply chain – both in the sphere of planning and reality – are burdened with risks that may be caused by emerging dangers.

The value of risk (its evaluation) in the supply chain can be written as (Sienkiewicz, 2015a; Zaskórski, 2015):

$$\text{RISK} = f\left(\text{DANGER}, \text{VERSATILITY}, \text{CONSEQUENCES}\right) \qquad (1.1)$$

or

$$\text{VaR} = P \cdot S_x \cdot P_d \cdot E_x \tag{1.2}$$

where:

VaR – risk evaluation;

P – probability of risk occurrence;

S_x – the value of possible losses;

P_d – risk vulnerability, which determines the degree to which the supply chain is vulnerable to threats and the level of potential impact;

E_x – exposure factor which determines the degree to which the supply chain is important from the point of view of the danger.

Both in Formulas (1) and (2), threats that affect the security of the supply chain are an important factor, and therefore it is necessary to predict their occurrence based on historical data and to detect (monitor) and identify them. Data collected in this way with the use of IT systems (such as OLAP) allow the forecasting of the effects, prediction of the forces and means to counteract them, and conduction of rescue (corrective) actions. The use of mathematical models allows for the quantitative assessment of threats, and the use of heuristic techniques (including expert assessment) helps to evaluate them qualitatively. Extremely helpful in assessing the "harmfulness" of threats to the security of the supply chain is their full identification through their division (classification) considering the place of the threat, its duration, physical properties and range.

Threats to the functioning of logistics systems can be divided into four groups (Gurtu & Johny, 2021):

■ the first group includes natural disasters and events caused by civilization causes, such as catastrophes, breakdowns and other events resulting from human action or neglect. This group of threats includes, among others: fires, floods and flooding; strong winds and hurricanes; thefts; epidemics of human diseases; epidemics of plant and animal diseases; radioactive and chemical contamination; as well as mining, construction and communication disasters; and energy network failures.

■ the second group includes events that violate the constitutional order of the state (states), such as terrorism, road blockades, illegal demonstrations, ethnic conflicts and mass migration.

- in the third group, there are mechanisms that are aimed at destroying or distorting information sent, processed and stored for the needs of logistic systems. Any disruptions in the flow of information make it difficult to efficiently and effectively manage logistics along the entire supply chain.
- the fourth group includes threats resulting from the effects of a financial crisis, which in fact affect every aspect, including processes and logistic systems. Even an economy with excellent development indicators does not provide security against crises, and in fact, anti-crisis instruments have not been fully developed.

These threats can have a destructive effect on the supply chain, disrupting the flow of material and information along its participants. These threats can be divided according to (Sienkiewicz, 2007):

- place of threat – subsystem:
  - roads for all modes of transport (i.e. road, rail, air, water, sea transport);
  - modal points of a logistic network often referred to as transport points (e.g. warehouses, independent container centers, airports, ports, logistics centers etc.);
  - auxiliary devices facilitating the operation of roads and transport points;
  - management (e.g. failure to fully identify threats and their results, overestimation of opportunities, misinterpretation of results, lack of tools for optimization and simulation of activities, failure to consider rising energy and transport prices, unexpected bankruptcies of logistics service providers, lack of control over employees who behave unethically by committing property fraud or other breaches, including in the selection of suppliers);
  - procurement (e.g. extended, suboptimal and over-absorbing tendering and purchasing procedures, inconsistent supplier selection criteria, supplier selection only on the basis of the lowest price, untimely purchasing process, poor quality, price or quantity, wrong assortment, bribery, corruption, no possibility of obtaining components for production, no buffer stock);
  - production (e.g. deficiencies in production systems, damage, wastage, theft of resources, lack of availability of professional personnel,

production breaks, breakdowns, fires, floods, catastrophes, product counterfeiting);
- distribution (e.g. ignoring new products and new producers, thefts, weather conditions, poor quality of finished products, economic crisis, disregarding the management of customer relationships and product flow in the supply chain);
- transport (e.g. disruptions caused by fire, explosion or accident of a means of transport, washing from the deck, impossibility of transfer due to weather conditions, inefficient means of transport, maladjusted internal transport, changes in transport regulations, thefts, catastrophes[2]) (Kolibabski, 2021);
- warehouse and inventory shaping (e.g. thefts, losses as a result of excessively high stocks, fires, floods, construction disasters, power grid and IT system failures, damage to the automatic identification system);
- handling of packaging (e.g. destruction of products during transport as a result of inappropriate selection of packaging, failure to deliver packaging on time due to unfavorable climatic conditions, environmental pollution);
- handling customer orders (e.g. disruptions caused by lack of stock, incorrect orders and invoices, inability to locate the product, untimely delivery, as well as damaged products delivered to the customer, no response to complaints and delays, fires, thefts, damage);
- informative (e.g. loss of confidentiality, integrity and availability, natural hazards such as fires, climatic disturbances, electrostatics, passive and active attacks, random errors).
- ■ duration:
  - short-term, sporadic;
  - long-lasting, increasing;
  - repetitive, cyclical.
- ■ physical properties:
  - material (e.g. introduction of a component causing so-called bioterrorism – anthrax, radioactive elements, poor quality of production, transport or storage processes resulting for example from the differences between quality systems used in the same industry, e.g. HACCP, BRC, IFS);
  - information (e.g. damage to the IT or automatic identification system, untrue production data on the packaging);

- energy (e.g. gas, fuel);
- intangible (e.g. financial, political or social crisis).
■ scope:
  - extensive – along the entire supply chain – local or global;
  - increasing (e.g. as a result of the delivery of poisoned food);
  - not increasing (e.g. as a result of stopping the shipment of defective products to mass recipients);
  - local – for supply and production, between two enterprises within one region.

The above breakdown is presented in Table 1.1.

The presented breakdowns of disturbances show a wide spectrum and multi-faceted nature of unfavorable activities that may occur in the

Table 1.1   Threats in Supply Chains – Division

Category	*Examples*	
Place of danger	• transport roads; • modal points; • supply; • production; • distribution;	• transport; • warehousing; • handling customer orders; • transmission media.
The duration of the threat	• long-term, increasing (poor quality of products in several consecutive deliveries); • recurring; • cyclical; • single, occasional (e.g. poor quality in a single delivery of goods in the amount above 0.5%).	
Properties	• material (e.g. food contamination, viruses); • informational (e.g. damage to the IT, or automatic identification system); • energy (e.g. gas, fuel); • intangible (e.g. financial, social or political crisis).	
Reception	• local (e.g. for supply or transport); • extensive (e.g. along the entire supply chain – incorrect data from the traceability system); • increasing (e.g. as a result of deliveries of defective products); • non-increasing (e.g. defective deliveries retained at the distributor's premises).	

Source: own elaboration.

functioning of processes in the supply chain. In terms of functions and levels of management, disturbances can arise from:

- inadequate assumptions for strategic planning, inadequate assessment of strategic options;
- loss of reputation and social responsibility through events triggering long-term criticism from the government or from the international media;
- inadequate or unreliable internal processes, production, storage and distribution technologies used, employees' activities, improperly functioning processes;
- external, unpredictable actions of customers, suppliers, competitors, new market participants, substitution services as well as changes in the external environment;
- poor relations with stakeholders and resulting from an inappropriate organizational structure of the system of delegating powers and responsibilities, as well as the lack of or inappropriate rules of conduct for employees and managers of organizational units;
- non-compliance with the provisions of generally applicable law, internal regulations and contractual obligations;
- inadequate level of physical security of assets and people;
- inadequate preparation of ICT resources (outdated and obsolete ICT technologies, inconsistent ICT strategy, disruptions in the functioning of the ICT infrastructure);
- functioning of the natural environment – permanent, serious environmental damage; loss of commercial, recreational or conservation utility, resulting in considerable financial consequences for participants in the supply chain.

An interesting typology of security threats that can be used for the supply chain was presented by P. Sienkiewicz in the article "Theory and engineering of systems security" (Sienkiewicz, 2015a). The threats were divided into three groups: related to human behavior, not related to human behavior and natural disasters.

1.3 Security of Supply Chains in International Requirements and Standards

Supply chain security management can be defined as a set of coordinated actions taken when threats (disruptions) appear, directed at the logistic resources of all participants in the supply chain, with the intention of achieving the goal, which may be supply security, risk reduction, meeting the conditions agreed by the owner of the cargo and protection of market position and brand. A helpful tool in these activities is domestic and foreign legal regulations. Some of them are presented below.

1.3.1 Specification for Security Management Systems for the Supply Chain – ISO 28000:2007

The ISO 28000:2007 standard was developed especially for companies and organizations participating in the supply chain. It enables the identification of threats and reduction of risks in the supply chain through the implementation of security processes aimed at reducing the risk of theft, smuggling and illegal cargo manipulation, and ensuring a response to threats from attacks by criminals, terrorists and others. It requires the organization to apply it to:

- formulate a security policy;
- carry out a risk assessment;
- develop a plan to manage and reduce the identified threats;
- implement a plan for safety management, monitoring and supervision of the system, taking corrective actions when required;
- systematically improve the developed undertakings and procedures through training and simulations.

The organization, in order to determine safety requirements, should consider (ISO 28000):

- business goals – including the security of supply, reduction of threats (theft, piracy, counterfeiting, acts of terrorism), meeting the requirements of cargo owners and protection of reputation and brand;
- national and international legal requirements;
- hazard identification and risk assessment.

After identifying the nature of an organization's activities, scale and other requirements, a security policy is formulated and a risk assessment is carried out. The risk assessment process enables an organization to identify assets and processes that are key to the further operation, identify real threats, assess gaps in existing security programs, estimate the likelihood of a threat and consider its consequences.

By using a risk assessment process, organizations can determine the probable extent of such a risk and then determine priorities (for identifying safety objectives and targets) that are used to establish safety management plans to mitigate the identified hazards (Williams et al., 2008, 254–281).

Safety management programs should be implemented and constantly monitored for effectiveness. This allows for the implementation of corrective actions, thus enabling the improvement of the system, which in turn reduces the level of risk during its next cyclical assessment. This standard can be used by companies to ensure a consistent approach of all actors in the supply chain and as a reference point for managing security in the supply chain (Sitkowski, 2009).

1.3.2 Business Continuity Management System – ISO 22301:2012

The standard specifies the requirements for a business continuity management system. The ISO 22301 system is designed to ensure the readiness for continuity of work in emergency situations in production lines and in logistics, as well as in natural disasters and IT failures. Business Continuity Management Systems (BCMS) includes (ISO 22301):

■ BCP (Business Continuity Planning) – continuity planning for critical business processes;
■ DRP (Disaster Recovery Planning) is planning a method of action in the event of a failure, catastrophe or other negative events.

The requirements set out in ISO 22301 are general and apply to all organizations or their parts, regardless of the type, size and nature of the organization. The extent to which these requirements apply depends on the organization's working environment and complexity.

1.3.3 Safety and Quality Assessment System – SQAS

This system is a tool for assessing and identifying the level of safety and quality of operational activities undertaken in the trade of chemical products, both inert and dangerous, subject to ADR, RID, ADN and HCDG (High Consequence Dangerous Goods) materials by entities operating in the logistics chain. The SQAS assessment is addressed to companies operating in the areas of land transport, road and railroad carriage, freight forwarding, chemical product distribution, warehouses, reloading terminals, railway tanker repair plants and tanker washes. The assessment is performed by independent, CEFIC accredited auditors (SQAS Accredited Assessors, 2021). Therefore, the SQAS system is aimed at (SQAS Accredited Assessors, 2021):

- companies participating in the TFL logistics chain;
- distributors of chemical products;
- companies operating in the transport of chemicals;
- owners of warehouses, as well as tank and tank-container washes;
- repair workshops for railroad tank cars.

The benefits obtained by a business after the implementation of SQAS include a guarantee for chemical companies that a given logistics service recipient meets international safety standards for employees, the population and the natural environment, which allows: the minimization of the risk in choosing a supplier; an increase of safety during the transport of chemical materials; increased competitiveness, also on the European market, thanks to a uniform evaluation system; minimization of accidents during the execution of an order; lowering of costs.

1.3.4 Container Security Initiative – CSI

CSI (*Container Security Initiative*) was launched in 2002 by the US Customs and Border Protection (CBP). It is an American initiative for safe container traffic in supply chains. The program covers US and foreign ports and assesses the risk level of specific containers containing goods that may pose a potential threat of a terrorist attack. Container inspection takes place at the ports of loading. They are x-rayed there. Once the containers arrive in the United States, there is no need to recheck them. The goal of CBP is to "extend the security zone outward so that US borders are the last, not the first line of defense" (Dworakowska, 2021). CSI is for the:

- identification of high-risk containers. CBP uses automated tools to identify containers that pose a potential terrorist threat, based on prior information and strategic intelligence;

- screening and assessment of containers before shipment (containers are checked in the supply chain at the port of departure);
- use of modern technologies (x-rays and detection) to detect threats.

1.3.5 International Ship and Port Facility Security Code – ISPS

ISPS (*International Ship and Port Facility Security Code*) is a set of recommendations and regulations whose main purpose is to improve the safety of shipping and to counter terrorism. It requires shipowners, ports and governments to develop and implement safety regulations and procedures. This stemmed from the belief that ships – like airplanes – can be a target and a tool of terror. The code entered into force in 2004. It has made governments, shipowners, ports and personnel responsible for detecting and countering security incidents. ISPS recommendations apply to maritime and port units involved in passenger transport and international trade. The basic assumption of the ISPS is the conviction that all units at sea can be targets of terrorist organizations. For this reason, the code covers (ISPS, 2021):

- passenger ships: ferries, cruise ships, water trams, floating hotels etc.;
- specialized units: mobile drilling units, adapted to drilling and exploring the seabed;
- cargo ships: general cargo ships, container ships, bulk carriers, specialist vessels etc., with a capacity exceeding 300 GT (gross tonnage);
- cargo and passenger ports serving vessels on international connections.

Under the ISPS Code, the ship management company is required to develop a security plan for each of them, based on the risk analysis performed. Such a plan must be approved by the administration of the flag state of the ship. In practice, the state may commission this to an authorized agency.

The plan must include (Forkiewicz, 2020): a description of measures to prevent the illegal introduction of weapons and other dangerous substances onboard the ship; identification of restricted areas and measures to prevent unauthorized access; measures to prevent unauthorized persons from boarding the ship; procedures for responding to ship safety threats; procedures for operating under different security levels; identification of persons responsible for compliance with the plan guidelines (company security officer, ship security officer); procedures to ensure the readiness of the ship and crew to act in a safety emergency (crew training, equipment maintenance). A ship security plan is a confidential document.

The ISPS: enables detection and prevention of threats as part of international cooperation, determines the distribution of roles and responsibilities, enables the collection and exchange of information related to security, provides methods of security assessment and ensures appropriate standards of protection. It obliges the ship's crew and employees employed in the port to (Ustawa z dnia 4 września 2008 r. o ochronie żeglugi i portów morskich):

- collect and evaluate the obtained information, conduct and maintain communication standards;
- prevent unauthorized access, weapons etc.;
- start the emergency procedure;
- develop a ship and port facility security plan and confirm the conduct of training and drills.

For the purposes of ISPS, there are three levels of maritime and port security (Ustawa z dnia 4 września 2008 r. o ochronie żeglugi i portów morskich):

- the first level – for which the minimum protection measures resulting from the security plan will be maintained at all times;
- the second level – for which, as a result of the increased risk of a security incident, appropriate additional security measures resulting from the security plan will be maintained for a specified period;
- the third level – for which additional security measures resulting from the security plan will be maintained for a limited period, related to the probability or immediate threat of a security incident, where it may not be possible to identify a specific target of an attack.

Depending on the likelihood of a security incident, different security levels and different security measures at each security level may be implemented at different port facilities within the same port.

1.3.6 Advanced Cargo Information – ACI

The ACI (*Advanced Cargo Information*) includes (ACI, 2020):

- data on the logistic unit (ship – its name, voyage number, port of landing, destination);
- data about the cargo – name of the goods, number of pieces, weight;

- exporter's and importer's data – name, address; container – number, its type; bill of lading – number) in electronic form, which are made available significantly ahead of the date of delivery of the goods to the country of import;
- providing current data to authorized parties anywhere via a web application;
- timely handling of import/export documentation, as well as detailed monitoring of the flow of imported/exported goods.

The benefits of using ACI include (Jażdżewska-Gutta, 2020):

- sending information online, via SMS and e-mail to system users – the physical flow of documents is eliminated;
- risk management and fraud prevention;
- lower costs of port agents;
- gathering commercial intelligence;
- ongoing monitoring of transactions;
- easier information management – data can be imported directly in real time, and forms can be completed and submitted online;
- 24/7 access to information;
- low costs of system maintenance.

1.3.7 *Authorized Economic Operator – AEO*

AEO (Authorized Economic Operator) is an institution of the Community Customs Code, which was introduced into the legal order of the European Union on January 1, 2008, in order to create a secure supply chain and to fight terrorism.

An authorized economic entity is an institution relating to all entities related to trade in goods with countries outside the European Union, i.e. to producers who keep bonded warehouses, carriers, forwarders, importers, exporters or customs agencies.

The standards that apply to the areas covered by AEO are: ISO 28000:2007 Security management in the supply chain; ISO/IEC 27001:2005 Information security management systems; ISO 9001:2009 Quality management systems (Koślicki, 2021). Granting the AEO status to an operator is nothing more than recognizing it as an authorized economic entity, i.e. a privileged entity who is entitled to many advantages when conducting economic transactions with foreign countries. An Authorized Economic Operator (AEO) is a business which has one of the following permits: AEO

C – customs simplifications; AEO S – safety and security; AEO F – customs simplifications/safety and security.

The AEO status granted in one member state of the European Union (EU) is recognized throughout the EU. The AEO certificate guarantees compliance with the provisions of EU law when conducting international transactions (AEO, 2021).

It should be remembered that the provisions of customs law do not impose on entrepreneurs the obligation to cooperate only with contractors with the AEO status. The above conditions and criteria, examined by customs authorities during the AEO certification procedure, are detailed in Art. 14h–14k of the above-mentioned Regulation of the Council establishing the Community Customs Code (CCIP). The AEO status is associated with specific benefits, the catalog of which depends on the type of certificate that is applied for.

In the field of customs control related to safety and security, the operator may take advantage of the following simplifications (AEO, 2021):

■ it is subject to a smaller number of physical inspections of goods and inspection of documents than other entrepreneurs;
■ if selected for inspection, it will be carried out as a priority;
■ the right to advance notification of the selection of a shipment for inspection;
■ entitlement to lodge entry and exit summary declarations with limited security data;
■ the possibility of requesting an inspection at a place other than the competent customs office.

1.3.8 Risk Management – ISO 31000

ISO 31000 is a family of risk management standards developed by the International Organization for Standardization. ISO 31000 provides a universal model for specialists and companies implementing risk management processes and aims to replace current standards, methodologies and models that vary depending on the industry, type of activity or region. Currently, the ISO 31000 family includes:

■ ISO 31000:2018 Risk management – Principles and guidelines;
■ ISO/IEC 31010:2009 Risk management – Risk management techniques;

■ ISO Guide 73:2009 Risk management – Vocabulary; guidelines for use in standards.

ISO 31000:2018 was introduced to the collection of Polish Standards as PN-ISO 31000:2018-08 Risk management – Guidelines, and replaced PN-ISO 31000:2012. It is available from PKN in English.

ISO 31000:2009 provides guidelines on how to deal with risks. The guidelines include (Zarządzanie ryzykiem, 2020):

■ avoiding risk by choosing not to start or continue activities that contribute to the risk arising;
■ accepting or increasing risk to seize opportunities;
■ elimination of the source of risk;
■ changing the probability of risk materialization; changing the consequences of risk materialization;
■ sharing the risk with another party or other parties; making a conscious decision to maintain the risk.

This standard allows for unifying the implementation of industry risk management standards, such as 14001 (environmental risk), OHSAS (occupational health and safety risk) or in ISO 27001 (information security).

In many organizations, a special program supporting the risk management process supports the implementation of the guidelines contained in the ISO 31000:2009 standard.

1.3.9 Corporate Risk Management – COSO

COSO (The Committee of Sponsoring Organizations of the Treadway Commission) is an American organization dealing with the development of good practices and education in the field of organizational transparency. In 1992, the COSO document on internal control was issued (Okuniewski, 2021).

In 2004, COSO II was published. The document includes an integrated enterprise risk management framework. The benefits of implementing this standard include (COSO II, 2020):

■ providing a systematized presentation of the process of integrated risk management (all concepts, rules and vocabulary have been clearly specified, criteria for assessing the effectiveness of risk handling have

been presented and guidelines for the improvement of the risk management system have been proposed);

■ supporting the management board, supervisory board, managerial staff
or the audit unit to make decisions by regular monitoring and evaluation of control activities in the company (the occurrence of unforeseen
situations is limited to a sufficiently low level);

■ adjustment of the risk management system to the company's operating
strategy and its "risk appetite" (decisions taken in response to risk are
rationally justified).

Corporate risk management consists of eight related elements that are
used to achieve the goals of the organization's strategy. These elements are
(Mechelewski, 2020):

■ internal environment – covers the nature of the organization and is the
basis for employees' perception of and response to risk; philosophy of
risk management and the acceptable level of risk; honesty and ethical
values and the work environment.

■ goal setting – objectives must be set before the managerial staff begins
to identify potential events that may impact their achievement. Risk
management ensures that management has procedures for setting goals
that are relevant to the mission and vision and are consistent with the
level of risk allowed by the organization.

■ identification of events – internal and external events affecting the
achievement of goals must be identified, distinguishing between threats
and opportunities, which are then considered in the process of setting
goals and building the organization's strategy.

■ risk assessment – analysis and assessment of the likelihood of occurrence of a given risk.

■ response to the occurrence of risk – managerial staff selects the type of
response: avoiding, accepting, reducing or sharing the risk, in order to
develop a set of actions to link particular types of risk to an acceptable
level.

■ control activities – policies and procedures established and carried out
to effectively implement risk responses.

■ information and communication – appropriate information should be collected and communicated in a form and timeframe that enable employees
to perform their duties. Effective communication also needs to take place
on a wider scale – down, across and up the organizational hierarchy.

- monitoring – monitoring of individual types of risk is carried out through continuous management actions, independent assessments or a combination of both.

1.3.10 *Information Security Management Systems – ISO/IEC 27001*

In a knowledge-based economy, information is a resource as much as matter or energy, as it has real value that contributes to the creation or increase of added value. Due to its importance and meaning, just like any material thing, it is subject to distortion, destruction, theft or loss. With the advent of new information technologies, new threats have arisen, such as (Szymonik & Bielecki, 2015, 119):

- computer viruses (disk, file, script viruses) and computer phone viruses; spyware (these programs collect information about the user and send it to their author often without the user's knowledge and consent – such information includes web addresses visited by the user, personal data, payment and credit card numbers, identity data, user interests);
- hacker intrusions;
- theft of credit card numbers;
- theft of logins and passwords;
- industrial espionage which may expose the institution to loss of competitiveness;
- reputation and substantial financial losses.

Numerous examples made available to the public prove the increasing frequency of loss or breach of information security in enterprises and therefore the need to establish a system that will protect all kinds of data against a wide range of threats to ensure business continuity, minimize business risk and maximize ROI and business opportunities.

Information security is achieved through the implementation of an appropriate security system, including policies, processes, procedures, organizational structure, as well as software and hardware functions. These safeguards must be established and implemented, and also monitored, tested and improved as necessary to ensure that the organization's security and business objectives are met. It is extremely important that this should be realized in conjunction with other business management processes. In practice, secure information means that three essential attributes of protection must be met (System Zarządzania Bezpieczeństwem, ISO/ IEC 27001, 2021):

- confidentiality – that is, ensuring that information is available only to authorized persons;
- integrity – that is, guaranteeing the accuracy and completeness of information and methods of its processing;
- availability – that is, providing authorized users access to information and related resources in accordance with their specific needs.

Information security in ICT networks and systems depends on the efficiency and effectiveness of the developed system, which includes (Bezpieczeństwo teleinformatyczne, 2021): creating a security policy for networks and computer systems; setting out rules for accessing resources; formulating safety standards and recommendations, and good safety practices; developing safety risk analysis procedures; developing response procedures and documenting security incidents; determining security classes of computer systems; monitoring of security status, monitoring of transmitted data; specifying tools for security analysis; updating operating systems and applications; defining service and user authentication mechanisms.

There are many legal regulations allowing the creation of a secure information management system. These include, among others, the international ISO 2700 standard which defines the requirements related to the establishment, implementation, operation, monitoring, review, maintenance and improvement of an Information Security Management System. This was announced in 2005 on the basis of the British standard BS 7799-2. In Poland, the ISO/IEC 27001 standard was published in 2007 as PN-ISO/IEC 27001:2007. On December 2, 2014, PN-ISO/IEC 27001:2007 was withdrawn and replaced with the PN-ISO/IEC 27001:2014-12 standard. In turn, this was replaced by the PN-ISO/IEC 27001:2017-06 (ISO/ IEC 27001, 2021) standard, published on January 10, 2018. This standard is based on a process approach and uses the Plan-Do-Check-Act (PDCA) model which is applied to the entire ISMS process structure. Attention should be paid to normative Annex A of this standard, which contains the required safeguards divided into 11 areas (Norma ISO 27001, 2021): A.5 – security policy; A.6 – information security organization; A.7 – asset management; A.8 – security of human resources; A.9 – physical and environmental security; A.10 – system and network management; A.11 – access control; A.12 – acquisition, development and maintenance of IT systems; A.13 – information security incident management; A.14 – business continuity management; A.15 – compliance.

An organization that wants to properly protect its information should apply a systemic approach in which it will comprehensively manage its information assets, infrastructure for their processing and information security risks. Currently, the best solution is the Information Security Management System standard.

1.3.11 Occupational Health and Safety Management System – ISO 45000:2018

The activities that are carried out in the supply chain include the storage and transport of goods and components, and ensuring the usefulness of place and time for them in accordance with their needs. In practice, this is carried out by people who should be provided with safe working conditions. One of the tools ensuring such standards is the ISO 45001 standard published in 2018 (it replaces the BS OHSAS 18001 standard), which (ISO 45001:2018, 2020):

- regulates issues related to occupational health and safety, constitutes the basis for preventing accidents and occupational diseases;
- guarantees safe and healthy workplaces;
- enables the introduction of effective protective measures that will contribute to ensuring safety at the workplace;
- makes it possible to increase the competitiveness of a business, which will positively affect its image among customers and employees;
- is based on the PDCA (Plan-Do-Check-Act) cycle.

The new ISO 45001 standard places great emphasis on the role of managerial staff in the management system. Top managers should demonstrate leadership and commitment to OSH management through (Najważniejsze zmiany, 2021):

- taking full responsibility for the prevention of accidents at work and work-related illnesses and ensuring safety and health in the workplace;
- ensuring that a health and safety policy is established;
- ensuring that the requirements of the health and safety management system are integrated with the organization's business processes;

- providing the resources necessary to establish, implement, maintain and improve the OSH management system;
- ensuring active participation of employees or their representatives, using consultations at all levels of management within the OSH management system.

When determining the risks and opportunities of the OSH management system and its intended outcomes, the organization considers hazards and risks related to OHS and others. The benefits of using ISO 45001 include:

- increasing trust in the organization as an employer that organizes work in a safe manner;
- increasing the organization's responsiveness to changing legal requirements and opinions of stakeholders;
- reducing the cost of accidents and downtime;
- reducing insurance premiums;
- reducing absenteeism and employee turnover.

Notes

1. In the most literal sense, security is indeed identical with safety and means the absence of physical danger or protection against it.
2. An example of a disaster was the blockade of a container ship in the Suez Canal from March 23, 2021, to March 29, 2021, which ran aground on one of the banks and got stuck across the canal, blocking it completely. Goods worth $9.6 billion flow through the channel every day; each hour of blockage costs $400 million.

Chapter 2

Contemporary Conditions of Supply Chains

2.1 Logistics 4.0 in Modern Supply Chains

Contemporary delivery chains adapt to the requirements of Logistics 4.0, which is defined as (Logistyka, 2021): a network of interconnections of independent logistics systems using large amounts of data, which determine the automation, organization and course of processes, and support for Industry 4.0. It includes mutual data exchange, digitization and cloud computing. Logistics 4.0 is nothing more than digitization and automation of the supply chain in terms of specific subsystems (Hompel & Kerner, 2015) leading to higher efficiency and quality of production (Müller et al., 2018). It is related to (Deniz, 2021):

- introducing innovations in the operation of warehouses where intelligent sensors are increasingly used to enable virtual planning of loading and unloading, based on special network modules and where data on the filling of the space are transmitted;
- increasing production efficiency which is combined with additional optimization and automation of data flow (information is exchanged inside companies and among all entities at the top and bottom of the supply chain);
- "tracking" (monitoring) of transport and shipments (automatic generation of messages to the customer, informing about the load, its weight and estimated time of arrival);

DOI: 10.4324/9781003286110-2

- joint planning of logistics in the area of distribution, production and procurement, in real time;
- automation and digitization of processes;
- fast, personalized deliveries;
- digitization of land, sea and air deliveries;
- extensive use of cloud computing to use online databases, in the online space, without the need to purchase (install) additional applications (programs);
- digital reflection of reality in logistics activities.

The important elements in the scope of Logistics 4.0, which shapes the image of modern, innovative supply chains, include seven areas: Internet of Things (IoT), big data, cloud computing, smart factory, 5G, automation and blockchain.

2.1.1 The First Area – The Internet of Things

The *Internet of Things* (IoT), which for the purposes of supply chains, can be defined as (Niyato et al., 2015; IoT w polskiej gospodarce, 2019):

- a network connecting wired or wireless devices characterized by an autonomous (not requiring human involvement) operation in the field of acquiring, sharing, processing data or interacting with the environment under the influence of these data. It is a concept of building telecommunications networks and information systems with a high degree of dispersion, which can be used, among others, to create intelligent control and measurement systems, analytical or control systems, practically in every field.
- The concept of IT architecture that enables cooperation (interoperability) of various ICT systems supporting various field applications and is based on the following layers:
  - equipment – devices (or items equipped with such devices), in particular sensors, actuators, but also controllers, smartphones, tablets, laptops or computers that are capable of communicating and processing data without human involvement or with limited interaction with humans;
  - communication – telecommunications infrastructure and (wired or wireless) telecommunications network, operating on the basis of

　　 any data transmission standards with any range (in this case the
　　 Internet);
　　 – software – IT systems of IoT devices and software for data exchange,
　　　processing, system management and security;
　　 – integration – sets of defined IT services ensuring software interoper-
　　　ability at all levels of architecture.
■ An ecosystem of business services, using objects capable of collecting
　and processing information (interacting), connected to form a network,
　ensuring interoperability and synergy of applications. Combining prod-
　ucts/services of Internet of Things allows for a better understanding
　of the consumer, the environment, products and processes, including
　logistics processes, identifying important events and reacting for imme-
　diate optimization or more precise personalization.

Analyzing the presented definitions, we can conclude that the implementation and use of IoT in practice improve many processes carried out in the
supply chain. The most popular solutions of the Internet of Things in logistics include (Internet rzeczy (IoT), 2021):

■ inventory tracking systems that assist logistics managers in planning
　replenishment and distribution. With the use of connected sensors,
　business owners will be able to ensure the safe storage of products,
　save time by locating the required item immediately and minimize
　human error. It is also the ability to trace the product from the ware-
　house to the customer's door, which increases the confidence that all
　stages of the supply chain run smoothly.
■ predictive analytics systems that help managers make informed deci-
　sions about warehouse management and supply chain planning. They
　are used to determine the shortest delivery routes, detect early signs of
　faulty equipment and remind staff when to replace items of equipment.
　Predictive analysis systems increase warehouse productivity and reduce
　delivery costs.
■ location management tools that allow real-time tracking of each vehi-
　cle's location, delivery status and estimated time to complete the pro-
　cess. It is also an instrument that allows determining the location of
　warehouse equipment (racks, trolleys, cranes, ventilation and air con-
　ditioning devices, fire protection devices etc.), tools for maintenance
　and repairs, which in turn improve the functioning of warehouse
　management.

- delivery by drone – an effective way to speed up and automate deliveries. In the supply chain, they can be used to improve warehouse navigation, provide customers with immediate store deliveries and solve last-mile problems.
- automated vehicles – these will be the main innovation in logistics, in the supply chain. Logistics companies are likely to be among the pioneers in the deployment of autonomous vehicles and those that will benefit most from this innovation. Vehicles will select the most convenient route, adjust the temperature and other properties in the vehicle to store the products in a favorable environment, and they will also have many other applications to suit each delivery.
- automated order processing and status updates that help companies reduce shipping staff, thus reducing overall logistics costs along the supply chain. Using connected bots for final-stage delivery helps reduce costs exponentially and also increases customer satisfaction.

2.1.2 The Second Area – Big Data

Big data as a key factor in Logistics 4.0 is an evolutionary method of collecting data from available sources in a fully legal manner and then their analysis (Business Intelligence), drawing conclusions and using them to implement the set goals defined for the needs of the supply chain. Big data is a combination of volume, diversity, speed and reliability that gives organizations an opportunity to gain a competitive advantage in today's digitized market (Schroeck & Shockle, 2012).

Big data implementation is all about skillful compilation of many types of data – structured and unstructured, internal and external, archival, current and future data – in order to gain new knowledge about the environment in which the supply chain operates along its top and bottom part, including first- and lower-tier suppliers (Czym Jest Big data, 2021).

There is no uniform definition of big data in the literature on the subject. The essence and meaning of big data reflect the content of its terms and are closely related to:

- collecting, processing and analyzing large amounts of data in order to obtain new knowledge (Blog poświęcony e-commerce, 2020);
- high-volume, high-velocity and/or high-variety information assets that demand cost-effective, innovative forms of information processing that

enable enhanced insight, decision making and process automation (Beyer & Laney, 2012);
■ data sets that cannot be managed with current mining methods or software tools due to the large size and complexity of the data (Fan & Bifet, 2012);
■ analyzing and coordinating relations, opportunities and profits between cooperating companies that were previously not considered because businessmen did not notice them;
■ data sets that are simultaneously characterized by a large volume, diversity, real-time streaming inflow, variability and complexity, as well as requiring the use of innovative technologies, tools and information methods in order to extract new and useful knowledge from them (Tabakow et al., 2014).

Analyzing the presented and available definitions of big data, from the point of view of value added to activities within the supply chain, we can present a number of assessments and postulates:

■ First: big data is a set of large volume, variability (diversity) that allows obtaining, collecting and analyzing (processing, inferring, visualizing) data from various sources to obtain specific benefits.
■ Second: big data is a popular term to describe the rapid accumulation and availability of both structured and unstructured data (it is not the size of the data that is most important) (Big data, 2021).
■ Third: the usefulness of big data results from the efficient and effective analysis of data in the context of its usefulness. Contemporary changes in the approach to data mining in the process of knowledge discovery require non-standard tools such as data cleansing, data integration, data selection, data transformation, pattern evaluation, knowledge representation.
■ Fourth: revolutionary changes in big data technologies and management approaches require changes in the use of data in the organization to support decision making and the development of innovative logistics processes.

In practice, big data improves the functioning of the supply chain, among other things, by:

■ increasing the level of integration of the supply chains and coordination of activities of its individual links at three levels: adoption of the assumptions of supply chain management, cooperation and coordination of activities, goals and measures of their implementation, and the use of IT systems to increase the quality and speed of information exchange;

■ matching (configuration) of the supply chain to the customers' requirements in accordance with their needs (personalization) with the use of tools for monitoring electronically recorded manifestations of their decisions and actions;

■ quick identification of inefficiencies (wastes) in the flow of materials and accompanying information along the supply chain and elimination of their causes;

■ effective elimination of unnecessary stocks, improvement of the quality of logistics processes leading to a reduction in value for target customers or an increase in logistics costs;

■ increasing agility (quick and effective adaptation of the supply chain to changes occurring in its environment) and its vulnerability to crisis situations (threats);

■ quick and effective search for new methods, technologies or environments for the implementation of specific logistic activities related to flows, processes, technologies, participants – links.

Big data for supply chains comes from many different sources, such as (Big Data Challenges of Industry 4.0, 2020):

■ design data for future logistics processes;
■ data on the various processes related to the movement of materials and the accompanying information;
■ data on the quality of the implemented logistics processes;
■ records of manual operations performed by logisticians;
■ information on logistics costs;
■ error detection and other system monitoring implementations;
■ information from customers etc.

Some of these data sources are structured (e.g. sensor signals), some are partially structured (e.g. manual operation records) and some are completely unstructured (e.g. image files). However, in all cases, most of the data is either unused or used only for very specific, tactical purposes. In addition to the typical functions related to data collection, the possibility of examining correlation relationships between data also deserves attention. This is particularly important from the point of view of large enterprises, i.e. with a high complexity of production and logistics processes (also related to security) and a high level of personalization of their products (Davenport et al., 2012).

2.1.3 The Third Area – Cloud Computing

Cloud computing – this term was first used in 1996 by S.E. Gillet and M. Kapor (1997). This concept refers to computing services (support) offered by external entities, available on request at any time and regulated as needed (Rosenberg & Mateos, 2011). Cloud computing is a data processing model based on the use of computing services provided by the service provider in the form of scaled servers, databases, networks with optimal bandwidth and security, software, analyses etc., via the Internet. The companies that offer these services are called cloud providers. The customer pays for the use of a specific service, e.g. for the possibility of using the IT infrastructure, in accordance with the previously signed contract, and thus does not incur any investment costs.

Cloud computing can be classified using various criteria. The first classification is in terms of the way clouds are designed, created and later managed. According to these criteria, the following types of cloud can be distinguished (Leończuk, 2012; Malinowska & Rzeczycki, 2016):

- public cloud, intended for the mass recipient, and its main advantage is its universal availability, which means that it can be used by anyone with access to the Internet (free email services are a typical example of a public cloud);
- private cloud, i.e. dedicated IT resources or a ready-made solution intended for one economic entity (dedicated resources should be understood as the latest IT technologies and highly qualified engineers);
- hybrid cloud, combining elements of both models;
- community cloud, in which resources are offered to a group of organizations with common goals implementing specific activities (the cloud can be owned by each of the organizations involved, by only one of them or even by an external entity);
- dedicated cloud, in which the service provider allocates a certain part of the cloud to the recipient who has exclusive access to it;
- virtual private cloud, in which a set of resources is made available on an ad hoc basis for the needs of the user as part of a service in a "public cloud", taking into account a certain degree of isolation of these resources.

Today's cloud technology goes beyond storage and scalability and underpins advanced growth capabilities such as real-time computing, forecasting and artificial intelligence, continuous learning and machine learning. Regardless of the industry, cloud technology acts as a key factor enabling companies to innovate new technologies, including artificial intelligence (Mell & Grance, 2015).

When implementing cloud computing for the supply chain, several aspects should be considered by answering the following five questions (Wydajna chmura obliczeniowa w logistyce i transporcie– co warto wiedzieć?, 2021):

1. When to move services to the cloud?
2. What logistics data can be transferred to the cloud?
3. Is it worth using the SaaS service?
4. What are the costs of logistics with cloud computing?
5. What are the most common challenges and needs?

When answering the first question, it should be borne in mind that cloud computing in the supply chain is a remedy for problems related to changing requirements for server space. It is a flexible solution, so the demand can be increased during periods of high performance and then restored to its former level. The scalability of the SaaS service in the cloud allows it to perfectly keep up with the pace of development of the enterprise which is a link in the supply chain. Thus, it allows investment in further modernization of IT infrastructure and the costs of its maintenance to be avoided.

The answer to the next question is simple because all the data on the coordination and interaction of supply chain participants along its entire length can be placed in the computing cloud. Not only do they allow improvements in its current functioning, but they also are an indispensable element facilitating the planning of the future in logistics. Moreover, data:

■ ensure continuous control over logistics processes in real time;
■ enable communication with all business partners and customers within a consistent interface and any device;
■ improve settlement and reporting processes.

In answering the third question, SaaS is a user-friendly software that provides supply chain links with the ability to connect to and use cloud-based applications via the Internet. Common examples include email, calendar and office tools (such as Microsoft Office 365). This solution allows service providers to be held responsible for: data security, system stability, necessary service work or backup, thanks to which the logistics company focuses on the main object of its activity. Cloud computing in logistics is also appreciated for its flexibility and scalability, and it additionally (Pagano & Liotine, 2020):

- allows costs related to building IT infrastructure to be avoided;
- offers unlimited space for data storage;
- guarantees continuous control over logistics processes in real time;
- is a place of efficient communication between all participants of the supply chain.

Returning to the next question, it should be clearly stated that the analysis of requirements, design, coding, testing, installation, operation and IT system decommissioning involves high expenses, which for many links in the supply chain may be completely unjustified. Modern logistics companies see an opportunity to increase their market competitiveness as part of cloud computing technology. With the implementation of the SaaS model and paid subscription, they gain access to the desired software, avoiding significant investments. A cloud SaaS provider takes care of all the technical aspects, offering an easy-to-use tool that helps to complete supply chain tasks – especially in terms of the transport process.

Answering the fifth question, it should be said that cloud computing is a modern, future-proof solution with many advantages, which include: scalability, ease of implementation, easier mergers and acquisitions, short implementation or commissioning time, lower risk of downtime and better security and privacy. Many logisticians and managers are not entirely in favor of taking full advantage of this service. They see many threats, which include: data security breach, misconfiguration of services, lack of architecture and security strategy in the cloud, insufficient management of identity, access and authentication details, a takeover of a privileged account in a cloud service, internal threats, lack of due diligence and errors at the level of copying, data migration and storage, errors at the level of the application and infrastructure layers, as well as of metadata structures, the ineffectiveness or insufficient effectiveness of the processes of monitoring the use of cloud services, abuse and unfair use of cloud services.

2.1.4 The Fourth Area – Smart Factory

Smart Factory – to put it simply, this is a modern type of production plant, based on cyber-physical systems, their integration with advanced production technologies and innovative methods of management and organization of production. The term covers a highly digitized environment in which devices and machines can improve the production process through automation and optimization. The benefits of this process go much further than physical production – they pertain to, inter alia, the logistics supply chain (What Is the Smart Factory and Its Impact on Manufacturing?, 2019). The main elements of a smart factory, which is the basic link in the supply chain, are shown in Figure 2.1.

The most important modern technologies that will lay the foundations for future intelligent factories, include big data analytics, industrial Internet of Things, advanced robotics and production automation, as well as the large-scale use of artificial intelligence and augmented reality. Currently, these technologies are already used in an increasing number of production companies, although the scale of their use still leaves much to be desired. The factories of the future will offer real benefits in various areas of the operation of companies, not only related to production itself, but also to the coordination and monitoring of the flow of materials and accompanying information across the supply chain. A smart factory can (Traczyk, 2020):

- use resources efficiently (including by reducing downtime, which increases the productivity of the entire supply chain);
- optimize logistics costs by monitoring losses;
- improve the process of planning and management of production processes, supplies and distribution in the supply chain;
- track flows in the supply chain;
- shorten the time needed for designing and introducing new products and services to the market, among others thanks to the possibility to monitor their basic parameters on an ongoing basis during their use by the customer;
- produce personalized products tailored to customer requirements, which results in better competitive advantages and efficiency of the supply chain;
- manage global supply chains geographically;
- build closer relationships with customers across the supply chain;
- integrate production, procurement, distribution, warehouse and transport processes across the supply chain.

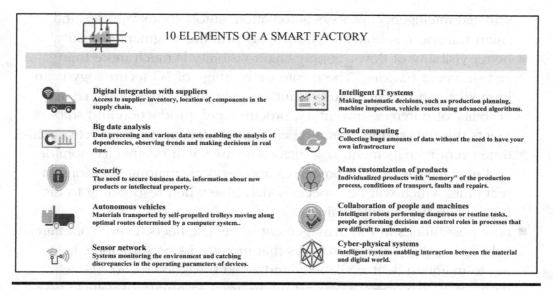

Figure 2.1   The elements of an intelligent factory, which is the basic link in the supply chain. Source: Compiled based on: www.tsl-biznes.pl/newsy/przemysl-4-0-w -logistyce/, May 22, 2021.

2.1.5 The Fifth Area – 5G Technology

5G technology, also known as the fifth generation of mobile technology, is a driving force in the operation of supply chains. It is a standard for data transmission in a cellular network with increased performance parameters, which include (Technologia 5G, 2021):

- throughput up to 20 Gbps downstream;
- throughput of up to 10 Gbps upstream;
- latency of up to 4 milliseconds;
- support for more devices (target 100 devices per 1 m^2);
- integration with wired or satellite systems;
- lower costs of infrastructure maintenance.

The main benefits of 5G technology for the operation of the supply chain are (Technologia 5G, 2021):

- the possibility of wide implementation in the monitoring and improvement of logistics processes with the use of such technologies as Internet of Things, cloud computing, remote-controlled vehicles, asset tracking and location solutions, electrification of transport and tools, blockchain, artificial intelligence, process automation, autonomous vehicles and smart transport, robots and drones, 3D printing, augmented reality.

- better visibility of flows. Supply chain visibility is much more than just shipment tracking. The greatest advantage of 5G technology is an immediate and accurate insight into supply chain operations, i.e. the visibility of purchase, inventory, procurement, production and shipments throughout the operating environment, supported by active real-time event management. Logistics companies will be able to monitor and manage the flow of processes and services, making decisions in real time, which will be especially desirable when responding to disruptions in the supply chain.
- new possibilities in the management of vehicle fleets. Every commercial vehicle is equipped with sensors that monitor its performance, helping to maintain fleet availability and avoid breakdowns. As 5G networks will also operate beyond urban areas, commercial vehicle fleets will become part of an always accessible transport network. Transport Management Systems (TMS) will enable real-time control of vehicle utilization to benefit the entire supply chain.

2.1.6 The Sixth Area – Automation and Robotization

Contemporary and future-proof supply chains are inextricably linked with *automation and robotization*. The concept of robotization, for the purposes of logistics, is closely related to automation and is often used alternately. However, the definition of robotization should be presented to explain the differences between these concepts. Robotization is "replacing human work with robots, and a robot is a device that replaces humans in performing certain activities". Automation, on the other hand, is the introduction of automatic devices to do transport, warehouse processes, order and customer service, packaging service, office work etc. The difference is subtle as it concerns the emphasis on replacing human labor with robots. Robotization is a form of process automation that involves replacing a human with a robot (Grzeszak et al., 2019).

Robotization is primarily intended to reduce the costs of logistics and thus increase the efficiency of the processes carried out in the supply chain. As it turns out, in Europe, there are an average of 114 robots per 10,000 employees (in Poland there are only 46 robots per 10,000 employees, compared to our neighbors, the Czech Republic – 146, and Slovakia – 169). And although Poland is not yet one of the leading countries with the highest robotization rate, at the end of 2020 it made its debut on the list of 15 countries in which robots are bought most frequently (the ranking is published by the International Federation of Robotics) (Polska dołączyła, 2021).

To improve the processes carried out in the supply chain, the following types of robots are used (Roboty magazynowe w erze logistyki 4.0, 2021):

- Industrial robots – these are machines that have been designed to completely replace the work of operators. Their task is to perform difficult and repetitive activities, most often related to the handling of massive loads. Examples of this type of equipment in warehouses are stacker cranes and industrial conveyors.
- Collaborative robots, also known as cobots, assist the operators in the warehouse. Unlike industrial robots, they work in close contact with humans. Their design ensures that they do not pose a threat to the operator's safety. They can be programmed to operate fully autonomously or in accordance with instructions received from an employee. In warehouses, cobots are used mainly for handling loads and packing goods.
- Business robots – they handle standard online applications or standard telephone calls. It is done by RPA (Robotic Process Automation) bots which are programs (sets of algorithms) that emulate an employee and carry out repetitive tasks that so far had to be performed manually. These include basic office tasks such as: completing and recording invoices, administration of data (e.g. sales results, personal data of candidates and employees, competition results), control of compliance of financial documents or preparation and distribution of reports within various departments of the organization based on numerous data collected in distributed systems of the enterprise.

Important conditions for the effective use of robotics in supply chains are (Automatyzacja połączona siecią…, 2021):

- having qualified personnel, trained as part of professional development in the use of robots.
- creation of business ecosystems in which cooperating companies exchange knowledge from various subject areas (IT, machine engineering, logistics etc.).
- holistic perception of processes carried out comprehensively by robots.
- extensive use of sensors to track the flow of materials along the supply chain.

- extensive use of sensors in inventory storage areas. With their use, it is possible to obtain real-time information on the status of items in the warehouse and to save this data in the warehouse management system. This ensures complete warehouse transparency and enables the automation of further process steps, e.g. picking. It should also be noted that the use of sensors along the flow of materials increases the accuracy and safety of logistics processes and also supports autonomous transport operations, and triggers automatic delivery orders in the event of exceeding the reserves (safety stock).
- having tools for the optimization of transport traffic. By combining transport traffic measurement systems with sensor systems, the use of vehicle load areas can be optimized. Data-driven comparison of transport capacity and vehicle loading enables higher workloads and more efficient route planning.

2.1.7 The Seventh Area – Blockchain

Blockchain in Logistics 4.0 has not yet been fully defined. In general, this technology is a distributed database, based on blockchains which are used to store and transmit information about transactions concluded on the Internet (Tasca & Tessone, 2019). One block contains information about a certain number of transactions; after it is saturated with information, another block of data is created, followed by subsequent blocks, creating a kind of chain. In the chain, on average, every ten minutes, a new block appears, in which information about various transactions can be sent, e.g. transactions related to trade, ownership, shares, sale, purchase, electricity generation, purchase or sale of currencies, including cryptocurrencies, i.e. electronic currencies (Pilkington, 2016; Biedrzycki, 2020).

There are specific areas for Logistics 4.0 in terms of applications and benefits of blockchain. In the context of the supply chain they are shown in Table 2.1.

This technology has some limitations and shortcomings, which include (Wodnicka, 2021):

- lack of sufficient legal regulations, which limits its practical use;
- dependence on Internet infrastructure, in particular on the policy of Internet providers;
- scalability, that is the ability to maintain acceptable performance in the face of increasing workload, which means that its performance will

Table 2.1   Features of Blockchain

Characteristic	Description
Data Availability	• Multiple business partners can work on the same document in real time without data loss. • All data stored is digital, eliminating the need for printed documentation. • Each user has the ability to track all previous information and changes. • There is no central institution responsible for data verification and sharing.
Security	• Blockchain is a decentralized technology and its data is made available via the cloud (cloud computing), which means that records are published using the Internet, but access to encrypted information is not automatic, as the business partner must verify access to specific data and express consent to it. • It is not possible to manipulate and falsify information in blocks because each new entry is information in a new block. • The distributed and encrypted nature of blockchains makes them difficult to hack (this is an opportunity to increase the security of the Internet of Things). • The possibility to view a specific chain only for people who have permission to open it and view the data contained in it.
Transparency	• Each business partner is required to upload up-to-date digital data. • Each of the business partners can constantly check and monitor the data. • Acceptance of transactions takes place based on consensus, which means that more than half of the nodes must confirm a given (commercial) operation and agree on the order of transactions. • The transaction register is public and uses a timestamp to indicate the time of the operation.

Source: Compiled based on: Tasca, P., Tessone, C. (2019). Taxonomy of Blockchain Technologies. Principles of Identification and Classification, *Ledger*, 4/2019, 1–39.

decrease with the increasing number of visitors to the website or the increasing amount of processed data;

■ very high energy cost of each transaction (electricity consumption per transaction corresponds to the daily energy demand of a typical American household);

■ the key issues facing this technology are its complexity and the small number of IT specialists who are able to create business solutions using it).

2.2 Supply Chain Management Strategies

The term strategy is not clearly defined and there are several definitions. Here are some of them:

■ Strategy is the art of planning the best way to gain an advantage or achieve success, especially in war (Collins Online English Dictionary, 2020).
■ Strategy which companies use to coordinate their decisions on structural and infrastructural elements (Bozarth & Handfield, 2007).
■ Strategy is the art of interpreting and finding the meaning and importance of events in the environment and in the organization itself (Obłój, 2000).
■ Strategy is primarily the choice of the battlefield and the weapon used. It is about choosing target customers and the offer addressed to them, as well as the means that will be used to reach them with this offer. Therefore, market segments (customers) and the company's offers are the battlefield (Brilman, 2002).

Most of the links that are elements of the supply chain have more than one level of strategy. Strategic decisions concerning the entire organization, including the supply chain, formulate a **business strategy** that can be defined as identifying the company's target customers and specifying the time frame for its implementation and its performance goals (Bozarth & Handfield, 2007). A business strategy is also a set of plans that include (Waters, 2001): organizational structure, geographic location, competitive position, level of diversification, growth policy, productivity, innovation and used resources. The main goals of a business strategy are: achieving efficiency, recognizing and seizing opportunities, mobilizing resources, securing a favorable position, meeting challenges and threats, directing efforts and behavior, and taking control of the situation (Business Strategy, 2021).

Enterprises that are links in the supply chain may use an offensive or defensive strategy (Hattangadi, 2019). An offensive strategy involves high risk but also high potential returns. It requires a research and development department with a high level of innovation, a strong marketing system and an efficient production system that can quickly turn innovative ideas into real products. This strategy is typically used by larger companies that may take economies of scale into account.

A defensive strategy is the opposite of an offensive strategy; it means low risk and lower profits. Companies using it do not bear the risk of losses to which a company dealing with the development and promotion of a new product is exposed. These companies try to reduce production costs and introduce to the market substitutes for new products offered by companies applying an offensive strategy.

At the enterprise level, the role and place in supply chain strategy can be clearly defined, regardless of whether the enterprise is a subsidiary of a corporation or operates autonomously. The relationship between business strategy and supply chain strategy is shown in Figure 2.2.

Business strategy is what defines the strategies of operation and of the supply chain, with the following activities as its essential elements:

- Operational activities (a set of people, technologies and systems within an organization, the primary goal of which is to provide customers with *its products*) and the supply chain (a network of producers and service providers who work together to process goods from raw materials to the level of end-user) are implemented within the same functional strategy indicating how the structural and infrastructural elements in the described area will be acquired and improved to support the implementation of the overall business strategy.
- Structural activities include (Bozarth & Handfield, 2007):
  - production capacity (e.g. size, type, timeliness of production capacity changes);
  - facilities (e.g. service facilities, production plants, warehouses, distribution centers, size, location, degree of specialization);
  - technology (e.g. manufacturing processes, material handling equipment, transport equipment, computer systems).
- Construction (ordinal) activities include:
  - organization (e.g. structure – centralization or decentralization, reward or control systems, workforce decisions);
  - material source decisions and procurement process (material source acquisition strategy, supplier selection, supplier performance control);
  - planning and control (e.g. forecasting, inventory management, production planning and control);

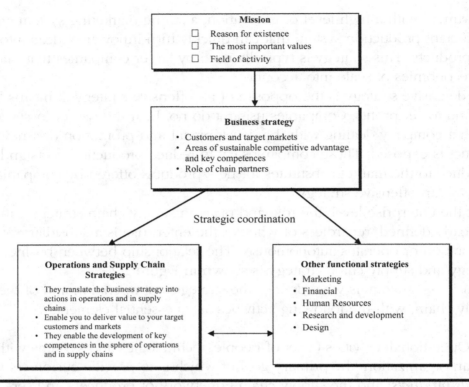

Figure 2.2 The place of supply chain strategy in business strategy. Source: Compiled based on: Bozarth, C., Handfield, R.B. (2007). Wprowadzenie do zarządzania operacjami i łańcuchem dostaw, *Helion*, Gliwice, 54.

- quality management (e.g. total quality management (TQM), continuous improvement, statistical quality control);
- product and service design (e.g. development process, organizational roles and suppliers).

There are generally three objectives for the strategy of operations and supply chain (Bozarth & Handfield, 2007):

- assisting managerial staff in choosing the right combination of structural and infrastructural elements based on a clear understanding of the dimensions of performance valued by customers and the necessary trade-offs;
- ensuring strategic coordination of structural and infrastructural decisions with the company's business strategy;
- supporting the development of key competences in the area of operations and supply chain.

On the basis of the material concerning strategy, business strategy, as well as operation and supply chain strategy, it is proposed to assume for further consideration that **supply chain strategy** is: identifying a network of producers and service providers who cooperate to process and move goods and specifying the time frame for implementation and sequence of events increasing the value of the product. The most frequently formulated goals of the strategic management of supply chains in terms of logistics are (Szymonik, 2014c):

- minimizing the total costs of the flow of products and information while maintaining the quality of delivery service required by customers (the so-called savings logistics);
- ensuring the shortest possible order fulfillment time and the highest possible reliability, frequency and flexibility of deliveries at the assumed level of flow costs (the so-called efficiency logistics);
- optimizing the level of inventories on the scale of the supply chain along with flexible adaptation to the preferences in the scope of servicing the supplies of particular market segments.

Based on the literature on the subject, it is possible to define the factors shaping the strategy of supply chains, which are presented in Figure 2.3.

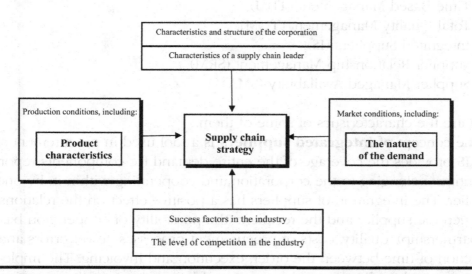

Figure 2.3   Factors shaping supply chain strategy. Source: Compiled based on: Ciesielski, M., Długosz, J. (2010), (ed.), Chain strategy delivery, Warsaw, 41.

The presented supply chain strategy applies to the entire corporation, enterprise within the corporation or an autonomous enterprise, and its most important factors are:

- market conditions (nature of demand);
- factors of success in the industry (the level of competition in the industry);
- production conditions, including product characteristics;
- the characteristics and structure of the corporation, including the characteristics of the supply chain leader.

Supply chain strategies are geared towards the end customer by synchronizing the flows of supply and demand (Siambi & Okibo, 2014). In the formulation and implementation of long-term activities in the relationship between the sender and the recipient, various concepts are used that improve the effectiveness and efficiency of the chain, and reduce the waste of time, place, quantity and quality.

The concepts that allow obtaining a long-term competitive advantage, while maintaining an appropriate level of satisfaction of all participants in the supply chain, include the following strategies:

- Quick Response (QR);
- Efficient Customer Response (ECR);
- Time-Based Management (TBM);
- Total Quality Management (TQM);
- Integrated Suppliers (IS);
- Supplier Relationship Management (SRM);
- Supplier Managed Availability (SMA).

Here are the characteristics of some of them.

The concept of **integrated suppliers** is a tool used in procurement strategy. IS provides the coverage of the entire demand for components reported by entities belonging to the corporation and cooperating within it, by one supplier. The integration of suppliers has a positive effect on the relationship between the supplier and the recipient (the possibility of cooperation based on partnership), quality, costs of procurement processes, fewer errors and reduction of time between the order, execution and invoicing. The implementation and application of the concept of integrating suppliers are aimed at integrating the participants of the supply chain (Gonzálvez-Gallegoa et al.,

2015). This concept, like any other, is burdened with the risk of having one supplier (no competitive pressure, loss of continuity of supply with disruptions in production on the part of the supplier etc.).

Supplier relationship management generally refers to the planning and control activities and information systems that connect a company to its suppliers operating at the top of the supply chain (Bozarth & Handfield, 2007). It is a collection of applications, such as Design Collaboration, Design Decisions, Negotiations, Procurement Process and Supply Collaboration, that enables enterprises to monitor data about suppliers and their operations. Software vendors specializing in SRM applications are trying to provide more functionality and reliability compared to ERP vendors. However, the situation is changing, as the most important producers of ERP systems, such as SAP or Oracle, are looking for ways to offer more products in the area of, among others, SRM.

There is an IT system on the market that improves the management of relationships with suppliers, known as SAP SRM. It is a solution that allows the return on relationships with suppliers across all categories of expenses, and regardless of time, to be increased. SAP SRM enables the reduction of the costs of materials sold and the rationalization of the supply base and ensures a quick return on investment. It is a solution that integrates operations within the entire enterprise, stimulating cooperation between suppliers by automating processes carried out with the participation of all suppliers in the purchase of goods and services and throughout the enterprise (Sethi, 2010). SAP SRM covers the complete delivery cycle – from the strategic source of supply to operational procurement and vendor collaboration – providing the benefits of using consolidated content and base data. SAP SRM makes it possible to cooperate with each of the suppliers – including all purchased goods and services in the cooperation.

The continuous optimization of supplier selection is also guaranteed, as well as the shortening of the duration of delivery cycles. Focusing on source identification and sourcing strategy is also beneficial (Szymonik, 2014). Supplier relationship management provides tangible business benefits in many areas (Szymonik, 2014):

- reduction of process costs:
  - limiting purchases outside established purchasing channels and processes;
  - reducing complexity through content consolidation;

- increasing efficiency by automating procurement processes;
- reducing costs related to integration and connectivity;
■ lowering of unit prices:
- consolidating requirements across various business units;
- reducing costs related to carrying out the inventory;
- obtaining better prices as a result of competitive tenders;
■ shorter delivery cycles:
- automating monotonous processes related to tenders and inquiries;
- improved procurement through online approval;
- faster confirmations and responses from suppliers;
■ optimization of the strategy for determining the source of supply:
- rationalizing and optimizing the supply base;
- easier access to supplier performance data;
- improving the quality of deliveries and reducing risk.

There are four critical factors that must be considered for successful SRM implementation (Odlaniecka-Poczobutt & Capota, 2009).

■ Integration is the first step (information about areas such as product life-cycle management, supply chain planning, enterprise resource planning and customer relationship management should flow from a single data source).
■ Second, suppliers must be able to operate directly in the buyer's system (connection must be affordable, scalable and relatively simple to implement and use). The range of interface capabilities available to suppliers – XML, EDI, web services, portals or email – means that their investments in connecting to the customer's system will not generate too high costs.
■ Third, once a single "view" of the supply chain is visualized, analytical tools can be added to help identify areas of best opportunities for both the buying organization and major suppliers. Business analysis tools support the decision-making process and can help increase the profitability of both parties.
■ Fourth, a collaborative culture (partnership and trust) must be beneficial in the entire supply chain, and suppliers must be seen as a source of competitive advantage, not cost. Properly managed supplier relationships can contribute to innovation and growth of the enterprise, while a poorly managed supply base increases costs and slows down the initiative for new products.

The presented concepts used in supply chain management strategy are tools that effectively allow an advantage to be gained over the competition by eliminating significant and difficult problems occurring in various areas of cooperation between links in the chain. Consciously made decisions aimed at compressing the time of response to customer needs may bring the desired effects in the form of increased added value, but when used with disregard for the environmental conditions and the internal potential of the supply chain, they generate the risk of exceeding the acceptable level of costs due to excessively complex cooperation structures or procedures (Witkowski, 2003).

Supplier-managed availability is an extension of the well-known older concept of VMI (*Vendor-Managed Inventory* – also referred to as *Supplier-Managed Inventory*), i.e. inventory management by the supplier (it is one of the best solutions when sales are high, on time and targeted to specific recipients).

VMI means an optimized operation of the supply chain, as a result of the management of manufacturer's (or, for example, distributor's) inventory by the supplier who decides on the time and content of supplies guaranteeing full availability of products. VMI is the process by which the supplier generates orders for the customer and depending on the customer's needs, based on the customer's information about demand. This type of management can be treated as a tool to improve procurement processes in the supply chain (Erikshammar et al., 2013).

SMA does not base its philosophy on stock but on the availability of goods. The technique is based on the belief that inventory flowing down the supply chain is not an end in itself. The real goal is to have a product available if and only if a specific location (a specific link in the chain) needs it. The shift in focus from inventory to availability allows the supplier to consider additional ways to deal with fluctuations in demand. The result is even lower stocks than when using the "standard" VMI. It may turn out that it is more economical for the supplier to invest in "redundant" capacity that is used only when needed, rather than keeping large amounts of inventory on the customer's side. The supplier can also benefit from faster transport when needed (Odlaniecka-Poczobutt & Capota, 2009).

A slightly different perspective on the efficiency of the supply chain in strategic terms is presented in an article published in *Logistics*, where five elements influencing its configuration are distinguished (Juszczak-Szumacher, A. Sadowski, 2010):

- operational strategy (production to stock, production to order, configuration to order – a combination of the first two, technical development to order);
- outsourcing strategy (identification of key competences and their excellence, the inclusion of external partners in logistics activities);
- distribution channel strategy (defining how products and services are delivered to customers or end-users);
- customer service strategy – determining sales volume, its profitability and understanding the needs of individual customers;
- asset network – establishing the location of plants and infrastructure along with the immediate and wider surroundings of the supply chain.

Production and purchasing strategies shape the supply chain strategy. It was described in detail by J.C. Cooper who distinguished four basic variants of global supply chains (Figure 2.4).

The dimensions of these strategies are the horizontal dispersion of production (assembly) and the degree of globalization of supply. According to J.C. Cooper, the strategy marked as A in the figure is characterized by the expansion of the assembly plant in many countries (e.g. Fiat, Opel). The supplies come from the home country or from a larger area. The opposite of this strategy is the concentration of production and sourcing in the home country marked as D (e.g. Mercedes-Benz).

The strategy marked as B is based on the concentration of production and global sourcing (e.g. Airbus). On the other hand, the strategy marked

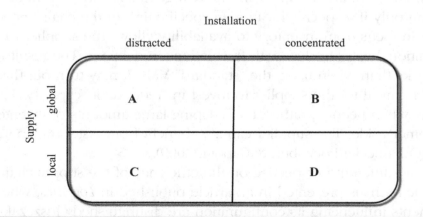

Figure 2.4 Variants of strategies for global supply chains. Source: Compiled based on: Ciesielski, M., Długosz, J. (2010), (ed.), *Strategia łańcuchów dostaw*, Warsaw, 44.

as C means both local production and local supplies (e.g. MacDonald) (Ciesielski & Długosz, 2010).

2.3 Factors Integrating Activities in the Field of Supply

The factors integrating activities in supply chains include trust, partnership and information. These factors are described below.

2.3.1 Trust

Modern organizations that are supply chain participants conduct their operations based on a changing environment. Unfamiliarity with the partner, creating ad hoc economic systems, often to perform just a single task or no legal regulations are only some of the problems that may arise in the management of the supply chain.

Activities in the knowledge-based economy (including in the supply chain) favor unethical activities such as:

- non-performance of obligations by an economic organization, company or individual – related within the supply chain;
- connecting an organization – especially within the supply chain, which is to undermine the good name of, and discredit another company on the market, most often of a global nature;
- conduct contrary to the interests of the home country, e.g. members of virtual organizations that want to circumvent embargoes, other legal restrictions or take advantage of tax reliefs;
- distorting information.[1]

Modern forms of operation in the field of e-business (e-logistics) require respecting mutual trust in all relationships and between all participants, both upstream and downstream of the supply chain.

This can be further expressed as trust in someone or something that was created by someone (e.g. a company, institution, virtual organization, supply chain). Trust means sharing the norms and values of another party and acting for the benefit of that party and not harming them (Collins Online English Dictionary, 2021).

The above-mentioned definition is one of many definitions of trust. Depending on the scientific discipline, for example, management, marketing, organizational behavior or IT, trust is defined differently, but most often the following terms appear in all of the definitions (Grudzewski et al., 2007):

- kindness – means concern and motivation to act in the interests of another party and is the opposite of opportunistic behavior;
- honesty – concluding contracts in good faith, telling the truth, keeping promises;
- competences – the skill and/or ability to do what is needed;
- predictability – refers to the actions of the parties (both desired and undesirable) that provide a sufficient basis for predicting future situations.

Mutual dependencies in the world of business and its management require considering mutual relations between the employee and the organization, between the company and other cooperating entities, especially the customer who has become demanding and capricious. This system will be effective when each of its parts (links) will participate in the creation of added value for the benefit of the whole (the entire supply chain).

Individuals, organizations and institutions that have been "favored with confidence" are not controlled, so often they are provided with a wider margin of non-conformist, innovative and unusual activities. At the level of society, individual cases lead to increasing mobilization, activity and innovation (Sztompka, 2005). And all of this is possible when the participants in this system view trust as a central factor for all transactions and processes.

Building trust and managing it is not an easy task, as often business participants do not know each other beforehand because they have not performed any transactions or operations before. An example is the Internet with an infinite number of buyers and sellers. Expensive middlemen who prolonged timelines and increased costs have been eliminated. Considering the low cost of data transmission and the gradual broadening of the bandwidth of this transmission, the number of transactions should be vast. However, practice shows otherwise.

It turns out that limitations, in addition to strategic factors (e.g. selection of a distribution channel), operational factors (e.g. remodeling of processes based on new IT technologies) and organizational factors (e.g. acquiring, developing and maintaining competences necessary to operate under new conditions) also include a lack of trust among both sellers and buyers (Brilman, 2002). In e-commerce, there is a concern about the loss of privacy associated with the use of a credit card or the use of customer information that is needed to complete the transaction (Gustavsson & Johansson, 2006).

E-commerce and e-service businessmen and managers in the supply chain seek to build trust by (Grudzewski et al., 2007):

- reducing subjective and objective uncertainty and risk faced by the counterparty in connection with the operation and transaction;
- convincing a potential customer to carry out an operation or purchase;
- increasing the loyalty of an already acquired customer;
- increasing the share of Internet services in customer's expenses, at the cost of reducing the number of operations performed with the use of both traditional distribution channels and other online stores;
- deepening the relationship with the customer;
- improving customer satisfaction;
- collecting data to deepen the relationship with the customer.

Communication is a good and helpful tool in building trust, and it can be considered its precursor because it involves formal and informal sharing (exchange) of important information, often of a strategic nature, between contractors (Hakanen et al., 2016). A high level of trust is achieved when communication is frequent and of high quality, i.e. the information provided is adequate, up-to-date, credible, understandable. To build trust through communication, it is important to use an appropriate communication strategy that includes frequency, duration, content, message channel and direction (Figure 2.5) (Grudzewski et al., 2010).

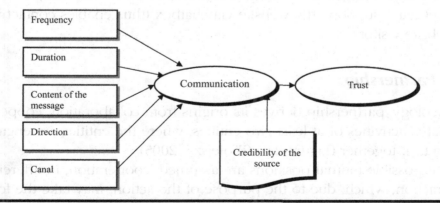

Figure 2.5   The impact of communication on trust. Source: Compiled based on: Nowacki, G., Olejnik, K., Walendzik, M. (2017). Ocena stanu bezpieczeństwa transportu drogowego w UE, *Autobusy,* **9, 116.**

The frequency and duration of communication relate to the amount of information transmitted. There are many definitions of "amount of information", but the most appealing one is that related to Shannon's information theory (Shannon, 1948).

Another good example of supporting trust and management in the context of source credibility is a set of tools supporting sales in-commerce. These include (Szarf, 2021):

- Brand24 – Internet monitoring (it works well for getting to know opinions about oneself, but also allows potential customers to be reached);
- Freshdesk – streamlines the handling of customer notifications sent via email, website and other channels;
- Hotjar – helps to optimize the usability of the website, helps in mapping, that is, visualizing the way customers move around the online store;
- Google Analytics – analytical tools for e-commerce managers (it has a dedicated module that allows virtually every activity performed by users on the website to be measured and analyzed);
- MailChimp – used to send newsletters and e-mails, offering ready-made message templates that can be changed and personalized;
- BaseLinker – a tool enabling the management of sales from various sources in one place;
- Landingi – an e-commerce tool that helps in the execution of temporary promotional campaigns;
- Wigzo – allows the transformation of data into user behavior forecasts;
- Crazy Egg – a tool for tracking user behavior on the website;
- LiveChat – supports the website via chatbox (thus enables contact with website visitors).

2.3.2 Partnership

In praxeology, partnership derives its origins from collaboration, cooperation, that is activities of at least two entities, where the entities are engaged in some task together (Figure 2.6) (Wołejszo, 2005).

Three possible mutual positions are assumed: cooperation, indifference or counteraction, which, due to the purpose of the action, may take the form of compatibility, contradiction or incompatibility (Klatka, 1972). Thus, it can be assumed that entity A cooperates (is a partner in Figure 2.7) with entity B if and only if causative behavior of A influences the results of causative

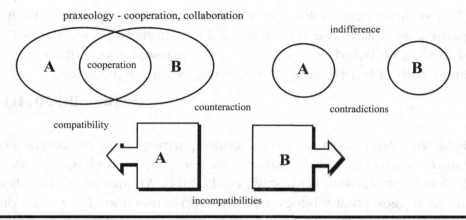

Figure 2.6   The lineage of partnership. Source: Compiled based on: Wołejszo, J. (2005). "Teoretyczne aspekty współdziałania", [in:] "Współdziałanie systemów dowodzenia wojsk operacyjnych i wsparcia krajowego", AON, Warsaw, 14.

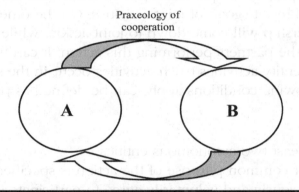

Figure 2.7   Dependencies between entities. Source: Own study.

behavior of B or if the action of B influences the result of the action of A in a similar way. Cooperation understood in this way covers both its positive and negative sides (Sokołowski, 1988). Partnership can be understood as the pursuit of shared goals and implementation of the assumed strategy aimed at their attainment or the distribution of risks, resources and skills among the parties concerned (McQuaid, 2009).

According to the Institute of Business Development, a partnership is

a mature form of being in a relationship and cooperating with others. Partners say: we are equal, we respect each other, we have common goals, we cooperate, we trust each other, we support each other, we openly name our expectations and needs, we discuss differences looking for solutions that are acceptable to both parties, we always use arguments and not strength. Such a partnership must be based on values because it is tested and verified at every turn. It is a challenge for individuals and organizations.

(Szymonik, 2014c)

The Economic Advisory Association defines partnership as the *division of labor and resources serving to optimize the use of a partner's skills to share profits, losses and liabilities* (Kupczyk et al., 2014). An analysis of the above definitions suggests that whenever partnership is mentioned, it means only such multi-entity activities (occurring in the supply chain) where participants consciously and voluntarily contribute to the achievement of a common goal or the goal of one of the participants of the action.

Therefore, the purpose of partnership is to ensure the efficiency of achieving the end result (goal) of joint activities. On the other hand, the essence of partnership will come down to joint action, while maintaining the autonomy of the partners performing this action. It can be assumed that only those multi-entity activities (such activities occur in the supply chain), in which the following conditions apply, can be defined as partnerships (Wołejszo, 2005):

- there are at least two autonomous entities;
- the agreed or common purpose of the action is specified;
- entities consciously and voluntarily agree to participate in the achievement of a common goal or of a goal of one of them;
- at least one of the parties must take steps to support the other.

According to the criteria defined above, actions taken by entities remaining in a relationship of business dependency or constituting elements of the same structure, e.g. of a consortium, holding or a group of companies, cannot be referred to as partnership. This, in turn, means that e.g. departments of a particular enterprise cannot be considered as a partnership because they constitute one entity set up to achieve predefined goals.

A concept often equated with partnership is the coordination of actions, i.e. "regulating collaboration and harmonizing relationships between factors of production in the process of attaining goals. It means temporal and spatial synchronization of particular actions" (Kopaliński, 2020). Coordination may be introduced in the field of, e.g. procurement, sale of products, services, warehouse management or transport, and the essence of the actions is that:

- each of the participants is assigned with a task within their specialty and capabilities;
- the organizer of the action seeks to maximize the use of the potential of individual elements;
- all activities of individual elements bring the organizational whole closer to the achievement of the assumed goal.

Coordination is also seen as one of the functions of management, along with planning, organizing, that is, acquiring and allocating resources, motivating, controlling and deciding. It is perceived as the activities ensuring the mutual cooperation of these functions (Rokicka-Broniatowska, 2006).

Partnership is also equated with the synchronization of activities, which is indeed essential for the efficient operation of a supply chain. This concept is defined as:

- bringing changes of several physical properties to synchronicity, simultaneity, temporal consistency (Kopaliński, 2020);
- temporal coordination of at least two phenomena (processes), i.e. striving for their timed, parallel, independent course or to their simultaneous completion (Kopaliński, 2020);
- making two or more phenomena, processes, activities etc., compatible in their temporal course (Kopaliński, 2020).

Synchronization of activities means their temporal coordination and is distinguished by the fact that:

- it is organized between, for example, links in the supply chain intentionally connected to perform a specific task;
- its participants are parts (links) of the same whole (supply chain), but due to specialization, they perform particular tasks.

Contemporary business partnership in the supply chain has been shaped and conditioned as a result of (Popławski et al., 2008; Romanowska & Trocki, 2002):

- the emergence of new organizational forms in business (e.g. large-scale, virtual, network enterprises, Industry 4.0, e-commerce);

- accelerated technological changes and their aging, requiring faster depreciation (decline) of capital and investment in know-how;
- difficulties in maintaining satisfactory profitability of the company, prompting the search for ways to reduce costs;
- the increasing complexity of many products and the diversity of technological processes;
- the growing number of legal regulations;
- intense competition on a global scale, which is a strong incentive for enterprises to seek market partners, that will make it possible to reduce the level of risk associated with specific undertakings (e.g. entering foreign markets, introducing new products etc.);
- joining forces by production and trading companies in the field of broadly understood market research;
- elimination of the boundaries of local and global markets as a result of the mobility of consumers who have their own models and preferences;
- abandoning all forms of intermediation in favor of direct purchases, often between the producer and final recipients (it is particularly visible in e-business).

Partnership between the links of the supply chain should be understood as "shaping economic relations between its participants based on the principles of trust, sharing risk and benefits, leading to additional synergistic effects and competitive advantage" (Witkowski, 2010). Supply chain partnerships result in benefits such as (Popławski et al., 2008):

- reduction of uncertainty;
- increasing flexibility;
- the possibility of easier access to scarce resources and skills;
- increasing the speed of action;
- obtaining information;
- organizing and maintaining a common base (of raw materials, energy, storage, transport etc.);
- use of more advanced technologies;
- greater production flexibility;
- greater possibility of reducing costs than in the case of classic solutions;
- creating innovative solutions.

Partner ties in the supply chain may have various arrangements, and the criterion for joining them may be the result of joint operational, financial or marketing activities. This generates a specific value chain, an important element of which may be the innovative potential of one of the cooperation partners or a group of cooperating companies. The natural inclination of each party to the agreement will be to strengthen its market position, which in turn will also depend on the position of partners, participants in the supply chain. Therefore, their common interest is to remain partners, bearing in mind that by acting in the system a synergistic effect can be achieved (Hammervoll, 2009).

In the literature on the subject, different classifications of partnerships in the supply chain can be found. Considering the time, intensity and scope of economic ties between the links, three types of partnership can be distinguished (Witkowski, 2010):

- the first type, usually consisting in short-term and limited cooperation in the field of coordination of activities and planning only within one plant or functional area of partners;
- the second type, which is a transition from coordination of activities to their integration between many plants and functional areas of partners in a long, but usually strictly defined period;
- the third type, characterized by a significant level of operational integration, which leads to the perception of the partner as an "extension" of one's own organization, without clearly defined deadlines for termination of cooperation.

Establishing partnerships between actors in the supply chain does not mean that everyone will "benefit equally". It is important that no one feels cheated, and the terms of the contract are also respected by the one who has the strongest position in this chain, e.g. in terms of capital. Therefore, when choosing and establishing a specific type of partnership relations between the links in the supply chain, it is first of all important to understand the relationships between the features of the purchasing process and the need for continuity of cooperation and mutual dependence of contractors (Witkowski, 2010).

Partnership requires continuous adaptation of organizational structures of individual links in the supply chain as well as competency changes in the understanding of the role and scope of influence of individual parts of this system, such as transport, purchasing, storage or information base. These changes should be aimed at (Brilman, 2005):

- creating planning and design structures;
- developing horizontal communication (without intermediaries);

- eliminating bottlenecks and reasons for withdrawing from others;
- creating formalized information flow systems (the same equipment, cooperating IT systems, common database, EDI – electronic data interchange, automatic identification – electronic product labeling etc.);
- creating conditions for frequent informal exchange of information;
- sharing information.

Partnership in the supply chain is a continuous process and requires improvement as the environment in which it operates is changeable and demanding. Organizing mutual relations is essential for the partnership and consists in (Brilman, 2005):

- accepting the fact that partner cooperation sometimes requires deviating from certain norms and standard practices previously used in logistics;
- maintaining continuity of contacts with the same contractors;
- sufficient legitimacy of those who are responsible for mutual contacts on both sides;
- respecting oral agreements and creating an atmosphere of mutual trust;
- ensuring formal and informal information flows;
- ensuring sufficient transparency of operation;
- establishing a single institution to make important decisions and settle disputes.

The basic elements of a partnership, from the point of view of each participant, are (Gordon, 2001):

- a database containing the most important information about the supplier and company indicators;
- evaluation of the supplier's share in the company's current and future revenues, based on which it selects strategic partners from among the suppliers with the relatively largest share;
- analyzing the current state of partnerships with all companies and defining goals that can be achieved by strengthening ties, especially with strategic partners;
- comparing vendor metrics (e.g. balanced scorecards, key performance indicators) and benchmarking in terms of their relevance to the enterprise;
- self-assessment of the enterprise in terms of the possibility of establishing partnerships with suppliers;

- identifying the benefits of deepening partnerships with suppliers, with particular emphasis on the best or strategic suppliers;
- choosing the method of planning the process of creating new value, as well as the methods of implementation, management, estimation and division of roles;
- choosing the method of managing the partnership;
- managing the process of introducing changes in relations between the company and suppliers.

The development of partnership relations between the customer and the supplier leads to the intensification of the phenomenon of externalization, i.e. the process in which a social unit externalizes the previously internalized (i.e. assimilated, recognized as own) values and norms (Synergius, 2020). Externalization means making processes available, resignation from a part of the added value in favor of a margin for the participants of the supply chain, funds and investment outlays improving logistic activities.

2.3.3 Information

A condition for success in any activities (including in the supply chain) is gaining an information advantage, understood as the ability to collect, process and share information, which will allow for example competition to be fought off or the logistic process to be improved. An information advantage can be gained, among others, by meeting the requirements of specific users, in this case, participants in the supply chain, e.g. by ensuring the qualitative characteristics of information, which include (Encyklopedia zarządzania, 2020):

- relativity – information responds to the needs and is relevant for the recipient;
- accuracy – the information is adequate to the level of knowledge represented by the recipient, it precisely and accurately reflects and defines the subject;
- timeliness – the cycle of updates is consistent with the content, and the pace of changes and the appearance of new versions is natural, in line with the passage of time;
- completeness – the information contains the optimal amount of data, which is sufficient to enable the transformation of the information into specific knowledge, the level of detail depends on the recipient's needs;

- consistency – individual elements, data, harmonize with each other, the form corresponds to the content, data updating is compatible with the objectives;
- relevance – appropriate presentation of information and description of the presentation enabling its correct interpretation;
- availability – information is available from anywhere and at any time;
- credibility – information confirms the accuracy of the data, contains elements ensuring the reliability of the message;
- connectivity – information is consistent with other information, interpreted in the right context, functioning in a familiar communication system.

Information is a complex concept, and in fact today no single, universally accepted definition of either *information* or *information theory* exists. In the literature on the subject, various approaches and definitions can be found, and thus:

- N. Wiener, the founder of cybernetics, believes that information is neither energy nor matter, but that its content is taken from the external world in the process of our adaptation and adaptation of our senses to it (Wiener, 1985).
- E. Niedzielski is of the opinion that information is a specific intangible good and a factor which – as a kind of "meta-energy" – may contribute to the transformation of the world economy (Niedzielski, 1986).
- P. Sienkiewicz describes information as a set of facts, events, features etc., specific objects (items, processes, systems) included in the information (message), formulated and presented in such a manner (form) as to enable the recipient to take a stance regarding the situation, as well as to take relevant mental or physical actions (Sienkiewicz, 2005).

The analysis of this and other information allows the identification of various functions of information. Depending on the situation, application or place of use of the information, it may (Rokicka-Broniatowska, 2006):

- be a driving factor;
- describe a specific part of reality;
- constitute a certain type of energy impulse (meta-energy) that moves greater amounts of energy and determines the spontaneity of human activities;

■ be a component of knowledge;
■ be a resource, similar to other resources, such as money, property, that have value and require incurring costs to acquire them and are used for achieving goals;
■ be a commodity that is produced on the market and for the market, is in demand and has a price;
■ be a psychological mechanism that regulates human behavior regarding the direction of action.

What cannot be measured or expressed in numbers cannot be effectively and efficiently managed, which is why the concept of the amount of information is used. And, since there is no unambiguous definition of information, there is no precise definition of the amount of information that can be proposed either.

As previously noted, it is assumed that the foundations of quantitative information science were laid by Claude E. Shannon for the needs of telecommunications. In its peculiar form, information theory is a branch of probability calculus and mathematical statistics. For elementary messages, the amount of information "I" related to the event x_i ($i = <1, N>$) occurring with a certain probability p (x_i) can be expressed by the formula (Rokicka-Broniatowska, 2006):

$$I(x_i) = \log \frac{1}{p(x_i)} = -\log p(x_i) \qquad (2.1)$$

Therefore, the following conclusions could be formulated:

■ the lower the probability of an elementary event, the higher must be the amount of information associated with it;
■ if x_i is specified, i.e. $p(x_i) = 1$ then $I(x_i) = 0$;
■ if there are two independent events x_i and x_j with a combined probability of $p(x_i, x_j)$ then $I(x_i, x_j) = I(x_i) + I(x_j)$.

The described regularities are true under the condition that the amount of information is associated with uncertainty as to the outcome of a particular experiment, each elementary message carries some information, and each of events x_i can be associated with the probability corresponding to it $p(x_i) = p_i$.

When considering a memoryless source with a set of elementary information $x_1, x_2, ..., x_N$ with the probabilities $p(x_1), p(x_2), ..., p(x_N)$, it is a situation in which subsequent elementary information selected by the source is statistically independent. The average amount of information emitted by the source H (X), called entropy, is defined as:

$$H(X) = -\sum_{i=1}^{N} p(x_i) \log p(x_i) \qquad (2.2)$$

In the considerations, it can be assumed that the amount of information contained in the message is the difference between the initial entropy (i.e. before receiving the message) and the entropy obtained after receiving the message. A message informs someone when it eliminates or reduces uncertainty with regard to some issue, and entropy is the measure of uncertainty. In general, it can be presented in the form of:

$$I(X,Y) = H(X) - H(X/Y) \qquad (2.3)$$

which means: the amount of information brought on average by the message from the set Y about the event (state) from the set of possible events (states) X is equal to the difference between the unconditional uncertainty as to the occurrence of one of the events (states) X and the conditional uncertainty as for this, after receiving one of the signals from the set Y.

For a specific user, informing is not an intrinsic goal but a means of achieving a specific goal or set of goals by making specific decisions or assimilating specific knowledge. **Information is useful**, i.e. has a certain utility value, if it increases the effectiveness of actions taken by the user, i.e. increases the probability of success or reduces risk. An example of a simple formula expressing usefulness is (Sienkiewicz, 2005):

$$U(I) = \log_2 \frac{P_1}{P_2} \qquad (2.4)$$

where:
P$_2$ – probability of achieving the goal before obtaining information;
P$_1$ – probability of achieving the goal after obtaining information;
U (I) – usefulness of information.

The main source of the value of information is its usefulness in making decisions. Information has value because, in each decision situation, it allows the effects of the decisions made with a higher probability to be assessed and thus enables them to be made more optimally (Brichler & Bütler, 2007). Estimating the value of information comes down to four steps:

- determining the best decision in both cases (of the presence and absence of information) – it is a first step;
- calculating the expected usefulness of the best decision in the presence of information – it is a second step;
- calculating the expected usefulness of the best decision in the absence of information – it is a third step;
- calculating the difference between the results of the second and third steps.

The more desired the effects of the decision inspired by the information in a situation of uncertainty, the higher the value of the information. The value of the information for the decision maker is also influenced by (Brichler & Bütler, 2007):

- degree of uncertainty of the decision maker in a given situation;
- precision of information;
- level of risk acceptance;
- cost of obtaining and using information (Oleander-Skowronek & Wydro, 2007).

The value of information is difficult to measure because:

- information has indirect usefulness (Oleander-Skowronek & Wydro, 2007);
- information is of variable nature, and resulting from its multifaceted nature, diversity and complexity, it can be used and interpreted in many ways by various users (Dziuba, 2007);
- information can reduce as well as generate uncertainty;
- information needs to be updated;
- the value of information depends on the scale effect; this value is an increasing function of wealth;
- the value of information decreases over time;
- the more often a certain type of information is used, the more it becomes valuable;
- information is worthless if it cannot be transferred (information can be transferred with the use of e.g. IT technology);
- it is an inexhaustible resource;
- it can be processed to obtain new information.

The above-mentioned features of information mean that subjective assessment will be the most adequate method of assessing its value, i.e. it depends on the person who uses it. The need to measure the value of information results from the following properties:

- information is a factor of production (Dziuba, 2007);
- information is purchased at a specific measurable cost, which may be significant in some situations;
- substitutes are available for each specific element of information and can be recalculated as more or less expensive;
- the cost of using the information can be significant;
- as every factor of production, information should be used optimally (Oleander-Skowronek & Wydro, 2007).

Information, like any other resource (funds, land, labor), can actually or potentially be used by its authorized (or unauthorized) owner at any time and place and for any purpose. It is a nondepletable resource, due to its inexhaustibility and impossibility to be worn out in the processes of its use.

So far, however, no satisfactory quantitative measure of the value of information has been found, because it is shaped by various factors, such as:

- unusual information resulting from the unusualness of an event or its unexpected occurrence, such as a financial crisis, supply disruptions as a result of strikes, poor weather conditions;
- confidentiality of information – for some reasons it is not made available – e.g. improvements introduced in motor vehicle engines, results of research and development works;
- persistent or declining usefulness of information, such as the value of procedural information, a blockbuster becomes an ordinary product over time;
- scope of information: the greater the number of recipients, the greater the value it acquires, e.g. the more consumers are informed about a new product, the greater the sales of the product.

The value of information plays an important role for policymakers who are increasingly operating under conditions of risk and uncertainty. The effects of their decisions cannot be classified as predictable (deterministic) but rather probabilistic with a low probability. Successful management, therefore, depends to a large extent on the value of information possessed by the manager. Currently, information is one of the most important commodities on the market and forms the basis of effective management (Bates, 1989). Information allows proper assessment of the condition or situation in which the entity has found itself, enables the forecast of the state or situation of the economic system in the future, allows correct assessment of the factors of the immediate and wider environment influencing the efficient and effective operation and, above all, it enables the right decisions to be made. It should be noted that the entity is not managed based on random information that is not valuable, accurate, reliable, up-to-date, timely, unambiguous, complete or reliable (Chmielarz & Turyna, 2009).

Good information based on new ICT technologies significantly affects the efficiency and speed of flows in the supply chain. The areas in the supply chain that are improved include (Brilman, 2002):

- speed of sending information, especially customer orders, with the use of e.g. email or 5G technology;
- organization of virtual meetings of sellers to exchange information, opinions about the market, about customer requirements, e.g. in the TSL industry etc.;
- providing reports, passwords, orders;
- internal, electronic catalogs for buyers and sellers to exchange information about products and prices;
- new customer service systems, networks, databases and process *re-engineering*;
- new services (e.g. GPS makes it possible to track the route taken by parcels);
- automation of calculations;
- electronic document management and document creation;
- reducing costs by switching to a new level of technology;
- new strategic opportunities for those who were limited by previously used IT tools;
- new methods of group work.

Note

1. More information in Section 7.4.

Chapter 3

Supply Chain Security Management

3.1 The Essence of Supply Chain Security Management

Supply chain security is inextricably linked with confidence, lack of hazards, calmness and non-threatening circumstances, as well as the process of obtaining, deploying and using resources to mitigate risk. It is the use of policies, procedures and technologies to protect supply chain resources (products, facilities, equipment, information and personnel) from theft, destruction or terrorism (Closs, 2004).

Supply chain security is inextricably linked with the crisis (a sudden breakdown of logistics processes), which is (Walas-Trębacz & Ziarko, 2011):

- defined as a "difficult situation" that either exists at a given moment or may yet occur, a major, negative situation unfavorable for the chain participants, which may result from various circumstances, an anomaly disrupting the everyday course of the stream;
- understood as an instability, or rather the instability of a situation, that precedes a sudden, decisive change;
- a situation in which there is a threat to the processes carried out along the entire supply chain (this also applies to situations where its continuity is broken altogether);
- a turning point for the better or worse, affecting the supply chain effects/losses;

■ the moment when it is decided whether the chain disruption is to continue, to be modified or to be terminated.

The originality of the supply chain crisis can be examined in relation to the following (Nogalski & Marcinkiewicz, 2004):

■ processes – attention is focused on the course of the crisis over time;
■ phases of processes – separation according to threat intensity;
■ places of origin;
■ problems, difficulties, difficulties in improvement and expansion concepts.

Considering the presented materials in the context of the essence of the supply chain crisis from the theory and practice point of view, it can be assumed that it is related to (Zelek, 2003):

■ a situation where activity is permanently disrupted;
■ a situation where the supply chain has or appears to have lost control of its activities;
■ a state of disturbed balance;
■ a state in which logistic processes encounter significant obstacles;
■ a state that may pose a threat to logistic processes;
■ a state that violates the continuity of the processes implemented in the upper and lower parts of the supply chain;
■ a violation of the financial condition, limiting its development possibilities;
■ a situation that puts at risk the achievement of the strategic goals of crucial supply chain links;
■ a situation characterized by an ambivalence of development and repair possibilities;
■ a specific breakthrough between two qualitatively different phases of the growth process;
■ a situation that may destroy the foundations of public trust and inner faith in the participants of the supply chain or damage its image and credibility.

To examine the essence of the problem related to the supply chain, it is important to introduce the concept of a "crisis", which includes objective elements (physical, internal conditions, unplanned situations – independent of contractors) and subjective elements (dependent on managers, quality, time-liness of developed procedures, documentation) influencing the realization of the flow of material and information. In general, a crisis in the context of the supply chain is associated with the state of:

- increasing destabilization, uncertainty as to the continuity of supply chain processes, resulting from threats, which are characterized by a violation of the planned course of the material flow and accompanying information, the possibility of losing control over management func-tions that trigger reactions above the generally acceptable level of risk in business activities;
- increasing destabilization, causing an intense, permanent and long-term deterioration in the functioning of supply chains (characterized by the escalation of the threat, loss of control over limiting the effects of an event (crisis) by individual links in the supply chain, disorganization, decision-making and competence chaos);
- organization (management) that leads to a breach of stability, delay or even a break in the supply of the material stream and information, and in the case of its existence in the long term (existence) for the needs of suppliers and recipients.

Crises in supply chains can be classified according to various criteria, namely (Zelek, 2003; Walas-Trębacz & Ziarko, 2011):

- adaptability (vulnerability) to changes caused by the crisis;
- the process nature of crisis management in supply chain links (it may be potential, concealed or open);
- supply chain life cycle phase (leadership, autonomy, decentralized crisis);
- warning time – i.e. the period between the first symptoms of a problem and the time a crisis emerges;
- area where the problem arises (bottom and/or top of the supply chain, first and subsequent row suppliers);
- causes/triggers of a crisis (natural, civilizational, social threats, terrorism);
- the sphere (area) of the organization that the crisis does or may affect, including management, supply, distribution, production, transport, investments, finances;

■ the multiplicity and variety of symptoms (symptoms) of undesirable situations among the participants of the supply chain, along its entire length.

Achieving the desired level of supply chain security, whether in theory or practice, requires its efficient and effective management during a crisis (hereinafter referred to as **crisis management**), which can be defined as a set of coordinated actions to be taken when threats (disruptions) arise, directed at logistic resources to achieve certainty of deliveries, reduce risks, meet the conditions set by the cargo owner and protect the market position and brand. In other terms, it is "the identification and management of risks for the supply chain, through a coordinated approach amongst supply chain members, to reduce vulnerability as a whole" (Juttner et al., 2003). Supply chain crisis management are actions that (Walas-Trębacz & Ziarko, 2011):

■ minimize the likelihood of a crisis – preventive measures in the pre-crisis period;
■ make it possible to control the crisis – preparatory actions – actions facilitating ones that enable the course of the crisis to be steered towards acceptable solutions – development of scenarios of possible development and course of the crisis;
■ make it possible to survive a given crisis with the minimum possible losses;
■ eliminate the effects of the crisis and create new resources less susceptible to various types of crises.

In crisis management, because of threats, one has to deal with an open system, and the features of the environment that affect its structure include such things as (Koźmiński & Piotrkowski, 1996):

■ the environment's complexity, meaning the awareness of how many elements it consists of and how varied these elements are;
■ environmental uncertainty, which is directly related to dynamics and instability, where there are four types of sources of uncertainty that characterize each system, including the supply chain:
  – uncertainty resulting from ignorance and inability to solve problems, especially unexpected ones;
  – uncertainty in the relations between supply chain participants due to the difficulty in recognizing phenomena and events that appear in a manner independent of the parties affected;

- uncertainty due to incompatibility between task network and information network, e.g. due to wrong or incomplete threat site data;
- uncertainty related to the ambiguity of regulations, including department, central government and local government regulations.

Managing the supply chain requires information that should be correct,
useful, selectable, complete, up-to-date, timely, communicative and available. In making decisions, every manager has specific information needs,
which are shaped by two basic factors (Rokicka-Broniatowska, 2006): the
type of task being solved – Q, as well as human knowledge and experience
(of the user U).

Information needs include, but are not limited to, opinions, forecasts,
diagnoses, factual data etc., which are necessary for the user in relation to
his specific purpose, as well as to predict the circumstances surrounding this
activity.

Information needs can be individual, i.e. related to a given individual and
group. They should be subjected to the objectification procedure, i.e. the
real requirements of users must be considered. These needs can be divided
into two subsets:

■ *Iu – information needed to solve Q and already available to the user;*
■ *L – information that is needed and not directly available.*

The shaping of information needs can be illustrated by the following diagram (Rokicka-Broniatowska, 2006):

$$< U, Q, M > \Rightarrow I \Rightarrow Iu \cup L$$

where:
   U – user of the information being sought;
   Q – problem (problem) solved by U;
   M – methods that U intends to apply to solve Q;
   I – information needed for U to solve Q when using method M;
   L – information (called information gap) needed to solve Q and which U
     does not have.

The L gap arises between the amount of information desired and that
which is available; it grows with the increasing complexity of the problem
(and this is what we deal with in crisis) and the amount of information.

3.2 Crisis Management Phases

When analyzing the events related to a crisis, it can be concluded that the boundaries between the subsequent "normal" (planned and implemented) and "undesirable" states are fluid and difficult to grasp. Overall, we can distinguish three phases of a crisis (Coombs, 2015). Certain symptoms of a crisis may appear significantly earlier and indicate the arrival of a crisis in the supply chain activities. This is often called **the pre-crisis phase**. In this phase, apart from the continuous monitoring of the situation, the main effort is focused on preparatory and security measures, which should consequently lead to the elimination (neutralization) or at least reduction, mitigation of the course and minimization of the crisis occurring in logistic processes. The duration of the pre-crisis phase depends on whether the crisis was foreseeable or not (predictable and unpredictable crises) (Skarżyński, 2000).

The next stage is the **crisis phase**, in which the threat may be of a one-off nature (e.g. tsunami, flooding of cargo, blockade of a transport route, gas explosion, avalanche) or of a continuous nature, with an extended impact duration (e.g. epidemic, drought, social unrest). The duration of the crisis depends on the nature of the crisis and the actions taken.

The post-crisis phase requires specific actions, forces and resources to remove or overcome the effects of a crisis. In this context, one can specify three groups of possible actions to be taken (Skarżyński, 2000; Szczurek, 2006):

- organizational activities aimed at restoring the pre-crisis supply chain functioning conditions, e.g. in supply, sale, transport, storage, communication and staffing markets;
- obtaining additional funds (sources of financing), e.g. budget, EU aid, sponsors, own funds;
- acquiring resources, e.g. in the field of internal and external transport, storage space, warehouse equipment, packaging.

Figure 3.1 shows a model presenting the course of a crisis and taking into account its severity over time.

In praxeological terms, crisis management in the supply chain is nothing more than proper management under pressure, which includes activities aimed at obtaining information necessary to explain the problem. Crisis management aims to reduce the likelihood of a crisis occurring in the first

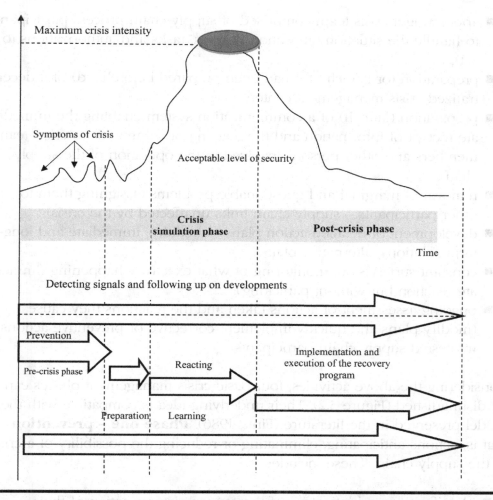

Figure 3.1   Phases of the crisis in the supply chain in comparison with anti-crisis measures. Source: Compiled based on: T. Szczurek, Problematyka podejmowania decyzji w sytuacjach kryzysowych, [in:] Świadczenia na rzecz obrony realizowane w sytuacjach kryzysowych, AON, Warszawa 2006, p. 58.

place, as well as work to minimize its impact should it occur and efforts to restore order after a crisis (Bundy & Pfarrer, 2015). Hence, these activities must include such things as (Szczurek, 2006):

■ assessment of the situation (finding out what exactly is happening, why it is happening, what might happen if no action is taken, how quickly to act, who else may be involved, what resources are available);
■ preparation of an initial plan of action and development of alternative plans for unexpected turnarounds in the different links of the supply chain;

- appointing a crisis team comprised of supply chain process participants to handle the situation (allocation of roles, tasks and authorizations to act);
- preparation (or launch, if it had been prepared beforehand) of a decentralized crisis management center;
- preparation (launch) of a communication system enabling the immediate receipt of information and the relaying of commands to crisis team members and other persons involved in the operation of the supply chain;
- removal of marginal and questionable problems (assigning them to other participants – supply chain links unaffected by the crisis);
- development of detailed action plans (schedules, immediate and long-term solutions, alternative plans);
- constant supervision, monitoring of what exactly is happening (immediate reaction but without panicking);
- ongoing assessment of actions taken and the reactions they cause (modify plans and quickly implement corrective or preventive actions in interested supply chain participants).

Considering the above activities, four basic crisis management phases can be distinguished (Figure 3.2). Their underlying idea is compatible with the model presented in the literature (Fink, 1986). **Phase one – prevention**, that is, actions anticipating, eliminating or reducing the possibility of a crisis in the supply chain. These include:

- identification and inventory of threats and determination of their sources;
- risk analysis of threats and forecast of their potential effects;
- continuous monitoring of phenomena that may constitute a source of threats;
- establishing priorities for the prevention phase;
- preventive action planning;
- preparation of appropriate legal regulations;
- securing financial expenses in the budget;
- supporting applied research and technology transfer;
- systematic employee training in effective management during unplanned situations at companies constituting strategic supply chain links;

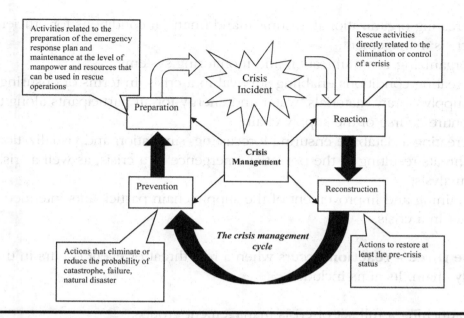

Figure 3.2   Phases of crisis management. Source: Compiled based on: E. Kołdziński, Wprowadzenie do zarządzania bezpieczeństwem, p. 15, http://www.uwm.edu.pl/, p. 15, 28 April 2021.

- creating a system of financial incentives and restrictions and the proper use of resources;
- ensuring proper management and coordination using modern communication channels.

Prevention refers to activities that eliminate or reduce disruptions in business continuity along the entire supply chain.

Phase two – preparation, in which the key element is the development of crisis response plans, which describe the actions to be taken, their time, actors responsible for their implementation and the manpower and means they are to use, as well as the legal basis of such actions (before, during and immediately after a crisis event). Preparation also includes the provision of backup supply markets, outlets, backup logistics infrastructure, establishing the crisis management site, providing crisis response personnel, as well as an inventory of resources useful for crisis response in the event of random events that may occur in the supply chain. Activities in this area include:

- developing emergency response plans, taking into account all links in the supply chain;

- creating organizational, technical and financial conditions for efficient crisis management;
- organizing communication and monitoring systems;
- creating conditions enabling survival in a crisis, in terms of ensuring the supply of raw materials, water and energy for all participants along the entire course of the supply chain;
- creating a database ensuring forecasting, simulation and visualization of threats resulting in the potential emergence of a crisis, as well as risk analysis;
- training and improvement of the supply chain participants intended to act in a crisis.

Phase three – reaction occurs when a real threat or event occurs in the supply chain. Its aims include:

- launching a full set of crisis management groups;
- launching preventive or minimizing actions in the event of discontinuity in the upper and lower parts of the supply chain;
- initiating appropriate procedures, depending on the existing threat, including directing appropriate manpower, material and financial resources contributing to the restoration of normal supply chain logistics processes;
- organizing and coordinating activities to help affected companies that operated as part of an active supply chain;
- ongoing updating in the database system of resources participating in integrated activities supporting the links of a given supply chain;
- collecting reports on the results of activities carried out for the benefit of the affected supply chain companies;
- coordinating and managing activities carried out to address a supply chain crisis until its causes have ceased to exist;
- keeping appropriate documentation (e.g. event log) on an ongoing basis.

The reaction phase requires:

- adherence to information circulation principles;
- gathering information and documenting activities;
- avoiding ill-considered activities;
- professional information;

- forecasting the development of events;
- predicting the effects of decisions made;
- considering the legal implications of decisions;
- ensuring the functioning of strategic companies from the point of view of their importance in the supply chain.

Phase four – reconstruction is the final phase of the crisis management cycle. While the reconstruction continues until all activities within the disturbed supply chain return to their original state, it does not end at that point. The experience gained and lessons learned from the course of the crisis make it possible to implement improved procedures, which can better protect the supply chain against potential future damage (material and personal) and ensure reduced losses. During the reconstruction period, attention should be paid to activities enabling the development of tools and instruments (including technological ones) in the future to increase resistance to disruptions that had previously occurred in the supply chain.

Reconstruction includes both short-term and long-term efforts. Short-term reconstruction is about bringing the supply chain back to minimum operational standards while long-term reconstruction can take many years. The time it takes to create a fully efficient and effective supply chain depends on the size of the losses incurred and the financial capacity of the entities involved. At the same time, the reconstruction of the supply chain should be carried out in a new (innovative) way, so that the newly created chain is less sensitive to another catastrophe. The tasks to be implemented in this phase include (Szymonik & Bielecki, 2015):

- estimating damage and losses resulting from the crisis;
- launching individual and collective assistance programs for the affected supply chain links;
- taking ad hoc measures to ensure the functioning of the supply chain using spare markets for supply, sale and logistics infrastructure;
- launching a financial assistance program for affected supply chain participants;
- preparing analyses and reports on response and reconstruction activities;
- modifying response plans, programs and procedures.

The security of the supply chain should be adapted to its potential threats and the desired level of security that must be provided to it.

3.3 Progressive Management

A complex system such as the supply chain requires a specific, individual and creative approach in management, which can be either progressive or conservative. The term "progression" means to increase or rise gradually, move forward; make progress (Cambridge dictionary, 2021). Progressive actions are distinguished and characterized by (Szymonik, Organizacja, 2011):

■ a tendency to solve problems independently and spontaneously, most often by applying trial and error methods;
■ a tendency to profess and proclaim ideas of progress and the ability to implement them;
■ departure from stereotypes, patterns and analogies.

Progressivity is the opposite of obsolescence, backwardness, schematicism, conservatism, orthodoxy and traditionalism (Słownik synonimów i antonimów, 2021).

One might be tempted to say that ideal progressive management anticipates a crisis and tries to eliminate it through real action before it occurs in the first place. And the main motto of such a model is – it is always better to prevent a problem than to remove its impact once it has occurred, both in economic and social terms.

This type of management is most desirable in the pre-crisis phase. It is there that, apart from the constant monitoring of the situation, the main effort is focused on preparatory and protective measures aimed at the elimination (neutralization), or at least reduction, mitigation and minimization of the effects of the crisis. The duration of the pre-crisis phase depends on whether the crisis was foreseeable or not (predictable and unpredictable crises) (Skarżyński, 2000). And it is at this stage that one should seek new solutions in terms of techniques, technologies and crisis management methods, which best suit the progressive action.

Risk inevitably accompanies progressive managers in making decisions, as it is them that must be bold enough to take uncertain actions, which may not necessarily comply with the opinions of others and the generally accepted principles. The result may be a success or utter failure, e.g. making it necessary to choose whether to remain on the market or file for bankruptcy. It is often the case that decisions made by a progressive manager handling a crisis can be compared to the decision-making process of a cardiac surgeon (Szymonik, Organizacja, 2011). By selecting a possible variant in a non-randomized way, the manager makes risky choices – often under time pressure – to "heal", e.g. the supply area or eliminate a major risk in the supplier market, like the one caused by Covid-19 in China.

Decision-making must be accompanied by creativity, the confidence of action and the relentless pursuit of the intended goal. It is a great responsibility not only for oneself but also for the whole, as is the case with the use of global supply chains.

Decisions are often affected by critique, concern, the possible loss of position, authority or even the job itself; they may also be accompanied by dissatisfaction among companies linked to material and information flows along the supply chain. It is crucial not to act rashly; decisions must be well-thought-out and must consider the effects of future actions. Much like a cardiac surgeon, a manager working under time pressure and using the available data, forecasts and simulations must utilize his personal knowledge, experience and intuition to choose a so far untested course of action and monitor its effects.

As the name suggests, a crisis is a state requiring immediate actions; it may soon be too late to act if one fails to do so at the given moment. Further, fixing errors is associated with significant expenses – and not only financial ones – as it also carries with it the loss of reputation among the cooperating supply chain links. A crisis requires one to be resolute and determined. It is no place for the so-called populists who promise solutions corresponding to the expectations of the majority of stakeholders to gain their support, as well as influence and power, without having any resources or improvement programs.

On the other hand, a manager cannot be given a free rein – his actions must be controlled to prevent abuse and the potentially irreversible negative impact of his actions. In these considerations, it is deemed that an irresponsible manager who believes in his infallibility may harm the business, unlike the person managing the response to a crisis that may arise in logistic processes, such as in the event of technical failures or natural disasters.

Progressive management should focus primarily on anticipating the emergence of crisis and using tools and instruments that would at least limit the effects. Innovative solutions should be the outcome of research and priority technologies (Table 3.1), and then the subject of practical training.

Progressive management in the area of supply chain operation should utilize wide access to internal and external security tools, including intelligence, police, judiciary, economic, financial and diplomatic resources,

Table 3.1 Research Areas and Related Priority Technologies

Research Area	Priority Technologies
Information technology	Data connection, collection and classification methods; image processing technologies, information and data management technologies, 5G technology
Artificial intelligence and supporting the decision-making process	Information and data mining, knowledge management, modeling and simulation, optimization and decision support technologies
Communication devices	Reconfigured communication, secure mobile communication, management of communication networks, broadband data lines
Information protection	Encryption technologies, data searching, access control
Computer technologies	Safe processing technique, high-performance processing
IT systems	Infrastructure supporting the management and dissemination of information, optimization and planning systems for the decision-making process
Scenarios and simulations of decisions	Developing advanced models and simulating human behavior, simulations for the decision-making process, predicting vulnerabilities of structures, evacuation and consequences management techniques, emission simulation
Integrated platforms	Unmanned platforms (land, sea and air, observation and navigation satellites)
Equipment based on sensors	Cameras, sensors, including technologies for the detection of specific chemical and biological hazards, passive devices with infrared (IR) sensors
Sensors	Multispectral sensors, processing of multispectral signals
Navigation, guidance, control and tracking	RFID (electronic product tagging) markings, tracking, GPS technologies, radio navigation, barcode-based tracking
Electronic authentication	Electronic tagging systems, "smart cards"
Simulators, training devices and artificial environments	Virtual reality, augmented reality, personnel training systems

(Continued)

Table 3.1 (Continued) Research Areas and Related Priority Technologies

Research Area	Priority Technologies
Forensic techniques – biometrics	Fingerprint recognition, face recognition; iris, retina, voice, handwriting, signature recognition
Biotechnology	Rapid analysis of biological agents and human susceptibility to disease and toxic substances, decontamination techniques, water testing and purification techniques, food testing and inspection techniques
Biological, chemical and medical materials	Chemical and biological detection techniques
Survivability and technologies that increase immunity	"Smart" clothes and devices, explosion-proof materials, specific architecture of critical buildings considering the effects of an explosion and shock
Light and resistant materials, covers	Light protective materials for people, "smart" fabrics, lightweight protective materials for places, the technology of protective and explosion-proof materials
Storage and distribution, energy generation	Electric generators, energy distribution
Space systems	Multispectral Earth Observation
Sociological sciences	Analysis and development of models of human behavior, population behavior, human factors in decision-making processes, teams

Source: Compiled based on: Z. Mierczyk, Nowoczesne technologie w systemach monitorowania bezpieczeństwa, [in:] Metodologia badań bezpieczeństwa narodowego "Bezpieczeństwo" 2010, t. II, AON, Warsaw, 2011, pp. 32, 33.

research results and modern technologies. Efficient, modern and effective progressive management requires information systems supporting the monitoring, identification and prevention of threats to citizen security, including information and decision-making processes and crisis management, as well as effective management of activities and crisis response.

3.4 Conservative Management

The word "conservatism" comes from the Latin *conservare*, which means "to preserve, save" (Konserwatyzm, 2021). Conservatism is defined as a strong attachment to tradition and reluctance to change (Cambridge dictionary, 2021). Thus, a conservative management method is distinguished by the acceptance of the general state, the value system, the slow introduction of new rules, as well as attachment to the existing, proven system. The implemented process of planning, organizing, leading and controlling the governing and executive bodies is carried out in a manner already developed, tested and approved by the management bodies of all supply chain links. This type of management is most useful in the following phases:

- crisis, where the threat may be one-off or continuous, with an extended duration (the duration of the crisis depends on the nature of the crisis and the actions taken);
- post-crisis, which requires specific actions, forces and resources to remove or overcome the effects of a crisis; three examples of enterprise groups can be mentioned in this context (Szymonik, Organizacja, 2011):
  - activities in the field of organizing, planning, staff selection, venue security, communications etc.;
  - obtaining funds (sources of financing), e.g. budget, international aid, sponsors, own funds;
  - acquiring manpower and technical means, e.g. qualified teams, materials and technical equipment, equipment, enabling the use of infrastructure (roads, ramps, airports, bridges, warehouses).

The reasoning for the usefulness of conservative management in the crisis and post-crisis phase is based on the proven adage that experimenting on and introducing new methods into a living organism, particularly innovative ones, may sometimes prove very risky and costly.

When making a systemic analysis of conservative and progressive management, several conclusions can be made (Szymonik, Organizacja, 2011):

3.4.1 First Conclusion

The ideal response to a crisis should be a combination of conservative and progressive management. Finding a compromise between them is the ideal way to make decisions in a crisis. Each decision should be considered by people working in the environment where the given solution is to be implemented and such people should provide their objective feedback on it. Decisions made under time pressure often turn out to be a failure. One cannot turn back time and the results may be unpredictable. Both our knowledge and experience enable more insightful thinking, allowing us to assess the situation more accurately and choose the most useful and satisfactory option.

3.4.2 Second Conclusion

The conservative way of managing is distinguished by the acceptance of the general state, the value system, the slow introduction of new rules, as well as attachment to the existing system; it is always based on traditional, tried-and-tested methods. Conversely, progressive behavior is very bold, innovative, modern.

3.4.3 Third Conclusion

Crisis management is a managing body activity that is an element of security management in the supply chain, which consists in preventing crises, preparing to take control over them through planned actions, reacting should they occur and removing their effects, as well as restoring resources and infrastructure. It is nothing more than a response to the crisis that occurs in the supply chain because of acts of nature and human activities. To solve this situation, one should always ask how to deal with the problem in a logical and orderly way. Given its complexity, it is not always possible to identify a crisis, including due to such factors as incomplete information, which is difficult to obtain. Therefore, the overall assessment of the situation must consider the interaction between different systems (including technological and human).

Solving a crisis typically involves making conservative decisions, i.e. doing what has already been done many times. This provides a learning effect – the more you do something, the faster and better you become at it. Conservative management is like a mechanism that provides a certain sense of comfort because its rational implementation often (but not always) proves the correctness of the procedure (the so-called predictability effect).

3.4.4 Fourth Conclusion

In a crisis, conservatives use well-established patterns based on "tradition", on principles. However, in cases where this does not bring the expected results, they are bound to try new solutions, thus creating a group of people with a progressive attitude. Both conservatives and progressives have their advantages and disadvantages, and as such, it is best to compromise and choose the best of both worlds. While the proven, conservative methods are often chosen in a crisis, there is no development without progress (or it is slow) and there occurs a tedious process of implementing whatever "must be done immediately". There is no such thing as strictly progressive or strictly conservative management. To face the nature of reality, elements of each approach must be used, irrespective of personal sentiments.

3.4.5 Fifth Conclusion

When managing a crisis, a set of interdisciplinary, professional, purposeful and coordinated interactions should be used, enabling the easier attainment of the goal. The interdisciplinarity of interactions results from the nature of the crisis experience and, in particular, from the phenomenon of the "spreading" of the crisis into both the immediate and more distant supply chain environment. Thus, it is vital that apart from routine, experience and proven methods (conservative behavior), crisis management should also take advantage of science and research, as well as the solutions they bring (progressive action).

3.4.6 Sixth Conclusion

Conservative management generally uses tried-and-tested procedures and methods of operation. On the other hand, innovations (progressive management) in solving difficulties are highly recommended, as they make it possible to examine the problem from many perspectives and find new solutions; however, this certainly requires higher costs and carries the risk of other unforeseen consequences that may result from the decision taken.

A good approach to crisis management is the modification of classic rules by introducing certain changes that take into account the existing situation in a dynamic way, which enables adaptation and corrections to the decisions made, contributing to the simplification of processes and the elimination of some of their stages. However, the decisions made are not always right, and therefore, it is necessary to dynamically adjust them depending on critical situations; one must be prepared for failures and be aware of the responsibility for the decisions made.

Modern supply chain management is based on information, yet not in terms of quantity, but rather quality. In crisis management, one should abandon the paradigm of quantity and use whatever makes it possible to react quickly and anticipate any unfavorable actions resulting from threats. This can be described as being "counter-surprised" with anything detrimental to business and the environment.

3.5 Risk Management

Broadly construed risk, including logistics risk, is considered as early as the supply chain strategic planning stage. On the other hand, the operational logistic risk concerns many logistics subsystems of the entire supply chain and results mainly from the imperfections of the day-to-day management focused on the supply, production or sale of goods.

When systematizing various types of logistics-related risk, it is worth taking a closer look at a group of companies that carry out joint activities necessary to meet the demand for specific products throughout the entire chain of goods flow, ranging from obtaining raw materials to making deliveries to the final recipient. Such activities include development, production, sales, service, procurement, distribution, resource management and support activities. The risk arising in contact between the supplier and the recipient is multifaceted (Kaczmarek, 2006).

Cost risk management requires specific actions to be taken by the controlling, production and transport planning departments, as well as consistent reduction of stocks. It is important to determine the optimal volumes of stored goods, which will keep costs as low as possible. However, in the case of certain customers, logistics may be affected by specific types of risks related to special production processes and separate sales networks, which cannot be transferred to other customers upon the loss of such special customers.

In Persian, *rozi(k)* means fate. In Spanish and French, *arisco* stands for both courage and danger. In English, *risk* denotes a circumstance causing a danger, though the word *hazard* is used more often to refer to the source of such danger. Many encyclopedias state that the word "risk" is derived from Latin, as the Latin verb *risicare* means to avoid something, like the Italian *ris(i)*, which denotes a reef that a (merchant) vessel ought to avoid. This is since the historically dominant concept of "risk" in most cultures applied primarily to sailors and traders (Kaczmarek, 2003). Today, *risk* is defined as follows:

■ an information deficit pertaining to the achievement of one or more goals (Kaczmarek, 2004);

- a potential failure to achieve project or contract objectives in a way that ensures compliance with the specific requirements regarding product parameters (characteristics), delivery schedule or costs (Kaczmarek, 2004);
- a possibility of failure to achieve the intended effects of economic activity, incurring unintended losses or higher-than-anticipated expenditures (Szymonik, Zarządzanie, 2013);
- the possibility of deviations from the intended effects of the action (Spekman & Davis, 2004), where these deviations are subject to the law of large numbers and can be predicted using the probability calculus (Szymonik, Zarządzanie, 2013);
- a situation where one cannot predict with certainty the outcome of choosing a given option, but has enough information to determine the likelihood of achieving the desired outcome (Stoner et al., 2001) through planning and proper risk assessment (Slack & Lewis, 2002).

Based on the above definitions, in relation to the supply chain, it is advisable to define risk as the conditions under which the mining, production, trade and service companies operating in various areas, as well as their customers between which the product and information streams flow, know the estimated probability of obtaining the desired result of their activity.

Risk applies to all product life cycle phases (from the idea to its implementation to product withdrawal) and processes (occurring in all phases of a product's life) that can be implemented throughout the entire organization or physical network starting at the supplier and ending at the final customer (Figure 3.3) (AQAP, 2000, 2003).

Potential risks can be determined based on the following (Klimczak, 2001; Iwasiewicz, 1999; Szkoda, 2004):

- analyzing contract review data;
- reviewing documentation, taking into account any changes;
- analyzing conclusions from previous similar contracts;
- brainstorming sessions;
- data from the department responsible for financing the contract being implemented;
- data from the supplier (mainly identifying the risk related to the suppliers participating in the contract performance).

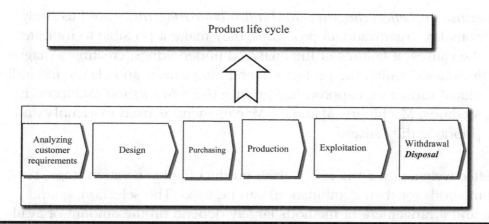

Figure 3.3   Risk sources in the product life cycle process. Source: Compiled based on: A. Szymonik, *Logistyka jako system racjonalnego pozyskiwania wyrobów obronnych*, AON, Warszawa 2007, p. 131.

The methods used in risk identification include (Iwasiewicz, 1999):

- brainstorming – identifying possible solutions to problems and potential ways to improve quality;
- what-when method – using a checklist of questions to be answered to provide a simple and general risk assessment;
- SWOT method – consists in identifying four groups of factors: strengths, weaknesses, opportunities and threats, which enables a thorough assessment of the development of the organization and potential risk areas;
- QFD method (Quality Function Deployment) – systematized procedures based on a diagram known as the "house of quality". The essence of this method is the proper determination of numerical values and qualification of data related to customer requirements and technical parameters of the product, as well as the technical parameters of the product and their interrelations, hierarchy of the importance of parameters and competition analysis.

The following techniques are used for the above methods:

- *flowcharts* – presenting the algorithm of the subsequent process stages, which may contribute to revealing the source of the problems;
- *Pareto-Lorenz diagrams* (related: ABC analysis, 80/20 graph) – based on the principle that 20–30% of the causes determine 70–80% of the effects, which means that most defects identified in the processes are caused by only a few reasons;

■ *cause and effect diagrams and a fish bone diagram* – used to study complex organizational processes; they make it possible to indicate the causes of failures of the analyzed undertakings; creating a diagram includes defining the problem, identifying causes and classifying individual causes into appropriate groups; the 5-M method (Manpower, Methods, Machinery, Materials, Management) is used to identify and prioritize the causes.

To effectively analyze the risk at each product implementation stage, several methods (or their combination) can be used. The selection, quantity, type and arrangement of methods largely depend on the amount of available data, know-how, skills and needs. While using too many methods can result in data scattering or data loss, choosing only a single method may not be enough to present a clear, complete and logical picture of the threats. Being aware of the common features, similarities, limitations and errors, it is advisable to analyze the differences in the methods presented, which may help make the right choice. Considering the variety of changes that affect the specifics of the products implemented, the ability to accurately select risk assessment methods is a serious problem that requires great flexibility, knowledge and experience in making decisions.

   Risk management in the supply chain can be defined as

> a logically ordered set of rules, principles uniformly and continuously applied to the activities of the network of organizations involved, by linking with suppliers and customers, in various processes and activities that create value in the form of products as well as services provided to end consumers

> **(Kaczmarek, 2002)**

or "an activity or practice of dealing with risk, along the entire supply chain" (AQAP, 2070). Yet another definition states that it is "an individual's perception of that total potential loss associated with the disruption of the supply chain of a particular item from a particular supplier" (Ellis et al., 2010). Supply chain risk management includes:

■ identification – the process of verifying the project, contract and supplier, including relevant systems, processes or products, to identify and document the risk involved;

■ planning – developing and documenting an organized, comprehensive and interactive risk management strategy that includes the allocation of appropriate resources to accomplish this task;

■ reduction – the process of implementing strategies and methods to maintain the risk at an acceptable level in relation to the requirements and goals of the implemented project or contract;

■ monitoring – the process in which the implementation of risk reduction measures pertaining to specific requirements is systematically monitored and assessed;

■ documentation – the process that records, maintains and presents the results of various risk management activities.

It can be assumed that risk management covers two areas:

■ estimation (includes risk identification and analysis);
■ risk management (includes risk planning, reduction, monitoring and documentation).

Risk identification in the supply chain can be performed in relation to:

■ Processes – considering the risk in various product life cycle phases:
  – In the design process, the risk may be related to the availability of human resources and infrastructure or instrumentation necessary to design and manufacture a defense product, along with the presence of requirements not specified in the contract or technical specification and the difference between the result and the actual defense product operating conditions.
  – In the supply process, risk may occur in the performance of the contract, which depends on supplies of materials, the performance of specific services, alternative sources of supply and the consequences of their use.
  – In the technical process, risk occurs when problems turn out to be more difficult to solve than anticipated, which manifests itself in potential threats related to the design, implementation, compatibility of parts and subassemblies and their operation or technical uncertainty of execution.
■ Products – in the technological area, this applies to such elements as the state of technology advancement, practical possibilities of fulfilling contractual requirements. In the operational area, it applies to additional

testing, as well as testing related to reliability, durability and maintainability. Safety of use is of paramount importance.

■ Suppliers – includes the organization of the quality management system, the scope and results of the supplier's pre-contract assessment, the results of assessing whether the supplier can meet the quality requirements, as well as of the financing structure and compliance with the implementation schedule.

Risk classification is a way of communicating the degree of likelihood and consequences (effect) associated with a particular risk area identified (AQAP, 2070). Both applicants and implementers recognize three levels of risk:

■ First – high – where there exists a high probability that a nonconformity regarding a system, process or product will occur. As a consequence, the system, process, or product will create dangerous conditions or a threat to the operating personnel, and the supplier will comply with the parameters, delivery date or costs critical for the project or contract.

■ Second – moderate – where there exists a probability of non-compliance in terms of the system, process or product. Consequently, the system, process or product will harm the use, reliability or serviceability of the product, and the supplier may not comply with the performance, delivery date or cost requirements important for the project or contract.

■ Third – low – where it is unlikely that a system, process or product non-conformity will occur. Normal process variation is present. There are no unfavorable process tendencies. The consequence of the resulting non-compliance will have a small effect on both the product and the supplier's ability to meet the project or contract requirements in terms of parameters, delivery date or costs.

For supply chain risk to be properly assessed and monitored, the following must be taken into account:

■ the implementation of every project carries risk, especially a brand-new one; proper risk management leading to its reduction to an acceptable level depends on the skillful and appropriate application of the method selected;

■ it is necessary to establish and formalize the risk assessment and documentation principles;

■ it is advisable to appoint a competent risk management team;
■ optimization of product implementation process costs is possible only through the effective identification of threats at the customer requirement review stage, as well as proper risk management to minimize them;
■ risk assessment should be an element of a functioning quality management system as there is no effective process management without risk management;
■ for risk management activities to be effective (implemented, maintained and improved), they should be treated as a continuous process, requiring data collection, analysis improvement and risk assessment throughout the product implementation process.

Effective risk management is impossible without risk assessment, which can be carried out either qualitatively or quantitatively, and makes it possible to estimate the probability of the occurrence and potential impact of the previously identified risks. The starting point for qualitative risk analysis can include such things as (Szymonik, Zarządzanie, 2014):

■ a risk management plan;
■ a list of identified risks along with their division into categories, considering logistic processes (including the design, supply and after-sales service stages) and logistics systems in the micro and macro dimensions;
■ a report on the progress in achieving the set logistic goals (e.g. 4W – the right place, time, quantity and quality or 7W – the right place, time, quantity, quality, price, product, information);
■ characteristics of the type of logistic solutions used in the implementation of activities related to the type of production (e.g. discrete, small series, serial, mass), organization of production flows (e.g. rhythmic and non-rhythmic, flexible production systems), location and distribution of individual devices participating in the production process (e.g. object, technological, mixed, manual, machine, mechanized, automated), product features (design, structure, complexity, processing degree, manufacturing technology), material inventory rules (e.g. joint inventory management, supplier inventory management, joint planning, forecasting and restocking);
■ characteristics of the accuracy of the data used in risk identification and description (these data should be assessed in terms of their reliability and availability);

■ a set of probability scales and measures of the impact of threat occurrence adopted at the company;
■ a list of assumptions made in the process of identifying and assessing risk sources.

Each management process requires the selection of the right tools to achieve the set goal. The basic tools and techniques used for qualitative risk analysis include the following (Wirkus et al., 2014):

■ a list of risk probabilities and consequences (either numerical or descriptive scales are used for both probability – e.g. very high, moderate, low and very low – as well as for risk effects – e.g. very severe, severe, moderate, mild and very mild);
■ risk probability and impact assessment matrix, which makes it possible to consider all the above-mentioned quantities and assess them (Table 3.2).

In the qualitative assessment of risk analysis, linear and logarithmic scales are used. In the case of probability, the scale starts with "0" – impossible event and ends with "1" – certain (deterministic) event. The entire matrix is divided into three areas, denoting the mild (the brightest area), moderate (middle area) and high-risk areas (the darkest area).

Quantitative risk analysis is often preceded by qualitative research. The input materials for the quantitative risk analysis include:

■ a risk management plan;
■ a list of identified risks;

Table 3.2 Matrix of Probability and Effects of an Event

Probability					
0.9	0.05	0.09	0.18	0.36	0.72
0.7	0.04	0.07	0.14	0.28	0.56
0,5	0.03	0.05	0.1	0.2	0.4
0.3	0.02	0.03	0.06	0.12	0.24
0.1	0.01	0.01	0.02	0.04	0.08
0	0.05	0.1	0.2	0.4	0.8
	Effects on the Process				

Source: Compiled based on: M. Wirkus, H. Roszkowski, E. Dostatni, W. Gierulski, Zarzadzanie projektem, PWE, Warsaw, 2014, p. 162.

- a list of risk hierarchies;
- a list of risks for further analysis;
- historical data;
- expert opinions and the results of other planning processes in the implementation.

The tools used for quantitative analysis differ in terms of their complexity. The most frequently used include:

- surveys (they are conducted among logisticians – decision-makers and experts – to determine the probability and impact of risk along the supply chain);
- sensitivity analysis (makes it possible to identify risks with the greatest potential impact on the course of the logistics process along the supply chain);
- decision tree analysis (establishes a diagram of consequences together with their specific probability and costs, including each of the possible logical event paths that may occur in the supply chain on a micro or macro scale during process implementation).

In practice, quantitative risk analysis is performed using the estimation method, also known as the Delphi expert consensus method. It is a subjective method as it is based on the experts' own judgment. It requires in-depth knowledge of the surveyed areas of the unit. Each of the group members assigns an appropriate level of risk to the previously selected areas. In this method, the level of risk assigned to particular areas and tasks is subjective as it is determined based on the evaluator's judgment. Risk analysis using the estimation method includes the following stages (Kulińska, 2011):

- an expert group is established;
- each group member, acting independently, i.e. without consulting with others, creates his own ranking list based on the assessment of risk severity; the number of points assigned to an item depends on the number of separate tasks;
- the task that should be implemented first receives the highest number of points; each subsequent task receives 1 fewer point – the last task on the list receives 1 point;
- points assigned to tasks by all group experts are summed up;

- task hierarchy is established in descending order, starting with the one that received the highest number of points;
- to express the obtained result as a percentage, the sum of points for all tasks is divided by the number of points received by the first task on the list and then multiplied by 100%.

The result of quantitative risk analysis for the achievement of goals in the supply chain may be a probabilistic analysis (including forecasts of logistic costs and task completion times), the probability of achieving logistics and time cost goals or the determination of trends characterizing the results of quantitative risk analysis (such information can be obtained by performing a quantitative analysis several times). The result of the planned risk responses is the process of developing procedure and activity variants that reduce the risks and increase the potential benefits for the formulated processes in the system that operates within the supply chain.

The risk response plan is a key step in the risk management process as it develops methods for responding to both favorable and unfavorable events. The effectiveness of planning the response to the risks of endangered tasks directly impacts the increase or decrease of the risk of implementing the planned supply chain processes. Any planned response must be proportional to the effects of unfavorable phenomena, eliminate the impact of a given threat in a cost-effective manner and be implemented on time.

Several strategies are commonly used in the risk response planning process. For each type of risk, the management plan should be selected in such a way that the actions taken are as effective as possible. The most popular strategies include (Szymonik & Bielecki, 2015; Wirkus et al., 2014):

- Risk avoidance – consists in modifying the logistics process implementation plan or the logistics system itself to eliminate a given risk (unfortunately, it is impossible to eliminate all threats in practice) or to favorably change the related conditions.
- Risk transfer – consists in transferring the effects of risk to another entity. This action is very effective in finance. It is usually associated with the need to pay a premium to the entity/person assuming the risk (e.g. insurance in the event of cargo loss, fire or in cases where cargo is washed off the deck).
- Risk Mitigation – the most common of all risk response strategies. It involves taking specific actions to reduce the likelihood or impact of a risk.

■ Risk acceptance – the risk is acknowledged and action is taken to minimize any consequences resulting from potential unfavorable phenomena. It is a deliberate decision by risk managers not to make any changes to the project plan related to the occurrence of a given adverse event. There are two basic types of risk acceptance: active and passive.

Passive acceptance is accepting a risk without taking any action to resolve the issues related to it. Active acceptance consists in acknowledging the risk but creating a special action plan in the event of an adverse event and, in some cases, the so-called plan of retreat.

The result of proper risk assessment and definition is a contingency plan. Developing an emergency plan beforehand may significantly reduce the costs of responding to the occurrence of a given unfavorable phenomenon. The outcomes of the risk response planning process are as follows (Szymonik & Bielecki, 2015; Wirkus et al., 2014):

■ risk response plan;
■ residual risk record (a list of risks that remain in the logistics system along the supply chain, following the implementation of risk avoidance, transfer and mitigation strategies);
■ secondary risk record – these are risks that arise due to the implementation of a risk response strategy and are a consequence of contractual provisions (contracts with the scope of responsibilities that are assumed by other entities participating in the implementation of processes occurring in the implementation of supply chain tasks);
■ amount of necessary reserves for logistics task implementation (these are the so-called financial and resource buffers reserved by managers in the event of unfavorable situations, e.g. in the case of rising fuel costs).

Based on the materials obtained from the Audit and Corporate Risk Management Office of a Polish petroleum corporation, one can conclude that critical elements in supply chain risk management, both in the micro (single link) and macro dimensions (along the entire supply chain), are as follows:

■ refined assessment methodology, considering the risks related to such things as:
  – strategy (e.g. selection of a key supplier, recipient);
  – finances in logistics costs (e.g. exchange rate changes for foreign purchases);

- business processes (e.g. risks resulting from inadequate or unreliable logistics processes such as procurement, storage, distribution, customer service and ordering, packaging);
- external factors (risk caused by activities outside the supply chain and related to the behavior of sub-suppliers, by competition, as well as political, legal and technological changes);
- IT (e.g. the risk resulting from improper management of ICT resources processed with the use of obsolete information technology);
- organization and management (e.g. risk related to relationships with stakeholders and resulting from an inappropriate structure of the supply chain, delegation system, authorizations, as well as inappropriate employee conduct);
- physical security (e.g. risk related to the protection of logistic loads during transport and storage – fire, theft, accidents, cargo getting washed off the deck).

■ developing control mechanisms for all supply chain participants for such purposes as:
  - risk prevention (preventive control);
  - risk materialization detection and impact mitigation (detection control);
■ control mechanism evaluation – the same for all;
■ creating a uniform model, which should include risk identification, risk assessment, gross risk assessment,[1] control mechanism assessment, net risk assessment, as well as development and implementation of corrective action plans, risk assessment monitoring and reporting;
■ establishing risk management coordination mechanisms and structures;
■ providing tools and methodological support for supply chain process participants;
■ corrective action plans aimed at improving the process of managing individual types of risk (by improving the existing or introducing new control mechanisms);
■ monitoring and reporting risk assessments by risk and process owners;
■ designating risk owners who:
  - answer to their superiors or a competent unit for risk level assessment;
  - are responsible for supervision and coordination of activities related to the development, implementation and execution of measures against risk;
  - identify and assess risk, develop corrective action plans with process owners, collect information on events that prove risk materialization, monitor the effectiveness of the risk management process;

■ designating process/sub-process owners who answer to their superior or another unit for:
  – coordinating the process of testing control mechanisms and risk assessment in their processes and sub-processes;
  – validating gross and net risk levels identified in the process and sub-processes and assessed as part of the self-assessment;
  – agreeing with the risk owners upon remedial action plans addressing the risks identified in the process and sub-processes, as well as implementing and monitoring such plans;
■ appointing persons supervising the implementation of control activities in the processes in which they participate and are obliged to work with the risk and process owners during the control mechanism testing period and assess the identified risk; this includes designing new control mechanisms (control owners are typically employees specified in corrective action plans as the parties responsible for plan implementation and control mechanism modification).

Risk management should be an integral part of the management process, which begins at the stage of organizing the logistics system and continues until the end of its operation. It must also be noted that having good analysis and assessment of adverse events and their impact without specific response plans designed to address such risks is simply not enough.

A vital link in the process of supply chain risk management is the logisticians, who should be prepared to react to unfavorable situations by acting to neutralize the effects of threats. Their conduct should be in line with the previously developed and approved procedures to facilitate the elimination of the given event's impact on the one hand, and protect the logisticians themselves against unjustified repercussions from their superiors or due to the applicable law on the other. It is worth remembering that we live in a world dominated by a culture that does not tolerate mistakes and failures.

3.6 Management Using Reference Models in the Supply Chain

The tool most frequently used for the description and comprehensive analysis of the supply chain is the *Supply Chain Operation Reference Model* published by the SCC (*Supply-Chain Council*). With its initial version released in the fall of 1996, the SCOR is a response to the increasing complexity of the business environment and the challenge of a holistic approach to supply chain management. The model is based on five main SCM processes: planning, procurement, production, delivery and returns, and identifies four levels of detail. The model does not consider such elements as administration, sales, technological development, design or after-sales service.

Competitors to SCOR include the *SCM Model* proposed by the Global Supply Chain Forum (GSCF) Association, which is based on eight main SCM processes (GSCF, 2021):

    I. Customer Relationship Management;
    II. Customer Service Management;
   III. Demand Management;
   IV. Order Fulfillment;
    V. Manufacturing Flow Management;
   VI. Supplier Relationship Management;
 VII. Product Development and Commercialization;
VIII. Returns Management.

3.6.1 Customer Relationship Management – CRM

In simple terms, CRM (Customer Relationship Management) is managing relations with current and potential clients – it is a set of tasks, procedures and tools necessary in contact with counterparties. Although the company management concepts that give paramount attention to the relationship with the buyer appeared many years ago, only recently did it achieve high popularity (itcube.pl/crm, 2204.2021).

Keep in mind that CRM is not just a technology-based phenomenon. Here are some examples of how experts see it (Szymonik, Zarządzanie zapasami, 2013):

First. CRM is a term used to describe known phenomena and behaviors. Take your local grocery store as an example. It has quite a few regular customers, and the store clerk is intelligent enough to roughly remember what their preferences are. Modern technology makes it possible to implement a similar model, but on a much larger scale.

Second. CRM is more a strategy than a process, designed to better understand and fulfill the needs of an enterprise's potential customers. Of course, we do have access to technological solutions that enable the collection of customer data and their consolidation at a central data warehouse.

Third. While the basics of CRM are very simple, their practical implementation differs from the basic assumptions due to the dependence of the company's management on technological solutions, as well as working under pressure to quickly achieve tangible results. There also occurs an inherent pursuit of solutions already introduced by the competition. This leads directly to the purchase of technology without a prior precise specification of assumptions, resulting in the project's ultimate failure.

Fourth. CRM is a customer-focused business strategy that necessitates changes in the enterprise's functioning, which must be supported by technological solutions. In other words, you first need to define your goals, reorganize your business to achieve them and only then start talking to your suppliers.

Fifth. CRM is a process aimed at profiting from customer relationships. To achieve this, marketing, sales and service departments should operate as one team and exchange information with each other. This is made possible by introducing an appropriate computer system.

3.6.2 Customer Service Management – CSM

It may sometimes prove difficult to find significant differences between such terms as *customer relationship management* and *customer service management*, but upon closer examination, it is evident that CRM is more a strategy than a practical action, whereas CSM is the actual implementation of all functions such as planning, organizing, motivating and controlling for past, present and future enterprise customers in the supply chain. As such, the responsibilities of the person managing customer service and customer relations at a company include the following (Szymonik, Zarządzanie zapasami, 2013):

- negotiations and contacts with key customers;
- working with partners and counterparties;
- consultations for both internal and external clients;
- managing teams working directly and indirectly with clients;
- monitoring and analyzing the quality of customer service and the systems used to improve it, e.g. SAP Customer Relationship Management Systems;
- supervising marketing information systems (including market research, market potential analysis, customer satisfaction surveys, service quality, supervising the usage and substantive content of customer databases);

- setting target segments for marketing, sales and after-sales service activities;
- marketing planning;
- actively working with other company departments, particularly marketing and sales departments;
- working with operational units;
- managing a loyalty program for the company's customers;
- achieving planned goals (in accordance with the previously adopted budget plan);
- standard-setting;
- conducting employee training, participating in conferences, symposia, as well as training sessions;
- taking part in the preparation of exhibitions and trade fairs and other events with the participation of existing and potential customers; participating in the team selection process.

3.6.3 Demand Management – DM

Managing customer demand is about balancing demand and supply possibilities. Today, many systems are used to support these activities on many levels, including SAP systems (Kondariuk, 2021).

Demand Management defines production planning strategies for all products for which there is an independent demand (i.e. originating from the market). The SAP system allows you to choose both basic production planning strategies, i.e. make-to-stock, make-to-order, assemble-to-order, design-to-order, as well as many variants that combine the features of these basic strategies. Thanks to this, it is possible to flexibly select a strategy suitable not only for the specific conditions of a given company but also for each manufactured and sold product.

The primary role of Demand Management is to define the quantities and deadlines for delivering finished goods to individual customers, which is aimed at maximizing customer satisfaction (ensuring the greatest possible product availability and the lowest possible cost of maintaining products catered to individual customer needs).

The sum of the required product quantities is called the total demand (demand program). This demand may comprise such things as (Kondariuk, 2021):

- customer requirements generated in the sales module as sales orders for a specific quantity of a given product required for a specific delivery time;

■ planned independent requirements, reflecting the demand for the organization's products not originating from a specific customer (such demand is the result of forecasting and long-term planning processes).

One of the most important planning and organizational decisions is defining and developing a model of reaction within the organization to market demand for a particular assortment. This greatly affects the remaining SAP planning components and has a significant impact on economic results, enabling the achievement of overarching goals for the planning processes. To create a demand program and manage it effectively, it is necessary to define the so-called *demand management strategy* for individual products.

The planning strategy represents a method of handling demand and determines when and under what conditions the organization takes action to meet customer needs. Using an appropriate strategy allows you to decide whether production activities are to be triggered based on sales orders (*make-to-order production strategies*) or whether it is economically justified that production not be directly triggered by unit sales (*make-to-stock production strategies*).

To achieve the overarching goal of your planning efforts, you should group your finished goods into assortment groups according to your individual planning needs. On the one hand, assortment groups should be as small as possible for greater *transparency and consistency* in planning processes, whereas on the other hand, there should be enough of them to handle all individual ways of dealing with needs (*flexibility*). It is worth noting that each assortment group will have a demand management strategy assigned to it.

SAP supports many strategies for responding to external demand in the organization. Such strategies are predefined but also configurable, and as such, the degree of their adaptation to the needs of specific organizations is very high. The division of all products into assortment groups and assigning them to individual strategies is a difficult task and requires extensive knowledge of the production process and experience in the field of SAP.

3.6.4 Order Fulfillment – OF

Order fulfillment is generally a process that begins with the receipt of the order and continues until cash is received. It consists of the following:

■ collecting orders;
■ order processing (configuration);

- price calculation;
- defining the completion date;
- order delivery tracking;
- providing the necessary information to customers and carriers;
- making the necessary changes to the database;
- consideration of returns and complaints;
- customer satisfaction survey;
- checking the confirmation of receipt of cash.

3.6.5 Manufacturing Flow Management – MFM

Delivering to the customers high-quality products in the right amount and on time is a major challenge for production and service companies. Understanding the basic principles of material and information flow management on a global scale is the first step to meeting high market demands and increasing customer satisfaction (Dubiel, 2021).

3.6.6 Supplier Relationship Management – SRM

The term refers to the planning, control and information systems that connect the company with its suppliers operating at the top of the supply chain (Bozarth & Handfield, 2007).

Effective supplier relationship management is an undoubted advantage of any dynamic enterprise, and over time, it is bound to become a requirement for every properly functioning organization – including the supply chain. A special role in the entire process is played by people who are indirectly related to the process of generating demand on the side of the recipient but are not necessarily responsible for making purchases themselves. The way the demand is created has a significant impact on how attractive the recipient appears to the supplier. Therefore, it is the recipient's responsibility to diagnose the current situation at their company, its organizational structure, as well as both the need and readiness for changes.

Among the IT solutions supporting supplier relationship management that are available on the market is the SAP SRM module (*SAP Supplier Relationship Management*), which allows you to increase the added value of supplier relationships in all categories of expenses, regardless of time (Mika & Godek, 2021). SAP SRM enables the reduction of costs of materials sold and rationalization of the supply base and ensures a quick return on investment. It integrates operations throughout the entire supply chain, stimulating cooperation between suppliers by automating goods and service purchase processes involving all suppliers. SAP SRM covers the full supply cycle – from strategic sourcing to operational sourcing and supplier cooperation – providing the benefits of using consolidated content and master data. Thanks to SAP SRM, it is possible to work with each of the suppliers in the scope of all purchased goods and services.

Supplier relationship management provides tangible business benefits in many fields, including (Pokora, 2021):

- further decrease in the total ownership costs;
- increase in revenues and profit;
- process efficiency improvement;
- supply chain risk management;
- improved innovation;
- development of competencies;
- joint problem solving;
- improved level of service;
- sharing expertise.

3.6.7 *Product Development and Commercialization – PDC*

The market development strategy consists in offering a new or improved product in a market currently served by a specific supply chain. However, such products must still fulfill their basic purpose in a given market. Changes in product characteristics increase the product's value for the buyer, causing increased demand and, consequently, increased sales of such products. Product development may take place through varying the quality of a given product, offering new models or product sizes. When using this strategy, supply chain participants must consider the necessity of technical changes in the product, as well as of testing the improved product and its increased promotion, which entails additional costs. However, practice shows that products offering qualitative improvements are also pricier, effectively covering the costs incurred by companies – i.e. supply chain links.

The process of planning new products typically includes the following stages (Kulasa & Kryzhanivska, 2021):

- seeking a new product idea;
- idea evaluation and selection;
- marketing analysis;

■ technical development;
■ market testing;
■ commercialization.

Figure 3.4 and Table 3.3 specify the stages of the new product development process.

The process consists of logically consecutive steps: idea generation, selection, idea selection, product development design and commercialization. The processes of developing new consumer products and industrial products are similar; however, there may be some differences in terms of searching for ideas and commercialization in certain cases.

When introducing new products, the following stages should be considered (Szymonik, Zarządzanie, 2013):

■ **When** – choosing the right time to enter the market can be a critical point in the process of commercializing a new product. In this respect, companies can opt for:
 – Being the first to enter – the advantage of this strategy is the ability to gain an advantage over competitors by blocking some distribution channels and achieving market leadership while the disadvantage is that if the product fails, the company risks losing its good reputation.

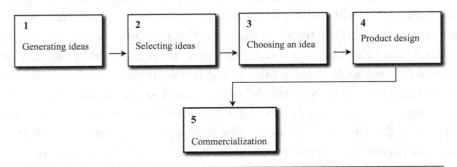

1) Seeking ideas and information in the environment,
2) Predicting sales, estimating return on capital,
3) Concept testing, verification of return on capital,
4) Research and development, model building, market test, economic analysis of production, product characteristics adjustment,
5) The final phase of new product development, where the decision to mass-produce and bring the product to market is made; it includes prototype production, marketing plan development, final return on capital assessment, commencing production, marketing plan implementation, full-scale production.

Figure 3.4 New product development process. Source: Compiled based on: E. Michalski, *Marketing, podręcznik akademicki*, PWN, Warszawa 2003, p. 206.

Table 3.3 The Stages of Commercialization

Stage	Actions
Idea stage	It assumes collecting information and verifying the potential uniqueness of the given invention, product, service, technology
Incubation stage	It concerns the subjective analysis of the commercialization potential, development opportunities, verification of property rights, as well as the preparation of a commercialization business plan and obtaining external funding
Demonstration stage (prototype)	Preparation of the final version of the subject of commercialization
Promotion stage	Preparation of the final version of the entity for commercialization
Maintenance stage	Further development and maintenance of products on the market

Source: Compiled based on: M. Koszembar-Wiklik, *Komunikacja marketingowa a komercjalizacja nowych technologii i produktów*, Zeszyty Naukowe Politechniki Śląskiej 2016 z. 93 No. kol. 1957, p. 256.

- Parallel entries – it consists in synchronizing one's entry onto the market with a competitor – i.e. if another company enters, so do we – the costs of promotion are distributed in some way.
- Late entry – you can delay your entry by waiting for a competitor to introduce their product to the market. This option allows you to save on the costs of consumer education and allows you to reveal possible product defects that can be eliminated. The company also learns the size of the market but simultaneously loses the benefits of being the first. If a new product is set to replace an older one, an enterprise may delay its introduction until the stock of the old product has been used up. The sale of seasonal products may also be put on hold until the onset of the relevant season.
- ■ **Where** – the company must decide whether to introduce a new product in a single locality, in several localities within a region or on the domestic or international market. Few companies have the resources necessary to introduce new products to their distribution network on a nationwide or global scale. Further, companies also work on how to gain market control over time. Small businesses choose an attractive city and run a swift market-entry campaign and then proceed to enter the markets of other cities

one by one. Larger companies launch their products in one region and then move to the next. Enterprises with a nationwide distribution network introduce their products straight to the nationwide market. As part of the gradual expansion marketing, the company must evaluate alternative markets in terms of their attractiveness, with the main evaluation criteria being the market potential, the local reputation of the company, distribution costs, media fees, the influence of a given area on other areas, as well as market penetration by competition. This allows the company to rank the most important markets and create a geographic expansion plan.

- **Who** – acting within the framework of gradually conquered markets, the enterprise must direct its distribution and promotion to the best groups of future customers. Presumably, the company has already identified its main future customers by this point. The main future customers purchasing new consumer products should be early adopters of the product who buy it frequently and in large quantities and who simultaneously shape opinions about the product and can be reached easily at a relatively low cost.
- **How** – the company must develop an action plan for introducing new products in gradually captured markets. Management can use network planning techniques such as critical path planning to prioritize and coordinate new product launches.

3.6.8 Returns Management – RM

The literature defines returns in various ways, including in the following ways:

- A return is a tangible property unsuitable for the user due to a defect or damage, which the user wishes to continue using once it has been repaired (Szołtysek, 2009),
- Returns may be quantitative (too much or too little goods delivered), qualitative (the goods are non-compliant in terms of the desired physical and chemical properties) or assortment-based (where the recipient receives goods other than those ordered) (Wanagos, 2010),
- Returns can erode profitability for a firm and can impact relationships with customers and end-users, as well as impact a firm's reputation with stakeholders (Mollenkopf et al., 2007).

While exemplary quality management helps to eliminate many sources of errors, returns remain a daily practice of supply chain participants. The reasons behind them vary and may include defective materials and products, errors, incomplete shipments, product seasonality, overstock, wrong recipient details, company bankruptcy, as well as other reasons. Returns can be divided into such categories as (Sadowski, 2010):

■ returns related to product servicing, repairs and spare part replacement;
■ consequence-free returns made during the warranty period;
■ returns made after ceasing to use the product (e.g. at the end of a lease term);
■ returns due to the end of the product's life cycle (*end-of-use*);
■ returns due to customers changing their minds;
■ returns made under guarantees and warranties;
■ returns upon the end of the product use period;
■ returns of returnable packaging, e.g. bottles;
■ returns of products destined for the secondary market, e.g. books, clothes;
■ returns due to the economic or physical wear and tear of products (*end-of-life*).

Although most shipments are delivered to the destination without errors, any possible returns generate additional costs and time loss, both of which are associated with a negative impact on work efficiency and customer dissatisfaction. For returns not to be a nuisance for customers, they should be managed properly by the company. Returns management is a deliberately organized and connected set of elements such as repairing, regenerating, transporting and storing goods returned by customers, as well as the relations between them and their properties that determine the reverse flow of goods (Lysenko-Ryba, 2020). In practice, this requires that a corporate officer be designated and procedures be developed beforehand, including in the scope of:

■ transportation routes;
■ returns acceptance methods;
■ deciding what to do with returned goods;
■ acknowledging the return;
■ analyzing the cause of the return and measuring its effects.

Note

1. Gross risk assessment – before the introduction of controls; net risk assessment – after the introduction of controls.

Chapter 4

Safety of Transport, Storage and Food Economy: The Example of Poland and the European Union

4.1 New Conditions Affecting Transport Safety

A modern economy cannot function without safe, sustainable, green and competitive land, air and sea transport. The European Union is making a lot of effort by developing a White Paper on Transport strategy and allocating funds for its development and environmental protection (Biała Księga Plan utworzenia jednolitego europejskiego obszaru transportu, 2021).

In the period of increased mobility of society, the transport policy considers new challenges and solves a number of problems in the European and global dimensions, which impact transport safety. These include:

4.1.1 Firstly

The Roadmap to a Single European Transport Area – Towards a competitive and resource-efficient transport system, published in the White Paper on Transport, is a far-reaching document with very ambitious goals. The overriding goal of future actions is to create a Single European Transport Area ultimately. It is to be an area with a highly competitive and resource-efficient transport sector. These expectations can be achieved in a situation

DOI: 10.4324/9781003286110-4

where (Biała Księga Plan utworzenia jednolitego europejskiego obszaru transportu, 2021):

- the number of conventionally fueled cars in urban transport is halved by 2030 and eliminated from cities by 2050; achieving essentially CO_2-free logistics in large urban centers by 2030;
- 30% of road freight over distances greater than 300 km is shifted to other modes of transport, e.g. rail or waterborne transport by 2030, reaching more than 50% by 2050;
- the European high-speed rail network is completed by 2050;
- a major part of medium-distance passenger traffic is by rail by 2050;
- a fully functional EU-wide multi-modal TEN-T[1] core network is created by 2030 and a high-quality and high-capacity network by 2050;
- all core network airports are connected to the rail network, preferably high-speed rail, and all major seaports are well connected to rail freight and, where possible, the inland waterway system by 2050;
- there is a transition to the full application of the "user pays" and "polluter pays" principles.

4.1.2 Secondly

Transport and its impact on the economy and human life meant that it became the subject of interest of important EU institutions and bodies, which include departments of the European Commission (executive body): Mobility and Transport and Maritime Economy and Fisheries; European Parliament's Committee on Transport and Tourism; Transport, Telecommunications and Energy Council; European Economic and Social Committee's Section for Transport, Energy, Infrastructure and the Information Society; European Committee of the Regions' Committee for Regional Cohesion Policy; European Investment Bank's Trans-European Networks; EU Agencies, including European Maritime Safety Agency, European Aviation Safety Agency, European Union Agency for Railways, Executive Agency for Competitiveness and Innovation (EACI), European Union Agency for the Space Programme. All Member States are obliged to participate in the work of these institutions actively and fulfill the obligations arising from the work of these bodies.

4.1.3 Thirdly

Several land, sea and air transport projects have been planned to create safe transport in the EU.

4.1.4 Fourthly

Rising petrol and diesel prices are a nuisance for transporters and consumers. The analysis of the consumer price indexes provided by Statistics Poland shows that in recent years, the prices of propellants and lubricants have most often increased compared to the previous year. The research shows the most important components of the functioning of a transport enterprise are the cost of:

- propellants and consumables;
- drivers' salaries (including business trips);
- employer's social insurance;
- road tolls.

The analysis of the available financial data is as follows (Waśkiewicz & Kamińska, 2018):

- The weighted average costs of 1 truck-kilometer in 2016 and 2017 in the surveyed companies of international road transport, in which the connections with the EU markets dominated the freight, amounted to PLN 3.85/truck-km and PLN 4.00/vehicle mileage. Compared to the average unit costs in 2009, the average unit costs in this area increased by around 33% by 2017.
- The structure of the weighted average costs of 1 vehicle-kilometer in 2016 and 2017 was dominated by the costs of propellants and consumables (39.1% and 38.6%, respectively), drivers' salaries (including business trips), the employer's insurance costs (24.7% and 24.9%, respectively) and road tolls (14.6% and 13.2%, respectively).
- By the end of 2017, compared to 2009, the average road tolls more than doubled, the average drivers' salaries (including travel) and the employer's social security costs increased by about 79%, and fuel expenses increased by about 36% on average.
- The weighted average costs of 1 truck-km in 2016 and 2017 in the surveyed companies of international road transport, in which the connections with eastern markets dominated the freight, amounted to PLN 3.83/truck-km and PLN 3.99/truck-km, respectively. Compared to the average unit costs in 2009, the average costs of 1 truck-kilometer increased by approximately 52% by 2017.
- In the structure of the weighted average costs of 1 truck-kilometer, in 2016 and 2017, the costs of propellants and consumables (36.9% and

36.8%, respectively), drivers' salaries (including business trips), the employer's social insurance costs (26.1% and 26.6%, respectively) and costs of insurance of means of transport and tax on means of transport (11.3% and 11.8%, respectively) were dominant. In the average costs of 1 truck-km, road tolls accounted for 12.4% and 10.1%, respectively.

■ By the end of 2017, compared to 2009, the average tolls increased more than fourfold, the drivers' salaries (including business trips) and the employer's costs of social insurance increased by 89%, the costs of insurance of means of transport and transport tax more than quadrupled, and fuel expenses increased by 46% on average.

■ The average freight rates in the surveyed companies, mostly the connections with other EU markets in 2016 and 2017, were PLN 4.04/truck-km and PLN 4.17/truck-km, respectively.

■ The freight rates in the surveyed companies, mostly the connections with eastern markets in 2016 and 2017, averaged PLN 4.14/truck-km and PLN 4.17/truck-km, respectively.

4.1.5 Fifthly

Traffic congestion paralyzes both road and air traffic. It costs Europe about 1% of its annual GDP; moreover, both the volume of freight and passenger transport will increase in the future (Szymonik, Zarzadzanie bezpieczeństwem, 2016). INRIX, an international information service for drivers, has published a report on the traffic situation in 200 cities in 38 countries. The capital of Colombia has become the undisputed leader in this ranking. Bogotá residents lose 272 hours in traffic jams each year. Rome came second with 254 hours. The capital of Ireland, Dublin, takes third place in this disgraceful ranking with 246 hours. The research results, published by INRIX, caused the greatest stir in Italy. Among the top 20 cities in the world with the most traffic are Rome (7th, 226 hours), Florence (14th, 195 hours) and Naples (17th, 186 hours). According to an indicator compiled by the European Commission's Joint Research Centre, the average number of hours per year in congestion per vehicle varies (Table 4.1).

The representatives of the Italian Green party emphasized that the hours lost by drivers in traffic jams are another factor, in addition to the dangerous level of smog which reduces the quality of life. As a solution to this problem, they indicate a drastic reduction of private cars in the traffic. In the discussed ranking, the capital of Poland took 20th place. Warsaw drivers

Table 4.1 The Average Number of Hours Spent in Congestion Per Year Per Vehicle in Selected Countries

Country	Number of hours
Finland	20
Poland	25
France	30
Hungary	28
Ukraine	40
Malta	75

Source: Compiled based on *Europejski semestr – zestawienie informacji tematycznych transport*, https://ec.europa.eu, March 7, 2021.

spend 173 hours in traffic jams a year. Kraków was classified in 78th place (125 hours) (Łubiński, 2021).

There is also a lot to do in passenger car travel. The time comes to abandon the individual approach (owning a car) in favor of collective (alternative means of transport), which will significantly help unblock crowded routes. In addition to professional car fleet providers, there are platforms supported by web or smartphone applications based on the peer-to-peer concept, i.e. enabling individual users to enter the market and exchange services without owning a vehicle fleet. Professionally managed fleets of passenger cars and bicycles are significant drivers of mobility in urban areas. Car sharing has long been a segment of urban transport, but it is still a niche service.

4.1.6 Sixthly

Infrastructure is not developed equally well in all EU countries. For example, most countries in the eastern part of the EU lack high-speed rail lines and traditional railways are often in poor condition. Moreover, even in the EU countries with a relatively good level of transport infrastructure development, the constant increase in demand for professional transport and logistics services for business entities means that the infrastructure does not always meet the expectations and economic development needs. Thus, similarly to Poland, in all EU countries, the level of infrastructure development is

Table 4.2 The Infrastructure Quality Assessment Based on Several Factors – Poland's Ranking

Description	2015	2018
Place in the world ranking (out of 140 countries)	63	27

Source: Compiled based on *Competitiveness Report 2019*, https://www.8-international .com//wp-content/uploads/2019/10/competitiveness-report-eight-advisory -2019.pdf, October 4, 2019.

perceived as one of the 15 basic barriers to the development of enterprises (Rolbiecki, 2012).

Despite the implemented infrastructure investments, the transport network in Poland is still of low quality and poses a serious threat to the effective functioning of supply chains. The research of the World Economic Forum concerning the global competitiveness of the economy also points to the infrastructural limitations in Poland. It should be emphasized that in the final three years (2015–2018), there was an evaluation with 36 items. The infrastructure quality based on a general quality assessment, the road networks, the railway network density, the number of air connections, the electricity network quality and the water supply system reliability is shown in Table 4.2.

4.1.7 *Seventhly*

The policy of the European Union is dedicated to the development of transport, which creates jobs, influences economic growth and does not harm the natural environment. Therefore, this branch includes rail transport, provided that it overcomes such obstacles as (Rabsztyn, 2013): equalizing domestic and foreign carriers in terms of law (domestic passenger transport is mostly closed to competition, and most domestic passenger trains run on the basis of contracts with state-owned carriers concluded directly, without tenders); simplifying the procedures for entering the market by new carriers by reducing administrative costs; unleashing the railway potential by replacing the national policies of individual countries with international actions (a network of infrastructure managers should be created to develop the Trans-European Transport Network (TEN-T) – a network of freight corridors and the European Rail Traffic Management System (ERTMS) – a European train control system); harmonizing standards and regulations in EU countries by transferring national powers to the European Union Agency for Railways

(ERA), which will allow wheeled vehicles to operate and issue safety certificates for all railways in the EU.

4.1.8 Eighthly

Competition – the European transport sector is confronted with increasing competitive pressures in the fast-growing global transport markets.

4.1.9 Ninthly

Transport companies implementing services on the national and European scale must pay special attention to the safety of people, cargo and processes in the supply chain, including ecological and social protection.

Human safety is a matter of concern for all modes of transport. Still, the most dangerous and socially costly, and, at the same time, the most widely used for the carriage of passengers is road transport (road accidents account for about 95% of all transport accidents) (Strategia rozwoju transportu do 2020 roku, 2013). Therefore, road safety is a priority in this regard. Its improvement requires taking actions that will significantly reduce the number of deaths. It should be noted that European roads are considered the safest in the world, and the number of road fatalities dropped by 23% from 2010 to 2019. Still, thousands of people die every year – pedestrians, drivers and passengers (Kwinta, 2021).

In rail transport, the fundamental factors influencing the safety condition are the technical condition of the railway infrastructure and the rolling stock, the functioning of railway crossings.

The improvement of traffic safety at railway crossings requires the implementation of the following intervention directions: observation (including filming) of crossings where the regulations are frequently violated; marking of particularly dangerous railway crossings with information boards; more intensive modernization of these crossings; elimination (if possible) of one-level crossings in favor of two-level crossings (viaducts and tunnels).

Civil aviation safety is currently perceived as a process of monitoring and maintaining a certain level of safety in three areas. First: systemic threats, which include (Krajowy Plan Bezpieczeństwa 2019–2022, 2019):

■ air traffic – total number of incidents, financing and resources of the national aviation supervision (CAA);

- standards set out in the "ICAO Annexes to the Chicago Convention applicable in Poland (in %)";
- the level of implementation of the National Programme for Civil Aviation Safety (NPfCAS);
- SMS effectiveness level of aviation organizations.

Second: European threats, which include:

- runway incursion;
- runway excursion;
- abnormal runway contact;
- fire, smoke & fumes;
- ground safety;
- controlled flight into terrain (CFIT);
- loss of control in flight;
- collision in the air and dangerous close-ups (mid-air collision (MAC)/aircraft proximity (AIRPROX));
- technical condition of SCF-NP and SCF-PP.3 aircraft (other than helicopters).

Third: domestic threats, which include:

- collisions with birds (birdstrike);
- wildlife hazard;
- unmanned aerial vehicle operations (RPAS);
- dazzling pilots with lights from the ground;
- glider towing related events (GTOW);
- incidents related to the transport of hazardous materials;
- helicopter events (HELI);
- FOD events.

Efforts for an effective maritime safety system will be based on the following directions: improving the standards of safe navigation by seagoing vessels; protecting shipping and ports against terrorist and criminal threats; developing the Maritime Search and Rescue Service (SAR) and improving cooperation of all services participating in rescue operations at sea; integrating VTS/VTMS and RIS; building and improving the National Maritime Safety System (including the Maritime Traffic Safety Supervision and Monitoring System (SMRM); the National Network of

Automatic Identification System (AIS-PL) Base Stations; the Early Warning System (EWS)).

In terms of ecological and social safety, transport is classified as one of the branches of the economy significantly contributing to air pollution (nitrogen oxides, carbon monoxide, volatile organic compounds, dust and solid particles) or greenhouse gas emissions. Therefore, the transport system based on sustainable development should maintain harmony between the system and its natural, cultural and socio-economic environment, involving the use of existing resources that enables their continued exploitation and preservation for future generations (McKinnon, 2016).

In the context of environmental protection, Polish transport has to cope with the challenges and external constraints on the horizon, such as the EU environmental protection policy, in particular the climate and emission limitations (including greenhouse gas emissions, as transport is responsible for roughly a quarter of the emissions). In the EU, these emissions in 2008 were distributed as follows: 12.8% was generated by air transport, 13.5% by sea transport, 0.7% by rail, 1.8% by inland waterway and 71.3% by road transport (Biała Księga Plan utworzenia jednolitego europejskiego obszaru transportu, 2021); the increasing struggle for access to increasingly limited resources of fossil fuels (oil, gas) translates into a rapid increase in fuel prices and thus deterioration of the economic efficiency of transport and the broader dimension of the competitiveness of the entire economy.

Future transport, which will have a slight negative impact on the environment, will be based on supporting: branch diversity and complementarity of means of transport within the system of national and international connections; transit organization solutions that pollute the environment the least; managing the demand for transport traffic; implementation of modern transport technologies reducing the negative environmental impacts (Gwilliam & Geerlings, 1994).

Practical measures will be directed at promoting energy efficiency through the development of intermodal transport in the carriage of goods; investing in a low-carbon economy through the elements of environmentally friendly transport (rail transport, sea transport and inland navigation); striving to create conditions conducive to shifting transport from road to rail, in particular at distances over 300 km; ecologically clean transport powered by alternative energy sources (e.g. fuel cells and hydrogen, electric, gas, hybrid, compressed air), along with a country-wide network of electric battery charging or swapping stations and hydrogen refueling networks; reducing transport congestion, in particular in urban areas, inter alia, by increasing the share of public transport in passenger transport, integrating transport in cities (including suburban commuting), optimizing and integrating urban transport and regional passenger transport systems, promoting pedestrian and bicycle traffic, organizing and developing delivery systems in cities and eliminating heavy cargo traffic and mass transport of dangerous goods through areas of intensive urban investment; promoting new forms of social mobility through: availability of travel information, integrated tariffs, delimiting residential areas without car access, developing teleworking system, wider use of video conferences, joint travel solutions and car sharing; modernizing and expanding (linear and point) transport infrastructure in line with EU and national environmental standards and requirements; modernizing all modes of transport (vehicles and other necessary devices and equipment) in order to bring them to the relevant EU and national standards and requirements of environmental protection; implementing innovative transport traffic management systems in individual branches and interoperable ones, contributing to the reduction of environmental pressures generated by transport (ITS – road transport, ERTMS – rail transport, SESAR – air transport, VTMS – maritime transport, RIS – river transport); implementing technical measures to reduce vibration and noise induced during the construction or modernization of transport connections and during the use of infrastructure by vehicles (e.g. freight trains in cities); continuous monitoring (indicators) of the impact of transport on the environment (Szymonik, 2013).

4.2 Safety Determinants of Transport Processes in Poland

4.2.1 General Introduction

In the most important documents concerning the national security system, i.e. the Constitution of the Republic of Poland, the National Security Strategy of the Republic of Poland of 2003, 2007, 2014, the Strategy of Development of the National Security System of the Republic of Poland 2022, much space is devoted to transport, emphasizing its role and importance for the proper functioning of the national economy and all security areas and sectors.

The White Book of National Security of the Republic of Poland includes a "transport" sector in the section concerning economic security to signify its rank and importance. However, the term transport is used in a different sense and context over 40 times in the same document.

It is also worth noting that all the above documents emphasize that one of the most important tasks of the state in the coming years will be expanding and modernizing the transport networks and ensuring a high level of transport services, which are not only crucial for the country's economic development but also the state security system. It is natural that a modern road and rail network, well-developed inland waterways, airports, seaports and infrastructure for accessing these ports, and an efficient public transport system enable the development of the Polish economy, strengthen its links with the global economy and are an essential component of security, and a nationally and territorially balanced development of the country (Strategia Bezpieczeństwa, 2014).

One of the main objectives of the EU transport policy, including Poland, is to increase the market share of environmentally friendly modes of transport, including rail, sea and inland navigation – integrated into intermodal transport systems – and reduce the share of road transport in European transport markets.

Despite many promoting initiatives undertaken by the EU and the Member States, intermodal transport is still uncompetitive compared to road transport, both in price and quality of services. The relatively low efficiency of the operation of intermodal terminals and the lack of unified and internationally compatible information systems in land and sea-land intermodal chains are among the fundamental barriers limiting the development of intermodal transport in Europe. Insufficient service capacity, long loading times, frequent incompatibility between the vehicles and the equipment for handling intermodal units, the insufficient scope of modern information systems for terminal customers – are the main weaknesses of intermodal terminals in Europe.

Economic development, demand for transport services, tariff elimination and quantitative restrictions in transport between countries are conducive to the need for freight and passenger transport in Poland (Table 4.3 and Table 4.4).

In Poland, more and more persons find employment in transport and warehouse management[2] in relation to the total number of employees, it is about 5% (Table 4.5). Marked increases in employment are visible in 2018 and 2019 compared to 2010.

Transport and storage management are significant factors creating growth of importance and competitiveness of the Polish economy. Moreover, they perform an important service that affects the improvement and development of the national and international economy. It should be remembered that

Table 4.3 Freight Transport as of December 31, 2019

Description	2010	2015	2018	2019
In millions of tons, including:	1795.6	1803.8	2191.9	2220.7
Railway transport	234.6	224.3	249.3	233.7
Car transport	1491.3	1505.7	1873.0	1921.1
Pipeline transport	52.6	54.9	55.3	52.4
Maritime transport	8.4	7.0	9.1	8.7
Inland water transport	5.1	11.9	5.14	4.7
Air transport	0.04	0.04	0.06	0.08

Source: Compiled based on *Concise Statistical Yearbook of Poland 2020*, Statistics Poland, Warsaw 2020, p. 319.

transport and storage have four critical functions in the economy – satisfying transport needs, ensuring the collision-free functioning of supply chains, improving the movement of people, positively impacting the growth of tourism. Income in global production in Poland, following Section H: Transport and Storage Management, is 7.7% of the total output (Table 4.6).

Table 4.4 Passenger Transport as of December 31, 2019

Description	2010	2015	2018	2019
In millions of passengers, including:	4883.1	4547.2	4626.7	4720.3
Public transport	4045.1	3843.4	3963.7	4032.5
Without public transport	838.0	703.7	663.0	687.8
Railway transport	261.3	277.3	309.7	335.3
Car transport	569.7	416.8	336.5	327.5
Maritime transport	1.2	1.3	1.5	1.7
Inland water transport	0.9	1.1	1.4	1.4
Air transport	5.0	7.3	13.9	21.9

Source: Compiled based on *Concise Statistical Yearbook of Poland 2020*, Statistics Poland, Warsaw 2020, p. 320.

Table 4.5   The Ratio of Total Employment in the Economy to Those in Transport and Storage (in Thousands) as of December 31, 2019 (Based on Average Employment)

Years/Number of employees	2010	2015	2018	2019
Total	13833.6	14055.8	15046.6	15275.2
Transport and storage	582.5	609.6	709.1	745.4
Shares (%)	4.5	4.3	4.7	4.9

Source: Compiled based on *Statistical Yearbook of the Republic of Poland 2020*, Statistics Poland, Warsaw 2020, pp. 245, 248.

Table 4.6   Global Production in Poland and Transport and Storage (2010 to 2019)

Year	2010 in PLN Million	2015 in PLN Million	2018 in PLN Million	2019 in PLN Million	2010 Shares (%)	2019 Shares (%)
Total	2897949	3583480	4309611	4610956	100	100
Transport and warehouse management	170127	242229	324727	356979	5.9	7.7

Source: Compiled based on *Statistical Yearbook of the Republic of Poland 2020*, Statistics Poland, Warsaw 2020, p. 697.

4.2.2 Road Transport

It should be emphasized that road transport coordinates and integrates individual elements of the economy into a single whole. It also results from the basic functions of road transport in the economy and the implementation of tasks within the fields and sectors of national security: consumption – the ability to meet transport needs by providing transport services; production – the possibility of satisfying production needs by providing transport services and thus creating conditions for such production activity and the functioning of the production; and integration – allowing the state and society to be integrated through transport services (it is a crucial factor of equalizing opportunities for various regions of the country). In addition, we observe the development of communication networks in Poland, particularly visible in road transport. It is most evident in the case of expressways (increase by 39% in 2015–2019) and motorways (increase by 7% in 2015–2019) (Table 4.7).

Table 4.7 Road Length in Poland (in km)

Years/Roads	2010	2015	2018	2019
Public roads (town and country roads)	406122	419636	424564	424915
Hard surface, including:	273760	290919	303957	307066
improved	249807	268366	281865	285259
expressways	675	1492	2077	2432
motorways	857	1559	1637	1676

Source: Compiled based on *Statistical Yearbook of the Republic of Poland 2020*, Statistics Poland, Warsaw 2020, p. 536.

Despite the significant increase in the length of motorways in recent years, considering the population per 100,000 and an area per 1,000 km², it should be stated that we are far behind countries such as Germany, Spain and the Czech Republic (Table 4.8).

Road transport grows fast. This is because it is quick and easy-to-use and beneficial for short-distance carriage of people; it enables delivering goods directly to the recipient (door-to-door), can be reached everywhere where there is no railway or ship access, allows high transport speed, motor vehicles easily adapt to various types of cargo, transport potential can be easily

Table 4.8 Motorway Lengths in Selected EU Countries as of 2017

Country	in km	Per 100,000 Population	Per 1,000 km²
Total in the UE	77596	15	17
Austria	1743	20	21
Belgium	1736	15	21
Bulgaria	734	10	7
Czech Republic	1240	12	16
Greece	2133	20	16
Spain	15523	33	31
Germany	13009	16	36
Poland	1640	4	5

Source: Compiled based on *Transport – Activity Results in 2019*, Statistics Poland, Szczecin 2020, p. 245.

Table 4.9   Condition of Motor Vehicles and Tractors (in Thousands) Registered as of December 31, 2019

Description	2010	2015	2018	2019
Total, including:	23037	27409	30801	31989
Passenger cars	17240	20723	23429	24360
Buses	97	110	119	123
Trucks and tractor units	2982	3428	3758	3883
Ballast and agricultural tractors	1566	1703	1785	1818
Motorcycles	1013	1272	1503	1587

Source: Compiled based on *Concise Statistical Yearbook of Poland 2020*, Statistics Poland, Warsaw 2020, p. 325.

adjusted to tasks changing in time and space. Falling motor vehicle prices also impact the development of road transport. The number of cars and tractors registered as of December 31, 2019 increased by almost a total of 9 million pieces compared to 2010, including about 7 million passenger cars, trucks, tractors, ballast and agricultural vehicles by 1.5 million pieces (Table 4.9).

Transport involves not only development and progress but also accidents that occur not only on Polish roads but also on company premises in the so-called internal transport, which is often overlooked. Road transport not only benefits the national economy but also causes accidents and losses in (Ocena ryzyka, 2013): people; economy, property, infrastructure (including critical infrastructure); environment. Effects on people include mainly the potential number of fatalities, injured or seriously ill (requiring hospitalization, evacuation, unemployment) and permanent disability and psychological effects. In addition, the impact on everyday life is indicated. In terms of indirect effects, social consequences (e.g. potential increase in unemployment) and permanent disability and psychological effects may also be shown. Comparing various modes of transport in the EU in the context of passenger death risk shows that air transport is the safest. On the other hand, most people die on road transport (Tables 4.10. and 4.11).

Effects on the economy, property and infrastructure concern both short-term and long-term effects. The analysis of the impact on property, including infrastructure, identifies the "disruptions" or "damage" that may occur. When analyzing the effects on property, attention should be paid to direct and indirect (domino effect) or postponed effects. If possible, estimated costs of losses and reconstruction costs are provided. Effects on the environment,

Table 4.10 Risk of Fatalities (Death) Depending on the Mode of Transport

Type of Transport Chosen by Users	Fatalities Per Million Passenger Kilometers
Airline passenger	0.101
Maritime transport	0.12
Railways	0.156
Buses	0.443
Passenger cars	4.45
Two-wheeled motor vehicles	52.593

Source: Compiled based on G. Nowacki, K. Olejnik, M. Walendzik, *Ocena stanu bezpieczeństwa transportu drogowego w UE*, Autobusy No. 9/2017, p. 116.

as part of the analysis of environmental effects, in addition to determining the adverse impact of a given scenario on the environment, it should be indicated which effects are reversible/renewable and which cause complete destruction/degradation of the environment. When describing these effects, it is vital to indicate possible time intervals. Transport safety is determined by the following basic indicators (Molková, 2009): human factor; mode of transport; environment.

They determine the level of road safety. The human factor is commonly regarded as the most important, and it most often influences the emergence of extraordinary events. The reasons for this may be poor health, insufficient prediction and inference abilities, insufficient knowledge and experience, various transient emotional states, time pressure, abnormal mental states. In the transport process, an individual acts as an active participant (car driver, airplane pilot, helmsman, dispatcher, traveler etc.) and a passive participant (a random passer-by, a person at risk of a road accident etc.).

The means of transport affect safety through their properties. They are determined by a set of design and operational factors and the care (systematic inspections) of the means of transport and their maintenance. In terms of transport safety, means of transport should be considered in the context of:

■ active safety enabling the prevention and repair of errors in the human factor or other traffic indicators (technical devices facilitating the control of the means of transport and increasing the quality and speed of the driver's response, including decision-making activities);

Table 4.11 Fatal Road Accidents in Europe – the Number of People Per One Million Inhabitants

No.	Country	2010	2018	2019	Change 2018–2019	Change 2010–2019
1.	Romania	117	96	96	0%	–22%
2.	Bulgaria	105	87	89	3%	–19%
3.	Poland	**103**	**76**	**77**	**0%**	**–26%**
4	Croatia	99	77	73	–6%	–30%
5.	Latvia	103	78	69	–12%	–39%
6.	Lithuania	95	62	66	6%	–38%
7.	Greece	113	65	65	–1%	–45%
8.	Hungary	74	65	62	–5%	–19%
9.	Portugal	80	66	61	–8%	–33%
10.	Cyprus	73	57	59	6%	–13%
11.	Czech Republic	77	62	58	–6%	–23%
12.	Belgium	77	53	56	6%	–24%
13.	Italy	70	55	55	0%	–20%
14.	Slovakia	65	48	51	7%	–25%
15.	**EU**	**67**	**52**	**51**	**–2%**	**–23%**
16.	Slovenia	67	44	49	13%	–25%
17.	France	64	49	48	0%	–19%
18.	Austria	66	46	46	0%	–26%
19.	Estonia	59	51	39	–22%	–34%
20.	Germany	45	40	37	–7%	–16%
21.	Finland	51	43	37	–14%	–24%
22.	Luxemburg	64	60	36	–39%	–31%
23.	Spain	53	39	36	–6%	–31%
24.	Denmark	46	30	35	20%	–20%
25.	Netherlands	32	35	34	–3%	9%

(Continued)

Table 4.11 (Continued)   Fatal Road Accidents in Europe – the Number of People Per One Million Inhabitants

No.	Country	2010	2018	2019	Change 2018–2019	Change 2010–2019
26.	Malta	31	38	32	–11%	23%
27.	Ireland	47	29	29	1%	–33%
28.	United Kingdom	30	28	28	0%	–3%
29.	Sweden	28	32	22	–32%	–17%
30.	Switzerland	42	27	22	–20%	–43%
31.	Norway	43	20	20	1%	–48%
32.	Iceland	25	52	17	–67%	–25%

Source: Compiled based on W. Kwinta, *Śmiertelne wypadki drogowe w Europie – zestawienie*, https://inzynieria.com/drogi/rankingi/59291,smiertelne–wypadki–drogowe–w–europie–zestawienie, March 20, 2021.

■ passive safety influencing the occurrence and magnitude of the consequences of a dangerous event (technical devices and passive elements aimed at protecting people at the time of an accident and immediately after it).

Based on the statistical data of Statistics Poland, we can identify several causes of accidents. There were 30,288 road accidents in 2019 (similar numbers have been reported since 2015). Details are shown in Table 4.12. There are still areas where there is no improvement (e.g. right of way not being respected). Nevertheless, positive downward trends can be observed in the number of accidents in 2010–2019.

The environment is a set of organizational, technical, socio-psychological and other conditions affecting humans and the means of transport. Creating an optimal environment for transport is a matter that covers many professional and scientific disciplines. The basic elements that make up the transport environment include transport facilities (transport routes and facilities, transport terminals etc.), transport devices (safety devices, auxiliary and service devices, road markings etc.), transport management systems (information systems, automation, organization of traffic management etc.), the surroundings of transport routes (obstacles, narrowings, objects distracting

Table 4.12 Road Accidents – Causes

Important Causes of Accidents	2010	2015	2018	2019
Failure to comply with road traffic regulations by vehicle drivers, including:	**30628**	**27307**	**27507**	**26534**
• failure to match speed to traffic conditions, including exceeding the speed limit	9222	6807	6219	6268
• right of way not being respected	7750	7235	7491	7252
• incorrect overtaking	1943	1472	1303	1252
Failure to comply with road traffic regulations by pedestrians, including:	**4427**	**2619**	**2113**	**1879**
• careless entering the road	2520	1733	1270	1142
Road user intoxication	3486	2211	2134	2089
Poor technical condition of vehicles	66	41	38	38
Accident victims, including:	**52859**	**42716**	**40221**	**38386**
• fatalities of accidents	3907	2938	2862	2909

Source: Compiled based on *Statistical Yearbook of the Republic of Poland 2020*, Statistics Poland, Warsaw 2020, p. 549.

attention etc.), meteorological conditions (transport time, season, current condition of transport routes etc.), transport law (laws and regulations, internal operating rules etc.).

It is not without reason that the most important documents regarding the road safety system devote a lot of space to the prevention of disasters, traffic accidents, "thanks to the use of modern transport infrastructure, modernized rolling stock parks and integrated transport management systems reduce costs in the economy, while contributing to lowering the pressure on the environment" (Strategia Bezpieczeństwa, 2014). In the White Paper, particular importance was given to road traffic safety control and transport protection by monitoring compliance with the applicable regulations concerning road transport and passenger and goods transport aimed at eliminating all negative phenomena in road transport as well as tasks in the field of compliance with order regulations, protection of human life and health and property in the railway areas (e.g. Road Transport Inspection, Railway Security Guard) (Biała Księga Bezpieczeństwa Narodowego Rzeczpospolitej Polskiej, 2013).

4.2.3 Railway Transport

Poland has excellent geographic and favorable spatial conditions for road transport, including rail transport. Analysis of rail transport after 1989 shows that development and modernization are not as visible as in the case of road transport. It is the case for several reasons. The end of the 20th century saw an economic slowdown, economic marketization processes, systemic transformation, privatization, fluctuations in the zloty exchange rate, imports exceeding exports, significant foreign debt.

In 2020, licensed freight transport was carried out by 84 companies based on licenses issued by the President of the Office of Rail Transport (Statystyka przewozów towarowych, 2021). According to the share of carriers by freight performance in the rail transport market in Poland, PKP Cargo S.A. took first place both in 2019 and 2020. The ranking of companies is shown in Table 4.13.

At the same time, the railway infrastructure in Poland was managed by nine entities, with the primary network of this infrastructure (93.2%) being managed by PKP PLK SA. Table 4.14 shows the volume of rail transport.

Analysis of the tables and data included in the Statistical Yearbook of the Republic of Poland 2020 and the Concise Statistical Yearbook of Poland 2020 shows that in 2019 rail transport in Poland:

Table 4.13 The Share of Railway Carriers by Freight Performance in the Rail Transport Market in Poland in 2019–2020

Company	2019 in %	2012 in %
PKP Cargo S.A	40.65	43.92
Lotos Kolej sp. z o.o.	10.36	9.79
DB Cargo Polska S.A.	5.09	5.66
PKP LHS sp. z o.o.	4.94	5.44
CTL Logistics sp. z o.o.	4.31	3.95
Orlen Kol-Trans S.A.	4.21	3.71
Freightliner PL sp. z o.o.	3.30	3.17
PUK Kolprem sp. z o.o.	2.52	1.89
Inter Cargo sp. z o.o.	2.32	2.33
PCC Intermodal S.A.	1.77	1.19

Source: Compiled based on *Statystyka przewozów towarowych*, https://utk.gov.pl/, March 10, 2021.

- only 14.0% of the total cargo transported was carried (Table 4.14);
- 7% of passengers were handled (Table 4.15).

Over the last few years, there has been a stagnation in rail transport of goods and passengers in Poland. It is not beneficial for the environment and proves the low use of intermodal transport, which has a positive effect on the protection of the environment. In 2019, there was also a significant decrease in the rolling stock, particularly in the number of freight wagons and passenger coaches (Table 4.16).

Railway transport is second only to road transport in terms of the amount of transported goods and passengers, and certainly the first in the area of safety and environmental protection. However, it is regrettable that the ERA data

Table 4.14   The Volume of Rail Transport

Description	2010	2015	2018	2019
Transport in million tons	179.6	1803.8	2191.9	2220.7
Railway transport	234.6	224.3	249.3	233.7

Source: Compiled based on *Concise Statistical Yearbook of Poland 2020*, Statistics Poland, Warsaw 2020, p. 319.

Table 4.15   Passenger Transport in Millions of Passenger Kilometers in Poland

Description	2010	2015	2018	2019
In millions of passengers	4883.1	4547.2	4626.0	4720.3
Railway transport	261.3	277.3	309.7	335.3

Source: Compiled based on *Concise Statistical Yearbook of Poland 2020*, Statistics Poland, Warsaw 2020, p. 320.

Table 4.16   Rolling Stock in Poland

Description	2010	2015	2018	2019
Electric locomotives	1905	1816	1734	1738
Diesel locomotives	2358	2217	2091	2149
Electric combustion units	1213	1330	1272	1245
Freight wagons	89270	86364	87696	87990
Passenger coaches	3795	2589	2434	2248

Source: Compiled based on *Statistical Yearbook of the Republic of Poland 2020*, Statistics Poland, Warsaw 2019, p. 537.

Table 4.17   Number of Significant Accidents on Polish Railroad Network in 2015–2019

Year	Number	% Compared to the Previous Year
2015	307	-8
2016	265	-14
2017	252	-9
2018	275	+54
2019	214	-22

Source: Compiled based on *Raportu w sprawie bezpieczeństwa*, UTK, Warsaw 2020, p. 25.

show that the Polish network is responsible for one-fifth of railway fatalities in the European Union when Poland's population constitutes only one-thirteenth of the EU population. However, it should be emphasized that the 2019 Safety Report prepared by the Office of Rail Transport indicates that the number of significant accidents shows a downward trend, as shown in Table 4.17.

In 2019, the number of significant accidents on the Polish railway network amounted to 214, which is a decrease of 61 (22.2%) compared to 2018, in which there were 275 significant accidents. This is the best result in the last five years. The reduced number of accidents results in fewer losses. Accident costs in 2019 were lower than in the previous year. Total costs in the reporting year amounted to EUR 141.17 million, a decrease of 19.1% compared to 2018 (Table 4.18).

The costs of significant accidents are calculated based on several cost categories, including:

■ loss of human life (in case of fatalities);

Table 4.18   Costs in EUR in 2015–2019

Year	Cost	% Compared to the Previous Year
2015	163 372 767	+2
2016	123 185 869	-24
2017	167 014 211	+36
2018	174 544 335	+5
2019	141 171 808	-19, 31

Source: Compiled based on *Raport w sprawie bezpieczeństwa*, UTK, Warsaw 2020, p. 26.

- damage to health resulting from serious injuries (in case of severe injury);
- material damage;
- environmental damage;
- train delays as a result of an accident.

Communication safety in rail transport depends on three groups of factors:

- technical (related to the railway infrastructure, including the condition of the railway, traffic control systems, e.g. active standby, automatic braking of trains, area braking, telecommunications systems, power systems and rolling stock);
- legal (related to the implementation of European and national legislation, internal instructions and procedures, the strict observance of which minimizes the risk of a railway accident);
- human resources (competences, qualifications and experience and professional development of railway personnel).

4.3 Telematics in Transport Safety

Transport telematics is a branch of transport knowledge concerning integrating information technology and telecommunications in applications for traffic management and control in transport systems, stimulating technical and organizational activities that enable increasing the efficiency and safety of these systems' operation. Its main goal is to improve the user satisfaction of these systems (Neumann, 2018). Individual telematics solutions cooperate, often under the control of an overriding factor.

Telematics in transport processes is identified with such concepts as intelligent transport systems and intelligent transport. Intelligent transport systems (ITS) cover a wide range of technological solutions aimed at improving transport by increasing mobility and road safety. These systems combine many elements and activities to enhance or improve the broadly understood transport in terms of communication, prevention, traffic control and management, incident detection, supervision or elimination of traffic violations, or reduction of fuel consumption by alleviating road congestion (Shaheen & Finson, 2013). ITS include:

- traffic management centers;
- integrated traffic management systems;

- traffic control systems, including traffic light control;
- public transport management systems;
- CCTV monitoring systems;
- ARTR video monitoring systems;
- speed supervision systems;
- variable message signs;
- dynamic vehicle weighing systems;
- vehicle height measuring systems, parking information systems.

Intelligent transport (IT) consists of two cooperating systems: intelligent road and intelligent vehicle, i.e. a vehicle equipped with devices that maintain continuous, especially wireless, information exchange with devices installed above/below the road or at the roadside. Each telematics system in transport can be described by defining its following structures (Bartczak, 2006):

- **functional** (supports electronic transactions as part of payments for the use of road infrastructure, provides information in situations that threaten the life and health of road users, manages traffic, including not only traffic on urban and rural roads but also extraordinary events in road traffic (incidents), supports the management of public transport operations, including the transport fleet, supports drivers operating vehicles (navigation), provides information to passengers before and during the journey, supports the observance of legal regulations on road traffic, supports the management of transport operations);
- **physical** (shaped by system centers, i.e. places where the collected data are stored and processed using computers, e.g. traffic control centers (TCC), traffic information centers (TIC), cargo and vehicle management centers etc.; roadsides, i.e. places where there are devices for measuring traffic flow, collecting tolls, providing information to drivers etc.; vehicles, i.e. places that are means of transport, where appropriate electronic (on-board) systems have been installed capable of electronic exchange of information with the environment, personal devices of a driver or passenger that enable them to communicate electronically with other elements of the telematics system, devices installed on loading units, e.g. containers, semi-trailers, which can transmit or receive information electronically with the environment; kiosks, i.e. devices available in public places that allow limited access to information resources stored in databases in the transport system);

■ **communication** (individual physical places of the telematic system, electronically interconnected within a specific communication system – the creation of an appropriate communication structure of the telematics system in transport requires selecting appropriate and commercially available information and telecommunications technologies).

4.3.1 Monitoring of Automotive Means of Transport

With the development of transport (in 2019, there were 31,989,000 registered motor vehicles in Poland, i.e. almost 25% more compared to 2015) (Concise Statistical Yearbook of Poland 2020, 2020) and new information and telecommunications technologies, it is possible to introduce integrated services consisting of continuous determination of the location of vehicles and automatic monitoring of domestic and international transport.

Growing congestion on roads and railways, variable weather conditions, road and rail emergencies have a significant impact on the quality and safety of transport operations. Mobile communication is becoming more and more important in transport and search and rescue operations.

Many companies, including Polish ones, produce many devices which, in combination with other techniques and technologies, constitute a system for determining vehicle position and data, which allow:

■ automatic transmission of information about the route of the means of transport (constant monitoring);
■ finding stolen vehicles, for example;
■ remote vehicle immobilization, e.g. in the event of theft;
■ providing information related to the transport of hazardous materials to the relevant services to reduce the likelihood of a disaster and prevent its consequences;
■ optimization of transport and operating costs (real-time data on speed, working time, stops and planning routes for safety reasons, i.e. traffic intensity, repairs, weather conditions, road surface condition);
■ online transport management (elimination of empty runs and unused cargo space, quick reaction in the event of unforeseen events, such as accidents or theft);
■ effective use of means of transport and human potential (timely unloading, quick response to disturbances in transport planning).

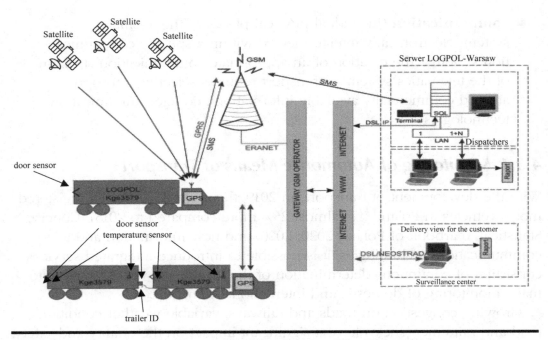

Figure 4.1 System for monitoring and identification of vehicles of transport bases. Source: Compiled based on W. Szulc, *Elektroniczne metody monitorowania ruchomych środków transportowych*, www.zabezpieczenia.com.pl/, March 17, 2020.

In practice, systems generally available on the market are used to monitor mobile means of transport, using the satellite global positioning system (GPS) in conjunction with the general packet radio system (GPRS) and the global system for mobile communication (GSM) using the 900 MHz frequency.

The operation of the existing satellite-based GPS vehicle tracking is possible thanks to a combination of advanced satellite, telecommunications and IT techniques. Satellite vehicle monitoring systems are composed of four basic subsystems (Figure 4.1) (Drewek, 2011):

- location (using satellites);
- data collection and processing – installed in a mobile facility, its tasks include, among others, receiving satellite signals (after processing by a microprocessor, these signals are data in the form of geographic coordinates and a speed parameter, a monitoring station receives this information along with reports on the condition of the facility);
- data transmission – uses conventional and trunked radio systems, mobile telephony, including packet data transmission, as well as satellite communication (this subsystem is responsible for ensuring two-way communication between the monitored facility and the monitoring center);

- management, responsible for continuous supervision of the facility and its management, both during its movement and stationary.

The presented system has many functions and allows (Szulc, 2020):

- real-time location of transport facilities using GPS;
- monitoring facilities using detailed digital city maps and road maps of Poland and Europe;
- round-the-clock access to current and archival information on the location of facilities;
- cheap and fast data transmission thanks to GPRS;
- alarm mode activation by the motion sensor system in the event of unforeseen tilt or movement of the vehicle;
- effective round-the-clock protection against vehicle and cargo theft;
- installation preventing unauthorized persons from accessing the GPS receiver and ensuring its undetectability;
- vehicle fleet management; support of the settlement of the costs of operating means of transport through automated data exchange (this feature is not common among other described systems).

Mobile means of transport monitoring system (Figure 4.1) includes:

- a surveillance center (ground part) connected to terminals installed in vehicles via the Internet;
- available positions (ground part) which cooperate with servers via LAN.

This makes it possible to obtain reports and send SMS by the base stations to the module located in the vehicle and to receive SMS sent in the opposite direction. In addition, GPRS communication is also possible via the GSM operator and the Eranet link. The algorithm structure for communication of the transport facility (mobile means of transport) with the monitoring system (supervision center) is shown in Figure 4.2.

The algorithm includes three main blocks: monitoring system (supervision center), GSM station, vehicle (mobile transport facility). In order to establish communication with the selected transport facility, the monitoring system connects with a GSM station via the Internet or SMS using a special terminal. Then the vehicle (equipped with a location and transmission controller) sends the necessary information to the GSM station via two alternative

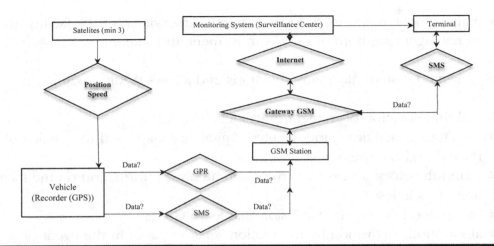

Figure 4.2   Communication algorithm between the transport object and the monitoring system (supervision center). Source: Compiled based on W. Szulc, *Elektroniczne metody monitorowania ruchomych środków transportowych*, www.zabezpieczenia. com.pl, March 17, 2020.

routes, i.e. GPRS or SMS. The GSM station sends the collected data to the monitoring station (monitoring center).

All data gathered by the computer marked with the number 11 come from sensors located in different parts of the means of transport (Figure 4.3).

The container detection and identification sensor – the presence of a container activates the RFID transponder reader located at the rear of the vehicle cabin. Depending on the loading method, each container is equipped with one or two RFID transponders. The reader identifies the unique code assigned to each of them. The collected information about

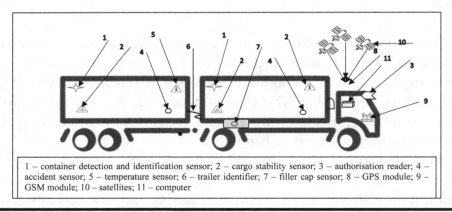

1 – container detection and identification sensor; 2 – cargo stability sensor; 3 – authorisation reader; 4 – accident sensor; 5 – temperature sensor; 6 – trailer identifier; 7 – filler cap sensor; 8 – GPS module; 9 – GSM module; 10 – satellites; 11 – computer

Figure 4.3   Diagram of a satellite vehicle tracking system. Source: Compiled based on W. Drewek, *Monitorowanie ładunków niebezpiecznych w transporcie drogowym*, Logistyka, No. 5/2011, p. 516.

the presence (from the presence sensor) and the unique code (transponder reader) of the container is transferred to the central processing unit (computer), from where, along with the information about the geographical position of the vehicle and time, it is sent to the dispatcher (or driver) (Moduł identyfikacji kontenerów i pojemników typu dzwon, 2021).

The cargo stability sensor (several may be mounted) allows checking if the cargo is physically present in the vehicle and in the same position as placed during loading. After loading, the container (packaging) is "detected" – waves reflecting from the surface of the packaging confirm its presence and distance from the edge of the loading box or container walls. The sensor controls and activates the RFID reader. The reader identifies the code assigned to each sensor (Drewek, 2011).

Accident sensors send an alarm signal to the GPS/GSM, giving the coordinates. An accident is understood as a collision or rollover of the vehicle on any axis. Immediately after one of the mentioned events, an alarm signal is sent to the central processing unit, which sends a message to the dispatcher's server and the phone number 112 (in European Union).

The filler cap sensor – a filler cap protection for trucks and machines; it is a device mounted on the fillers of the petrol tank to monitor and control the opening or closing status of the filler cap. The operation of the device is based on RFID technology so that any interference attempts will result in an SMS or email notification. Its installation consists of replacing the existing cap with a special casting permanently attached to the filler cap (Szymonik, Ekonomika, 2013).

The temperature sensor, e.g. refrigerated trailer – the data are sent to the system and combined with other information about the monitored vehicle are valuable material for analysis. Mounting such a sensor in a refrigerated truck enables continuous temperature control of transported goods. On the one hand, we have independent and remote control of the aggregate's operation; on the other hand, it allows us to protect ourselves against contractors' accusations of transporting goods under inappropriate conditions. A digital sensor ensures high measurement accuracy and does not require any additional calibrations.

The trailer identifier is a chip mounted in the socket of the spiral coupling linking the trailer (semi-trailer) with the tractor. It is used in cases where interchangeable use of trailers (semi-trailers) is possible. It allows creating lists of trailers' works.

The opening sensor is most often a transponder (a chip with a unique number read by radio). It allows the opening of flaps, doors etc. to be controlled.

4.3.2 Intelligent Road Transport Systems

Intelligent transport systems (ITS) cover a wide range of technological solutions aimed at improving transport by increasing mobility and safety in passenger and freight traffic. It means systems that constitute a comprehensive collection of various technologies (telecommunications, information technology, automation and measurement) as well as management techniques used in transport to increase the safety of road users, increase the efficiency of the transport system and protect natural resources (Akgun et al., 2019).

Telematics systems use various devices, computer programs and systems (Wikipedia, 2021):

- electronic communication, connecting individual elements of the telematics system (wide area and local networks, mobile telecommunications networks, satellite systems);
- obtaining information (measuring sensors, video cameras, radars);
- presentation of information for telematics system administrators (large-format screens and dedicated stands of system operators);
- presentation of information for system users (traffic lights, radio and Internet communication systems).

Telematics solutions are developed in various transport sectors. For example (Inteligentne Systemy Transportowe, 2021):

- In railways, we have the European Rail Traffic Management System (ERTMS), which includes two subsystems: the European Train Control System (ETCS) and the Global System for Mobile Communications – Railway (GSM-R).
- In air transport, we are talking about the Single European Sky ATM Research (SE-SAR) (it is simply a new generation European air traffic management system, which is an important technical component in the creation of the Single European Sky (SES)).
- In maritime transport, the SafeSeaNet system is being developed, which is the central component of the vessel traffic monitoring and information system within the European Union, i.e. the VTMS.
- In inland waterway transport, we have the River Information Service (RIS), providing harmonized river information services on inland waterways in the EU.

Directive 2010/40/EU of the European Parliament and of the Council of July 7, 2010 on the framework for the deployment of Intelligent Transport Systems in the field of road transport and for interfaces with other modes of transport outlined six priority actions:

■ ensuring multi-modal travel information services available throughout the EU;
■ providing real-time traffic information services available throughout the EU;
■ data and procedures for providing users free of charge, as far as possible, with a minimum amount of universal traffic information related to road safety;
■ harmonized provision of interoperable eCall service across the EU;
■ providing information services for safe and secure parking places for trucks and commercial vehicles;
■ providing reservation services for safe and secure parking places for trucks and commercial vehicles.

The benefits of using intelligent transport systems are manifold. Research shows that the use of ITS (Inteligentne Systemy Transportowe, 2021):

■ increases the capacity of the street network by an average of 22.5%;
■ improves road traffic safety (reduction in the number of accidents by an average of 60%);
■ reduces travel times and energy consumption (by nearly 60%);
■ improves the quality of the natural environment (reduction in exhaust emissions by an average of 40%);
■ improves travel comfort and traffic conditions for drivers, public transport and pedestrians;
■ reduces costs of road fleet management;
■ reduces costs related to the maintenance and renovation of road surfaces;
■ increases economic benefits in the region where ITS solutions are applied.

Access to current information is possible thanks to modern technologies that are visible in the vehicle and on external boards or monitors. These include:

■ GPS – one of the satellite navigation systems;
■ dedicated short-range communications (DSRC), a technique based on data transmission in a short distance, was used in high-tonnage

transport to collect tolls for specified road sections (toll collection system – viaToll);

■ wireless networks (GSM/EDGE, Wi-Fi), similarly to the technologies used for traditional Internet connection, allow for fast communication; mobile telephony – ITS applications can transmit data via 4G and 5G networks (the advantage of mobile telephony is live video);
■ radio communication systems (DAB, RDS-TMC);
■ traffic monitoring devices (sensors, detectors, controllers, video detectors); television surveillance apparatus (surveillance cameras);
■ devices and systems for monitoring and measuring weather;
■ variable light boards;
■ geographic information system (GIS);
■ road databases;
■ electronic cards.

In many countries, transport system improvement consists not only of building roads, improving existing ones but also of applying new techniques and technologies (e.g. sensors, chips, wireless technologies etc.).

4.3.3 Intelligent Transport Systems in Rail Transport

The European Railway Traffic Management System (ERTMS) is an important instrument for rail transport. It is one of the key projects to ensure the greatest possible interoperability of transport, especially railways in Europe (Szymonik, International, 2014). The ERTMS enables increasing the level of safety of train traffic; increasing the capacity of the railway line; reducing the risk of accidents, renovating communication facilities and adapting them to international standards; improving the quality of transport in connection with the possibility of launching additional services.

The ERTMS deployment is dictated by economic and safety reasons. The benefits of its application include (ERTMS, 2021):

■ increase in transport capacity of existing lines;
■ greater safety for passengers;
■ higher speeds – the system enables trains to run at speeds up to 500 km/h;
■ lower production costs – one proven, common system for the entire European Union is easier to manufacture, install and maintain, contributing to the improvement of railway competitiveness;

- lower maintenance costs: ERTMS level 2 does not require trackside signaling, which significantly reduces costs;[3]
- common supply market for infrastructure managers – customers can order components anywhere in Europe, which makes the market more competitive;
- greater reliability: the use of ERTMS improves the reliability of transport and its punctuality.

The ERTMS includes the Global System for Mobile Communications – Railway (GSM-R) and the European Train Control System (ETCS). Both systems are essential components of the European policy of removing barriers to transport, both in terms of the technical ones concerning rail networks within the EU borders and building a common market for rail products and services.

The ETCS enables cab signaling and continuous control of the driver's work. Under Polish regulations, driving a train at a speed exceeding 160 km/h requires cabin signaling. The ETCS adapts to the needs of the railway line by deploying the appropriate ETCS level. The first, second and third tiers are downwards compatible, which means that a vehicle equipped with a higher tier can run not only on the lines of this ETCS tier but also on the lower tiers (Szymonik, International, 2014).

The GSM-R is a railway version of the GSM operating in the 900 MHz band and providing users, apart from the "talking" channel, with a digital radio channel for data transmission and performance of functions intended for specialized railway applications. The GSM-R, in addition to the technical communication function for railways, is also a transmission medium for the ETCS levels 2 and 3, through which travel permits issued by a Radio Block Centre (RBC) are sent to individual trains within the area of a given RBC. Updated information is also sent via the GSM-R in the ETCS level 1 system, using the radio infill function.

According to the International Union of Railways (UIC), the GSM-R is installed at different levels in Europe. German and Italian railways lead in this respect.

4.3.4 Railway Transport Monitoring Systems

Rail freight is governed by slightly different rules, regulated by PKP. But more and more often, it is required to monitor entire train sets and the goods they contain (it does not concern railway traffic control). The problem also concerns the safety of services and the means of transport themselves.

The monitoring system of means of transport in rail traffic may be of great importance in the case of the carriage of valuable goods or goods requiring special supervision for other, for instance, strategic reasons. Due to this type of purpose, the class of users may include customs services, the police, Railway Security Guard (SOK), border guard and security companies, specializing, for example, in the transport of money, special cargo (e.g. radioactive materials), coal (e.g. from Silesia into the interior of the country) etc. The tools used in telematics in road transport are valuable here. These include the following systems (Wydro, 2021): electronic communication, connecting individual elements of the telematics system (wide area networks, local area networks, mobile telecommunications networks, satellite systems); obtaining information (measuring sensors, video cameras, radars); presentation of information for telematics system administrators (GIS, access control systems); presenting information for system users (traffic lights, radio, Internet technologies – WWW, SMS).

The most important functions of telematics systems are information handling functions. This applies to its acquisition, processing, distribution along with transmission and use in various decision-making processes. Telematics systems and applications are designed for specific processes.

A tool to be widely deployed and used in rail transport is the global navigation satellite system (GNSS), which consists of two basic elements: the space segment and the ground segment. In addition, there are broadly understood control segments, considered by some to be parts of the ground segment (Teunissen & Montenbruck, 2017).

The analyses carried out by the Community of European Railways and Infrastructure Companies (CER) and UIC identified more than 40 areas of application of the GNSS in rail transport. Simply put, they can be divided into five basic groups (Szymonik, Ekonomika, 2013):

■ GNSS in railway engineering, construction and modernization of railway systems, inspections, diagnostics and servicing;
■ commercial applications, mass market, comprehensive information and management;
■ basic security systems;
■ applications increasing safety – steering assistance, protection of basic systems;
■ automation of processes related to the management of rolling stock and rail traffic and precise coordination using GNSS as a time source for other systems.

GNSS applied in practice:

- improve geodetic measurements necessary for the modernization and construction of high-speed railways;
- assess the quality of the works performed or the technical condition of the track;
- conduct inspections of large railway networks using digital cameras coupled with GNSS receivers installed on locomotives (this enables simple, unattended documentation of the condition of the railway network and its surroundings);
- accurately determine the location, speed and time, allowing the train passengers to see at their individual passenger terminals or on the general monitors the map of the route covered with an indication of their current location and find out at what speed they are moving and if the train runs according to the timetable (passengers planning a change will find out whether their trains will depart according to the timetable and from which platform and people waiting for the train will be informed of the exact time remaining until its arrival);
- enable the tracking of wagons thanks to RFID transponders and gates along the train route, which allows wagon owners, shippers and cargo recipients to know where they are and when they will reach their destination (using the so-called Automatic Vehicle Identification (AVI) systems in rail transport);
- allow the risk during the transport of toxic substances, explosives and flammable materials, as well as nuclear waste and fissile materials, to be reduced by supervising the movement of cargo along its entire route, choosing a safe route and staging areas, reducing transport time, detecting irregularities and threats, quick location in case of threat detection, shortening the reaction time to the incident, using appropriate forces and means to counter the threat.

4.4 Warehouse Management Security

Warehouses are not only associated with the manufacture of goods and services but also with the maintenance of various means of supply, including strategic reserves, to secure the needs (of departments responsible for military and law enforcement, public services, rescue services, those in need of help) in terms of materials in times of peace, crisis and war.

Stockpiling covers three basic phases of undertakings: **build-up** of stock levels – the period between introducing a given product to the market and reaching the standard stock; **maintaining** stocks – the period of stock management, including supervision of the proper distribution of stocks, their quality condition etc.; **recall** of products that are not useful to the user (e.g. technical or moral obsolescence) (Doktryna Logistyczna, 2004).

An important sphere for the functioning of the warehouse is its security based on system analysis, which can be treated as (Sienkiewicz, 2015):

- ownership of the warehouse, which describes its resistance to the emergence of hazardous situations), with the focus being on the unreliability of the warehouse's security, i.e. its susceptibility to the emergence of dangerous situations;
- ability to protect stocks and warehouse infrastructure against external threats.

Warehouse security depends on three groups of factors, i.e. technical, legal and personal (Table 4.19).

Technical factors affecting safety in warehouses are related to appropriate equipment and infrastructure that ensure proper storage, internal transport, order picking, sorting, shipping and proper protection of the facility. The infrastructure also determines the safety of people working in the warehouse and the material resources deposited. The infrastructure includes:

- administration buildings (e.g. management and administration office);
- warehouse buildings and structures enabling the storage and protection of stocks; warehouse equipment (shelves, means for manipulating products, measuring and control devices, fire protection devices and others);

Table 4.19 Factors Determining Warehouse Safety

Factor	Description
Technical	Warehouse equipment and infrastructure
Legal (organizational)	Documentation and its implementation as well as procedures minimizing the risk of an accident or material loss
Staff	Competences, qualifications and experience, professional development of employees

Source: Own elaboration.

- means of transport for moving products both within the company and between suppliers and recipients;
- loading and unloading facilities; internal roads and access roads, mainly for cars but also for wagons; packaging with protective, storage, transport, handling, information and advertising functions; reusable loading units such as pallets or containers;
- buildings and offices related to performing auxiliary and additional functions (e.g. service station, petrol station, social and living rooms, banking service, insurance);
- safety equipment and measures, such as ESFR sprinkler systems, vents, emergency exits, emergency power supply – battery room, fire and smoke detectors, 24/7 security – monitoring using intrusion and assault signaling systems, video surveillance system, fire alarm system;
- "robot security guards" – the device consists of four cameras, microphones and a thermal imaging camera and acts as a security guard; it can also detect a fire and chemicals hazardous to health in the air (Figure 4.4).

In the age of IT and electronics, it is impossible to ignore the solutions that support the monitoring and online control of the stockpiles in terms of quantity, value, types and expiry dates. The helpful tools and instruments in this area include:

- download light indicators;
- radio-frequency identification (RFID) – uses radio waves to transmit data and power the electronic system that makes up an object tag through a reader to identify the object;

Figure 4.4   A robot security guard. Source: Compiled based on *Poznaj innowacje ID Logistics*, https://logistyczny.com/, January 22, 2021.

- voice systems – ensure easy two-way communication between an IT system, such as WMS, and its user, such as a warehouse employee;
- barcode readers, commonly known as scanners – convert the light reflected from the barcode into an electronic signal readable by a cash register or computer;
- RF terminals – provide wireless online information exchange via radio; such terminals are often equipped with a barcode scanner; vehicle-mounted computers and portable computers have an advantage over handheld devices (larger screens and keyboards); they are equipped with a graphical user interface (GUI) – generally, vehicle-mounted devices use an external – wired or wireless – barcode reader to process data).

Today, closed-circuit television (CCTV) systems are often used for 24/7 security. It is a set of technical and software measures designed to observe, detect, record and signal conditions indicating the existence of a risk of damage or threats to people and property. CCTV can be a separate surveillance system, or it can also be included, for example, in larger burglary and assault signaling systems or access control systems.

The **technical factors** affecting the safety of the warehouse also include mechanical security, i.e. all kinds of fixed partitions (structures, walls, gates, fire doors, burglar-proof doors), providing additional protection of particularly important (valuable or dangerous) supplies stored.

The **legal (organizational) factors** include the development of documentation and its implementation as well as procedures whose strict compliance minimizes the risk of an accident or material damage.

During the documentation preparation, it is crucial to consider what will be in the warehouse (type of means of supply, stock) and the rules and legal regulations specifying the conditions for storing such resources. The documentation includes the scope of duties of a warehouse operative; fire instructions for the warehouse; occupational health and safety instruction; warehouse information sheet; instructions on warehouse maintenance; instructions for instruments measuring humidity and temperature; instructions on airing the warehouses; instructions on alarm signals and their types; evacuation plan for property stored in the warehouse; composition of the emergency and rescue group (measures and means to evacuate property); quantitative list of warehouse equipment (applies to permanent equipment); diagram of the arrangement of equipment in the warehouse (storage plan); warehouse metrics with up-to-date data; instructions on what to do in the event of a spill of a dangerous substance; warehouse operation regulations; name list of persons authorized to approve material circulation documents; recording of temperature and humidity (also in electronic format); patterns of seals; records of people entering the warehouse facility; warehouse inspection records; records of property transferred for repair (maintenance); records of deposits; other (as needed).

Adequate procedures are vital to ensure the proper functioning of the warehouse through effective and efficient prevention of threats and reacting to the occurring threats, i.e. taking actions that minimize their adverse effects (outcomes).

The typical organizational procedures related to warehouse functioning include (Skowronek & Sarjusz-Wolski, 2008):

- technical conditions for the operation of the warehouse and its equipment;
- fire protection;
- burglary protection;
- staff work safety;
- acceptance and delivery of material goods;
- inventory of stocks;
- distribution of stocks in the warehouse;
- warehouse records;
- documents of receipt and issue of goods;
- other information activities.

Procedures should minimize the risk of an accident in a warehouse, where its causes may be:

- problems with the correct operation of lifts during operation;
- bravado and irresponsible behavior of employees;
- rush – time pressure; poor organization of work – non-compliance with work regulations;
- no reaction (foresight) to prevent events caused by inappropriate behavior of other employees and users of communication routes;
- incorrect position of the forklift operator or excessive effort – inappropriate positioning of the limbs causing fatigue or affecting operation.

Logistics procedures for large-area warehouses are IT-supported by the WMS, which performs tasks in the following areas (Instrukcja o zasadach

i organizacji przechowywania oraz konserwacji uzbrojenia i sprzętu wojskowego, 2013): registration of goods receipts from external deliveries and
own returns to the warehouse and goods releases from the warehouse;
updating and managing the inventory according to the assumed criteria;
indicating the places of storage of deliveries, the location of stocks and the
completion of releases; generating delivery and release documents; generating orders; control of compliance of the delivery/issue with documents;
control of loading of external transport means; warehouse turnover control;
identification and location of goods; inventory of stocks; selection of means
of transport for shipments.

The procedures regulating the material liability of employees for the
entrusted property are not without significance for the safety of the warehouse. The legal basis for liability is contained in the Polish Labour Code
and three regulations. Under article 124 of the Polish Labour Code:

1) an employee entrusted with the obligation to return or to calculate:
   (1) money, securities or valuables, (2) tools and instruments or similar
   items, as well as personal protective equipment, work clothing and
   footwear, is responsible in full for damage caused to this property;
2) the employee is also fully liable for damage to property other than
   mentioned in 1), entrusted to him with the obligation to return or calculate it.

The employee may be released from liability for damage to the entrusted
property if he proves that the damage was caused by reasons beyond his
control. As part of property liability, we can distinguish individual and joint
property liability.

In addition to legal regulations, it should also be noted that the warehouse operatives who bear property liability for the entrusted property have
appropriate training, professional and moral qualifications and certain professional experience. Persons appointed to the position of warehouse operative should not have addictions (drinking, gambling) and should not have a
history of convictions for theft, fraud or other economic crimes.

For the safety of warehouses, the procedures included in the plans for
the physical protection of warehouses are important. The optimal solution is
to sign a contract with professional companies such as specialized security
and protection services to protect persons and property, which are obliged
to cooperate with the police, the state fire services and the municipal
police. Such protection employees have the right to check IDs (within the

boundaries of protected areas) and apprehend persons, use physical force as a means of direct coercion, including such measures as truncheons, handcuffs, paralyzing gas, stun guns, firearms. The employees of these companies conduct ongoing control of the entry and exit of warehouse employees and third parties and the entry and exit of motor vehicles to and from warehouse premises.

A critical factor in the safety of a warehouse is the staff working there. It is a team of people working in warehouses and performing activities directly related to its operations. According to the qualification schedule, workstations in warehouses include warehouse manager, senior warehouse operative, warehouse operative, warehouse worker. The number of employees and their qualifications depends on the purpose and size of the warehouse. When selecting employees, one should consider their competences, qualifications and experience, and when they are already employed, one should not forget about their professional development (Richards, 2014).

Another crucial factor related to safety is the observance of health and safety regulations by the warehouse staff and people using it (e.g. drivers who deliver and take logistic loads to and from the warehouse). The numerical data (Tables 4.20 and 4.21) compiled by Statistics Poland in the analysis

Table 4.20 Persons Injured in Transport and Warehouse Management

Year	Total	Including Fatalities	Including Heavy	Including a Different Effect	Days of Incapacity for Work
2017	6873	56	38	6779	316273
2018	6884	32	26	6826	305198

Source: Compiled based on *Statistical Yearbook of the Republic of Poland 2020,* Statistics Poland, Warsaw 2020, p. 170.

Table 4.21 Estimated Material Losses and Losses of Working Time due to Accidents at Work in 2019

Description	Estimated Material Losses Caused by Accidents at Work/in Thousand PLN	Loss of Other People's Working Time due to Accidents at Work/in working hours
Total	85816.4	33374
Transport and warehouse management	45155.9	2480

Source: Compiled based on *Wypadki przy pracy w 2019,* Statistics Poland, Warsaw 2020, p. 167.

of accidents in transport and storage prove that this is a significant problem from the social and economic point of view.

In 2018, the number of persons injured in transport and warehouse management, amounting to 6,262 and the number of days of incapacity for work – 316,273 – prove that there is still a lot to be done in health and safety in the organizational and procedural areas.

For people organizing work in warehouses and responsible for the safety of warehouse employees (and even the safety of third parties), it is important that there are no separate regulations directly related to occupational health and safety when storing and stockpiling materials. Such a situation makes it necessary to use many legal acts at the same time, from general health and safety regulations, through industry regulations, to technical standards and in many situations, the principles of good warehouse practice. General requirements for broadly understood transport and storage works are specified in Chapter 4 of the Regulation of the Minister of Labour and Social Policy of September 26, 1997 on General Provisions on Health and Safety at Work (Rozporządzenie ministra pracy i polityki socjalnej..., 2003).

It is also necessary to know how to identify threats and apply appropriate preventive and corrective measures to reduce the effects of threats. Legal requirements in the field of warehouse structures, rooms, transport equipment used, rules for the storage and stockpiling of various types of materials are specified by numerous legal acts and technical standards, in particular covering safety issues in the areas of (Zieliński, 2015):

- construction and health and safety requirements for storage rooms;
- lighting and heating of warehouses;
- requirements for storage roads, general fire safety conditions;
- warehouse equipment – rules for safe storage, safety rules for open and semi-open warehouses;
- health and safety rules during warehouse transport, organization of mechanized warehouse works;
- storage of industrial gases;
- storage of liquid gases in cylinders, storage of hazardous chemical materials.

An important factor influencing the safety of people and stocks in the warehouse is proper fire protection. These are methodically, realistically developed instructions, collected, efficient fire protection equipment and systematic training guarantee a sense of security against the

Table 4.22   Warehouse Fires in Poland in 2015–2019

Description	2015	2018	2019
Total, including:	1117	1206	1053
small	891	946	827
medium	167	175	174
large	42	57	40
very large	17	21	12

Source: Compiled based on *Biuletyny informacyjne PSP za 2019 r.*, pp. 56 and 57, www.straz.gov.pl/, February 26, 2021.

consequences of possible fires in the warehouse. The causes of fires include (Živanić et al., 2019):

- arson by a dissatisfied employee, competition;
- failure to comply with the basic fire protection regulations;
- faulty electrical, heating and air-conditioning system;
- self-ignition;
- lightning and other causes.

The number of fires and their size is presented in Table 4.22.

The presented material on warehouse fires indicates several important aspects: each fire is a danger to people and material goods stored there, each fire is a loss and disruption of processes carried out by warehouse management, including the functioning of supply chains; on average, we have about 1,100 warehouse fires in Poland per year.

4.5 Ensuring Food Security

Food and packaging, just like any product, should meet the needs of producers, logistics and consumers by having certain characteristics: physical (e.g. dimensions, weight facilitating transport and storage), chemical (e.g. the composition of raw materials and their impact on the body, environment), technological (e.g. easy to manufacture, storage), organoleptic (e.g. pleasant to touch, taste, smell), functional (e.g. easy to open, prepare for consumption, disposal, easy to "follow"), economic (price, cost of preparation, disposal, transport), aesthetic (e.g. color, safety) (e.g. not harmful, healthy, easy monitoring of product quality, protection against thieves, destruction).

The presented requirements are all important, but those that impact human health and life and natural environment protection deserve special attention. As reality shows, there are products on the market that should never have been there in the first place. Food safety is increasingly important and affects consumers and businesses around the world. While most foods are safe, concerns about safety and product recall are of the utmost importance. According to 2015 estimates by the World Health Organization (WHO), 600 million people a year, or almost a tenth of the world's population, suffer from various diseases after eating contaminated food. As food safety requirements increase, having recognized safety certifications is increasingly important as it helps producers ensure that their products are as safe for consumers as possible. Incorporating product inspection equipment into company-wide product inspection programs can play a critical role in supporting compliance with stringent industry standards (Szymonik & Chudzik, Nowoczesna, 2020).

Form 2012, Corteva AgriscienceTM, DowDuPont's agricultural division and the Economist Intelligence Unit (EIU) publish the Global Food Security Index (GFSI) results. The survey covers 113 countries, and the economic and physical availability and food quality are considered. In 2018, Poland moved up to 26th place (from 27th in 2017 and 29th in 2016), with a total score of 75.4 (in 2017, it was 74.2 and in 2016 – 74.1). Poland was recognized, in particular, for its nutritional standards, food security systems, farmer access to financing and food security (Polska na 26. Miejscu, 2021).

4.5.1 *Food Security in Legal and Organizational Requirements*

In the European Union, the food safety strategy is based on three pillars: law, advice based on research and practical solutions, and control and implementation. Food safety legislation in the EU is comprehensive and covers: hygiene of foodstuffs, hygiene of food of animal origin, organization of official controls on products of animal origin intended for human consumption, official controls carried out to verify compliance with feed law and food and animal health and animal welfare rules. The list of the most important normative and legal acts is presented in Annex 4.2.

Ensuring food safety is related to implementing food safety management systems, such as the principles of Good Hygienic Practice (GHP), Good Manufacturing Practice (GMP) and the HACCP system. It is a legal requirement defined, inter alia, in (HACCAP, 2020): the Act of August 25, 2006 on Food and Nutrition Safety, Regulation of the European Parliament and of the

Council No. 178/2002 of January 28, 2002 laying down the general principles and requirements of food law, establishing the European Food Safety
Authority and laying down procedures in matters of food security. In the
light of the latter regulation, all food operators, regardless of the size and
profile of their operations, are required to have an implemented and functioning HACCP system from January 1, 2006. Hazard Analysis and Critical
Control Points (HACCP) is a food safety management tool and a universal
method of systematic assessment of the possibility of hazards and determining the methods of their elimination during food production.

In practice, there are additional food safety standards, such as (Szymonik
& Chudzik, 2018):

- International Food Standard (IFS) – developed in 2002 by representatives of the German retail trade. In 2012, an updated "IFS Food version
  6" was released, which came into force on July 1, 2012. The IFS system
  is a specific standard recognized and developed for all food producers,
  mainly for the needs of retail chains and their brands. The main purpose of this system is to confirm the safety and quality of the product
  and its compliance with applicable laws and standards. IFS unifies the
  requirements and introduces transparency in the supply chain, from
  raw material to the end product.
- BRC is a global standard developed by the British Retail Consortium,
  required by a growing group of hyper- and supermarkets throughout
  Europe. The standard was developed to ensure the highest possible
  quality of delivered products. The main benefits of introducing BRC
  are reducing the number of products of inappropriate quality; controlling both the supplier and the recipient; reducing the number of audits
  carried out by recipients; unification of food safety requirements; documentation confirming the repeatability of the product of the expected
  quality. In January 2015, version 7 was published and came into force
  on July 1, 2015.

Not without significance for food safety and hygiene management is the
PN-EN ISO 22000:2006, which introduces a unified and globally harmonized
standard in food safety and hygiene while facilitating the implementation
of the HACCP system and integration with the ISO 9001:2008. Standard
22000: 2006 applies to all organizations directly or indirectly involved in
the food chain, i.e. producers of food, feed, cereals, food additives, farmers,
companies providing food and catering services, retailers and wholesalers,

companies providing cleaning services, transport and distribution, suppliers of equipment, cleaning and hygiene products, packaging materials and other materials in contact with food.

Food safety and quality management according to the system under ISO 22000, contains specific requirements for ensuring food safety, concerning (Kielesinska, 2014): communication in the supply chain – internal and with suppliers and customers – to ensure the identification and supervision of security threats; quality system management – the applied and updated system should be included in all activities related to the management of the company; monitoring of operational prerequisite programs – material management plans (e.g. raw materials, chemicals), cross-contamination prevention measures, pest control, personnel hygiene, utilities supply, waste disposal; verification of HACCP principles – with an emphasis on the analysis and monitoring of risk control measures as the key to the effectiveness of the system.

Additionally, the following standards were developed for the needs of logistics (Szymonik & Chudzik, 2018):

- **IFS Logistics** is a standard for companies with physical contact with packaged food products (transport, packaging of packaged food products, loading, unloading, storage, distribution, pallet storage). This standard applies to the road, rail and sea transport as well as freezing and cooling processes.
- **BRC Global Standard for Storage and Distribution** is a standard in storage and distribution. It concerns logistics processes carried out in supply chains, including storage, distribution, transport, contract services, packaging, cooling, freezing, defrosting.
- **BRC/IoP (Packaging and Packaging Materials)** includes requirements for hygiene, production environment and packaging testing. The standard includes requirements not only for food packaging materials but also for all packaging manufacturers (including the following sectors: glass, plastic, wood, paper, aluminum, steel). The standard specifies two levels of hygiene risk, which depend on the end-use of the packaging material. Food packaging has the highest level of risk, while non-food packaging has the lowest.
- **IFS Broker** is a standard for the quality and safety of products at the stage of their purchase, storage and resale by importers, brokers and trade agencies. Thus, it is used by trade agencies, importers, brokers or other entities that deal in selling food products.

The implementation of procedures included in normative and legal acts and other standards and norms would not be possible without (Szymonik & Chudzik, 2018):

- early warning system for the notification of direct or indirect hazards to human health derived from food or feed;
- risk assessment (denotes a scientifically based process consisting of four steps: hazard identification, hazard characterization, risk assessment and characterization) and management;
- crisis management, defined as a biological, chemical or physical factor in a food or feed, or the condition of a food or feed that may cause adverse health effects.

4.5.2 Food Security in Practice

Interviews with experts responsible for food production suggest an unquestionable maxim that today a product for direct or indirect consumption is to be tasty, properly balanced, of the highest quality and freshness. Achieving the presented parameters is extremely difficult, experts found, due to (Szymonik, Bezpieczeństwo, 2015):

- constant changes in the perception, production, distribution caused by new techniques, technologies, intensive agriculture (high profits, use of efficient machinery, use of chemicals, fertilizers, insecticides etc.);
- functioning, with a growing tendency, of super and hypermarkets, mass catering companies and street outlets selling food (meals);
- environmental changes – its functioning is exposed to contamination (intentional or not), most often caused by civilization factors;
- extended supply chains resulting from the sourcing of cheap raw materials from global suppliers and the search for distant markets;
- the actions of competitors, sometimes unethical.

All this contributes to the increased likelihood of the spread of poor quality food, sometimes contaminated, often threatening human health and life, and negatively affecting the natural environment.

To ensure the highest level of food safety, the surveyed companies deployed the HACCP and IFS systems. They allowed a number of instructions and procedures to be developed that ensure that the food produced is safe and friendly to humans and the environment. The main purpose of meeting the requirements of these standards is:

- involving senior management in responsibility for food safety and quality;
- increasing the awareness and skills of employees who have the requirements that the product should meet;
- organizing the competences and responsibilities of people responsible for food production or nutrition.

In the area of logistics processes, several issues are important that should be considered, according to experts, so that the shifted material flow, from raw materials, through the production and distribution of food, is monitored and properly managed, and thus safe. Here are some of them.

4.5.2.1 First

Supplier selection procedures should be developed and approved. Purchased materials and services that impact food safety and quality should be monitored and checked, and the measures used for this should have clear evaluation criteria. Supplier assessments should be systematically analyzed in the context of risks.

During the performance of warehouse processes, particular attention should be paid to the fact whether received goods, including packaging and labels, are in accordance with the specification, storage conditions for raw materials, semi-finished products and finished products that should meet the relevant requirements and not lead to cross-contamination; timeliness of tags, facilitating proper management (first in, first out (FIFO) or first expired, first out (FEFO)).

4.2.5.2 Second

One should keep in mind that all participants in the supply chain – suppliers, producers, distributors, retail chains, shops, but also transport companies and logistics operators are responsible for tracing the origin of the food, as contamination or spoilage of food can occur anywhere in the chain. A helpful tool in traceability is the use of GS1 standards, which enable (Sokołowski, 2020):

- unambiguous identification of goods based on unique GS1 numbers;
- automatic collection of goods and loads moved in the supply chain based on scanning standard barcodes;
- transmission of information via commercial electronic documents.

In this way, it is possible to ensure the proper flow of information in the backward and forward tracing.

4.2.5.3 Third

Based on the threats and risk analysis and the intended use of the products, the company must have a specification for packaging materials. They must comply with the requirements set out in standards and legislation; be useful for each product (e.g. organoleptic, storage, safe for the product, people and the environment); favor the tracing process; good, readable, in accordance with the requirements, indelibly marked; be subject to systematic, documented control.

4.2.5.4 Fourth

Vital links in ensuring food safety are properly implemented maintenance and repairs that may not adversely affect the product; properly designed, prepared and operated social facilities; special cloakrooms for staff, contractors and visitors; washrooms, fully hygienic toilets (e.g. touch-free equipment, hand disinfection, appropriate hygiene equipment, signage explaining the requirements for handwashing, containers opened without using hands).

4.2.5.5 Fifth

Much attention in food companies is paid to food defense and external controls. The activities carried out under this project include appointing people who are responsible for the food defense: systematically analyzing the hazards and types of risks associated with them; developing procedures that are systematically checked and tested in practice (e.g. during training or additional training); securing the entire company against unauthorized access.

4.2.5.6 Sixth

According to experts, the best procedures, instructions, modern techniques and technologies will be useless if people fail during an open examination or controlled observation. The main issues are related to the possibility of food contamination by production (seasonal) workers over whom there is no great control. The vast majority of them are not Polish, and their verification during employment is practically not subject to any rules, apart from financial aspects. There is also a lack of sufficient quality control of the production process from the biological point of view in terms of very heavy contamination, e.g. with anthrax or radioactive elements, because such guidelines and procedures are not applied (Szymonik & Chudzik, 2018).

Notes

1. TNT-T (Trans-European Transport Networks) – an EU program for road, rail, water and air networks.
2. Section H "Transport i gospodarka magazynowa" in line with the Polish Classification of Activities (PKD), used for the needs of Statistics Poland.
3. ERTMS has three levels.

Chapter 5

Technologies Supporting Supply Chain Safety Management

5.1 IT Support

Safety management of the supply chain operation is a theory and practice, which boils down, among others, to implementing modern solutions facilitating the prevention, preparation and response to threats to logistics processes. These tools are IT systems developed with online technologies. They make it possible to forecast and determine the storage place of stocks, plan material needs, select transport, route, reduce costs, manage infrastructure (including storage) and fixed assets, which facilitates the implementation of projects for the subjects of security. An extremely helpful tool in the optimization and effectiveness of logistics processes implemented for supply chain security is automatic identification, which allows online tracking of products (parts, components) – what, how much and where we store, secure critical infrastructure, including access to buildings and systems, creating new levels of security for consumers in the banking sector and differentiated services based on fast and effective customer authentication at the point of use. Nowadays, the quality, resistance to disruptions, usability and timeliness of information are not without significance for supply chain safety management.

The set of determinants of supply chain safety management includes the broadly understood civilization progress, the foundations of which is technology, which contributes to creating better and better solutions and new products. Some of them may be helpful in managing the security of logistics systems for the benefit of the subjects of security. These include IT programs.

These programs used in logistics systems can be divided into three categories: universal (a module supporting a specific logistic process or multi-module systems for specific links in the supplier-recipient relationship), specialized (intended, for example, for integrating the chain), auxiliary (supporting the work of various company departments, managing documents, contacts with customers, facilitating the calculation of logistics costs) (Szołtysek, 2010).

IT programs in logistics facilitate process planning and provide the necessary data online for making decisions in the event of disruptions in the material flow.

There are typical IT systems that support logistics processes. These include the following: efficient consumer response (ECR), customer relationship management (CRM), supply chain management (SCM), warehouse management system (WMS), transport management system (TMS), logistics resources planning (LRP), enterprise asset management (EAM), returnable packaging management (RPM).

The systems that support logistics management within the supply chain also include solutions and modules such as material requirements planning (MRP), manufacturing resource planning (MRP II), enterprise resource planning (ERP), which enable complex planning and simulation operations along with optimization – advanced planning system (APS).

Identification of IT systems used in logistics shows that system manufacturers attach increasing importance to building scalable applications, i.e. those that will "grow" along with the length and capacity of the supply chain. Usually, they offer their customers a new application, externally very similar to the one provided so far but functionally extensive, using a modern, efficient database. As a result, supply chain participants who decide to purchase and deploy a program appropriate to the current situation can easily replace the software in the future as their needs increase (Chow et al., 2005).

The new program is similar in use, so the employees do not have to re-learn it. In addition, the time and costs of the system deployment are significantly reduced. An important tendency in enterprise management support systems is their systematically increasing flexibility. Modern software is becoming easier to modify.

The research results indicated that the necessary conditions for IT integration within multinational and cooperative supply chains are: IT technologies existing in companies and supply chains, uniform identification standard, automatic identification, electronic communication, including electronic data exchange, integrated IT system, securing the information against interference by unauthorized persons and guaranteeing its credibility (Edwards et al., 2001).

Comprehensive IT system integration can be done using various strategies depending on the type of business. The goal of such integration is to optimize the entire supply chain and then its individual participants. The fulfillment of this condition requires that the information system provides: the possibility of obtaining information at any desired point of flow along the logistics chain, the information availability for all cooperating partners, the information accuracy, a satisfactory speed of information flow and its timeliness, the ability to process information to support the decision-making process, the ability to automate activities related to production, acquisition and processing of information and decision-making (Zhu et al., 2011).

5.1.1 Efficient Consumer Response (ECR)

ECR is a supply chain oriented to the customer. It is a modern strategy for servicing the supply chain based on a partnership of its participants consisting of the synchronized management of supply and demand with the involvement of technologies supporting the flow of products, information and financial resources to increase the competitiveness of the entire supply chain and maximize the benefits of all its participants while increasing the satisfaction of the final recipient.

The concerted effort to maximize the efficiency of the entire chain, rather than the traditional focus on the efficiency of its individual links, leads to lower total system costs, stock levels and capital employed while increasing value for the end customer. Their activities focus on modern management methods and technical means to shorten the travel time of the product from the production line (warehouse, distributor) to the recipient and reduce costs. As a result of these activities, the customer receives an acceptable offer with a satisfactory level of service.

In practice, the ECR concept is the basis for building a modern supply chain management strategy. Manufacturers, distributors, retailers and service providers (logistics, IT, research) cooperate to meet the customer's needs better, faster and more effectively.

The implementation of the ECR strategy assumes using modern management methods and new technologies to shorten the travel time of the product from the production line (warehouse, distributor) to the recipient.

The ECR concept is based on three pillars (ECR w praktyce, 2021): ensuring the required level of service, eliminating costs that do not add value, maximizing effects and eliminating barriers along the entire supply chain.

5.1.2 Customer Relationship Management (CRM)

One of the systems supporting the company's operations (distributor, warehouse etc.) is customer relationship management (CRM). The CRM functions include (Rokicka-Broniatowska, 2006; Halicka, 2010): collecting and processing archival data regarding cooperation with the recipient, contacts, orders, activities of sales representatives and employees who are in direct contact with the recipient; automation of organization and delivery management; configuration of orders (products) at the individual request of the customer – CRM systems support agents at the point of sale and enable the compilation of selected elements of products and services; preparing offers; searching for relevant data; preparing sales and market analyses and forecasts; managing technical support departments and call centers; taking care of the customer, the supported recipient (service and possible complaints, technical support); market communication – searching for contacts with business partners; administration – daily organization of tasks (deadlines, contacts, reporting, presentations). The CRM software consists of three elements (Figure 5.1) (Lotko, 2003).

They include operational CRM (used to consolidate data about the customers, the recipients, their needs, behavior or history of cooperation); communication CRM (includes only solutions supporting contact with the customer, recipient), analytical CRM (helps to understand the customer's actions, carries out all contact processes with the client and recipient and performs all other processes in the organization that are important from the point of view of the client and recipient).

The CRM improved with new online technologies, i.e. so-called e-CRM, enabled extending the scope of customer relationship management to the online environment and reducing related costs (Szymonik, Informatyka, 2015). The customer is at the center of attention not only in the traditional economy. Network CRM, like the traditional one, is customer-oriented and performs the same functions. However, it requires separate rules of conduct and different technology. The way of customer service has changed completely.

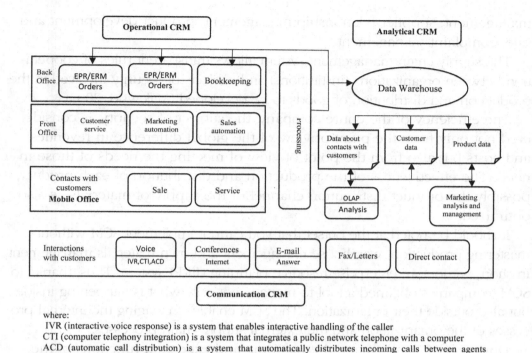

Figure 5.1 **CRM architecture. Source: Compiled based on J. Stasieńko,** *System infor-matyczny wspomagający zarządzanie relacjami z klientami,* **p. 228, https://docplayer.pl, February 28, 2021.**

5.1.3 Supply Chain Management (SCM)

Supply chain management (SCM) systems include IT solutions that serve a company, the subject of security, to manage a supply chain network. Internal SCM covers issues related to acquisition, production and distribution. External SCM integrates the company, the subject of security, with its suppliers and customers (David et al., 2004).

SCM solutions are used primarily in the product design stage, selecting sources of supply, forecasting the demand for products and controlling their distribution. They contain specialized tools that enable the supervision of individual logistic activities of the company.

In conclusion, the supply chain management model is based on eight complementary business processes supported by IT tools (Ciesielski & Długosz, 2010): customer relationship management, customer service management, demand management, order fulfillment, production flow management, supplier relationship management, product development and sale, complaint management.

The supply chain management system allows transparent rules of cooperation between organizations (institutions) and subjects of security involved in the production and distribution of goods to be developed (Majewski, 2002).

The efficiency of the entire company, the subject of security, is considered not only from the point of view of the global difference in revenues and costs but also from the point of view of meeting the needs of those in need. The effectiveness of the production and distribution of each product, possibly the product distribution channel or the supply of materials, is also optimized.

It should be noted at the outset that you cannot implement SCM without mastering production, warehouse management and own materials management, in short, without an enterprise resource planning (ERP) system. Thus, thanks to SCM, companies obtained a tool to manage not only what is happening inside but also outside their organization. The SCM enables managing the internal processes of the organization and the external supply chain processes.

During SCM deployment, the planning and execution functions of the supply chain are considered in more detail. The SCM enables the development of a model of the entire supply network and identifies all its constraints. Then, using this model, one can synchronize activities and plan the flow of materials throughout the entire supply chain. Based on this, supply to demand is adjusted, and workable plans for sourcing, production, stocks and transport are created.

The SCM planning considers many locations, their mutual dependencies, the global logistics chain and partners of a given company. Collaboration on a global scale is new to most companies and requires organizational changes. It involves implementation and strategic, tactical and operational planning. As a result, SCM impacts business processes even at the lowest level.

Real-time planning, advanced simulation methods and optimization possibilities with SCM guarantee a completely new process flow, different from an ERP system. Therefore, the SCM users need to be well-versed in the operation of the entire supply chain.

5.1.4 Warehouse Management System (WMS)

A warehouse management system (WMS) is an IT solution for managing the material flow in warehouses or distribution centers, commonly referred to by logisticians as a system for managing a high-storage warehouse. It supports the implementation and control of the flow through the warehouse and provides information about this flow and the creation of documentation accompanying this flow (Ramaa et al., 2012).

WMS solutions are often modular. They are based on the main program, which is responsible for such aspects as storage management or goods management. In terms of the WMS architecture, the modules that define the storage machines are important. The main WMS modules include such elements as (Pisz et al., 2013; Majewski, 2002): delivery service, input supervision, shipping service, output supervision, forwarding support, changes inside the warehouse, inventory, reports, packaging, classification of goods according to ABC and XYZ methods, which allows the warehouse space to be managed and speeds up the input/output operations.

Different warehouse management systems have several functions that make up their specificity and accurately describe their operation mechanism. These include (Szymonik, Informatyka, 2015): maximum use of warehouse space, reduction in time spent on carrying out activities related to the delivery and ordering of goods, increase in the turnover of stocks and assets, improvement of the quality of services provided by producers, reduction in possible errors thanks to advanced control and quick solving of potential problems between producers and suppliers, high flexibility and mobility of data exchange with the system, easier access to data, complete supervision of orders, the ability to manage warehouse traffic, facilitating the creation of documentation concerning the preparation of goods for shipment and automation of this process, application of barcode or RFID technology for marking goods and logistics units, recording stock levels based on locations, batches or expiry dates, automation of the inventory process.

In companies providing logistics services, the WMS is often a technology supporting the operation of an ERP management system. These systems should exchange data efficiently based on unified standards of information transfer. New software types usually ensure the handling of diverse data in individual IT subsystems of companies and their easy transfer from module to module. This, in turn, allows the movement of products in warehouses using the WMS to be fully automated.

Some ERP vendors offer WMS functionality as one of the modules integrally built into the ERP suite or partially support it as part of warehouse management modules.

5.1.5 Transport Management System (TMS)

A transport management system (TMS) is software that allows carriers from the TSL industry to process in electronic form the data necessary for effective transport management (Verwijmeren, 2004).

The TMS cooperates with the fleet management system (FMS), which is responsible for data processing, such as information on the condition of the vehicle, driving and rest times, loading and unloading times, service time, driver behavior on the road or the level and status of loading or unloading. The heart of the FMS is an open database structure. The onboard computer collects the necessary information about the driver, vehicle and cargo (Szymonik, Informatyka, 2015).

The main TMS functions performed together with the FMS (Pisz & Łapuńka, 2013): optimization of deliveries through consolidation of orders, transport and delivery planning, management of drivers, vehicle fleet and suppliers of transport services, monitoring transport events, handling of atypical forwarding orders thanks to defining features for various industries, according to individual needs, comprehensive handling of orders in the supply chain; handling contracts for transport services and the transport fleet, preparation of analyses and reports, the ability to define by the user price lists for transport services and settlement of transport services, reporting of transport costs, selecting carriers, including the most popular ones, and optimizing routes based on cost comparative printouts, easy integration with ERP/WMS master systems, selection of available vehicles (all by default), selection of orders (all for a given day by default), length of unloading (globally or for the customer), maximum number of stopping points on the route, maximum driver's working time and tolerance for exceeding the working time, maximum vehicle load capacity and vehicle load tolerance.

The system stores and warns about the expiry of deadlines related to, among others, vehicle insurance; technical and warranty inspections; tachograph validity date; events, e.g. tire replacement etc.; the validity of documents.

5.1.6 Logistics Resources Planning (LRP)

Logistic resources planning (LRP) systems are employed to plan logistics needs (resources). They integrate the functions of MRP and DRP modules because the information provided within them complements each other. The use of such a solution results from the tendency of modern logistics to abandon optimization methods for large stocks and focus on eliminating them and shortening the order fulfillment cycle. The main advantages of LRP include the possibility of reducing the costs incurred by individual partners in the supply chain thanks to ongoing corrections of demand forecasts, which also improves customer service (Yan-yan Li & Long, 2013).

In the LRP system, the demand forecast data concerning individual points of sale, including the time distribution of demand in individual cells of the distribution network, are transferred as a schedule to the manufacturing company. The DRP module is used here. At this stage, the indicated data are utilized to plan material needs for a fixed period, which in turn is the area of MRP application. The MRP module allows material stocks to fit the demand resulting from the main production schedule to be reduced, which should reflect the current market demand. In this way, the level of material stocks and the volume of distribution stocks are simultaneously reduced (Szymonik, Zarządzanie dystrybucją, 2015).

5.1.7 Enterprise Asset Management (EAM)

Enterprise asset management (EAM) systems support maintenance in manufacturing companies and manage tenants, contracts and spaces. They help monitor the long-term value of the property and sustainable development or ecological initiatives (Sinha et al., 2007). Generally, it can be stated that EAM facilitates (Figure 5.2): keeping records of assets, managing assets, keeping inventories.

The EAM systems have an advantage over the modules that are ERP components, which only allow the recording of assets and the generation of

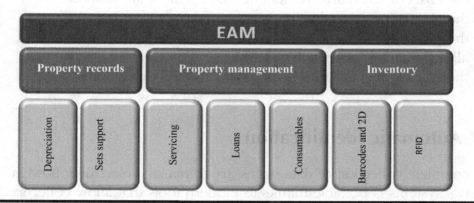

Figure 5.2 EAM areas of responsibility. Source: Compiled based on A. Szymonik, *Informatyka dla potrzeb logistyka (i),* **Difin, Warsaw 2015, p. 86.**

relevant documents, bypassing processes such as further asset management and asset inventory. However, a casual approach to the last two elements can often contribute to inappropriate use of the fixed assets and equipment, thus causing losses to the company (Szymonik, Zarządzanie, 2016).

The most popular EAM systems used by metal industry companies, for instance, are produced by IFS, SAP, Neuron and Junisoftex. They find application in (Szymonik, Zarządzanie, 2016): purchase and warehouse management (to handle purchase requirements, access stocks, e.g. spare parts or consumables), movable property management, including fixed assets (register, equipment, costs, locations, inventory numbers), space or tenant management (i.e. space, assignment of equipment and resources to space, premises, tenants, lease contracts, removals, space optimization), handling reports (e.g. incidents, problems, resource reservations), vehicle management (i.e. register, technical, registration and insurance data, service, equipment), management of planned works (e.g. planned works – preventive), property maintenance, maintenance works, service and organization contracts.

5.1.8 Returnable Packaging Management (RPM)

It is a logistics support service for customers who use returnable packaging. It fully manages the packaging flow between company locations, suppliers and customers. Thanks to one central control center for this process, fast information flow based on real quantitative and location data is ensured. As a result (Zarządzanie opakowaniami zwrotnymi, 2021):

- the costs of returnable packaging management are reduced;
- the circulation of packaging is tightened (monitored);
- the problems with the packaging administration are minimized;
- all information is accessible online;
- there is support in terms of products and EU regulations.

5.2 Automatic Identification

The complete collection of data necessary to manage electronic flow in logistics systems is possible thanks to modern tools that allow collection, analysis and transfer of data within each company and institution and in their relations with the near and far environment. In economic practice, automatic data capture (formerly AI, Auto ID, AIDS) systems are used. This tool involves automatic, direct input of data to IT systems or other micro-processor-controlled equipment using special devices (without a keyboard) (Kudelska & Ponikierska, 2009). These devices, e.g. readers or scanners, ensure quick and error-free data entry into the system. In practice, ADC systems consist of:

- download light indicators;
- optical character recognition (OCR) – a set of methods or software for extracting text from a raster image file (OCR usually recognizes text in a scanned document);
- radio-frequency identification (RFID) – a solution that uses radio waves to transmit data and supply the electronic system that constitutes the tag of the object by the reader to identify the object (it enables reading and sometimes also writing the RFID tag);
- voice systems – solutions that use voice technologies to ensure easy, two-way communication between an IT system, e.g. WMS, and its user, e.g. a warehouse worker who picks goods for release from the ware-house (instead of paper orders or instructions displayed on the screens of mobile terminals, employees use the most natural form of communi-cation, i.e. voice);
- barcode readers, popularly known as scanners, are devices that convert the light reflected from the barcode into an electronic signal readable by a cash register or a computer (depending on the type of reading mecha-nism, there are laser and diode/CCD barcode readers);
- RF terminals – wireless online information exchange via radio, such terminals are often equipped with a barcode scanner;
- vehicle-mounted computers and portable computers have an advantage over handheld devices (larger screen, larger keyboard); they have a graphical user interface (GUI) – generally vehicle-mounted devices use an external – wired or wireless – barcode reader to process data).

The ADC systems improve, among others, the following operations: receipt and issue of materials and goods with automatic control of deliveries, accounting of turnover with automatic updating of inventory stocks, storage and movement of materials and goods with automatic registration of their location (from where to where), picking and completing deliveries for pro-duction or consumption and goods outside companies or institutions with automatic release control, inventory-taking etc.

Depending on the specific needs, the following methods are used in ADC (Hałas, 2012): optical (barcodes, recognition of graphic signs, letters, images), magnetic (magnetic tapes, magnetic ink character recognition), electromagnetic (including electronic tags read by radio – RFID), biometric (voice, fingerprint, iris recognition etc.), tactile (smart cards), voice (headphones and a microphone and computerized speech synthesizer).

The above solutions allow collecting and sending data to IT systems that analyze, store and make it available to interested parties. In practice, mixed solutions are employed. They combine various methods into one system prepared for specialized projects based on information technologies.

5.2.1 Barcodes

Among the optical solutions, barcodes are widely used, especially in logistics, as the most accessible and cheapest, and therefore recommended as the basic ADC tool to improve logistics management (Hongying, 2009). So far, several hundred types and varieties of barcodes (linear barcodes, including reduced, two-dimensional, complex, composite) have been developed, but only a few found widespread use, primarily in logistics, serving as universal, international standards.

In logistics, barcodes are used to identify goods, perform warehouse operations, mark products, track shipments, register documents in the logistics system and record fixed assets of the logistics system. Barcodes enable, above all, a radical increase in the speed of data entry into the IT system and the elimination of errors.

The construction and use of barcodes based on international standards have made them readily used in the ADC systems. The ADC solutions based on barcodes are found in a stationary system – communication with the IT system database through media such as optical fiber or cable, and mobile – communication with the IT system database via radio links (WLAN, Wi-Fi standard). Mobile systems – (portable) electronic device that allows data processing without maintaining a wired connection to the network. A mobile device can be carried or transported. Stationary systems transmit data on a read-write basis. They are designed to work independently and are equipped with special tripods or housings that enable them to be attached to the ground. They are often used on checkout counters because of the cashier's freedom of movement and the possibility to scan codes regardless of their position (vertical, horizontal or at an angle).

The ADC systems consist of scanners (barcode readers), terminals, printers. Scanners can be divided into stationary, wireless, portable (mobile). The barcode reader can read one-dimensional (1D) – laser or diode readers and two-dimensional (2D) codes – vision scanners (imagers). Where mobility and independence are a priority, the ideal solution is to use portable (mobile) computer terminals (also known as data collectors) equipped with a barcode or RFID tag scanner. Data collectors have a built-in barcode reader, keyboard, LCD display, memory and operating system, e.g. Windows CE or Windows Mobile. They are designed to collect, store and transmit data.

The ADC system includes printers for placing barcodes on labels and the information contained therein, which is then used to mark the appropriate item or product. Printers with different technical parameters are available.

5.2.2 *Electronic Product Code (EPC)*

In product labeling (including packaging), a breakthrough occurred when a new method called Electronic Product Code (EPC) was used. Alternative names include radio-frequency identification (RFID), RFID tag, transponder (Bolan, 2008).

The first applications of RFID date back to World War II. The identification, friend or foe (IFF) system, developed by the British, was used to identify aircraft. It can be considered the predecessor of RFID. In 1948, Harry Stockman wrote a paper that introduced the concept of passive RFID systems. In the 1950s and 1960s, scientists in the United States, Europe and Japan researched radio waves to identify objects remotely. The first commercialization of RFID technology concerned anti-theft systems. In the 1990s, RFID became a part of everyday life and business. Since then, thousands of companies working on the development and application of RFID technology have been established worldwide (Szymonik, Zarządzanie zapasami, 2013).

Famous global companies that use RFID for electronic product tagging include Walmart, Target, Albertsons, Metro, Tesco, Max & Spencer, Procter & Gamble and Gillette. Soon, RFID technology will replace the barcode system for labeling goods, which will increase the efficiency of transport, storage and selling goods. An example of a successful deployment is the American retail chain Walmart. RFID is increasingly used in logistics, public transport, security systems and the digital payment market (Szymonik, Zarządzanie zapasami, 2013).

A radio-frequency identification system includes a base station to which an antenna is attached that radiates the energy necessary to power the transponder. The same base station antenna is used to communicate with the RFID transponder, making it possible to read and write data to/from the tag. The base station is connected to an external computer via a wired interface. The base station communicating with the transponder uses the radio interface.

The transmitter and receiver circuits are tuned to the same frequency. The RFID transponders can be divided into read-only (RO) and read-write (RW). The latter has the option of content modification.

Based on power supply, transponders can be divided into active – with an independent power source that provides energy for microprocessor chip and a transmitter with antenna; passive – without an independent power source, electric energy needed for momentary powering of microprocessor chip comes from electromagnetic field emitted by the reader; semi-passive is a cross between active and passive tags. The range of interaction also depends on the range of radio waves used in RFID systems.

An EPC is built in such a way that it is possible to identify all individual products and goods in the supply chain. The most commonly used tags include those following the GS1 standards. These include Serialized Global Trade Item Number (SGTIN), Serial Shipping Container Code (SSCC), Serialized Global Location Number (SGLN), Global Returnable Asset Identifier (GRAI), Global Individual Asset Identifier (GIAI). For product packaging identification in logistics, the first two tags (SGTIN and SSCC) are applied most often.

In the business world, the EPCglobal network was created by GS1 based on global standards. It encourages solution providers to develop software and hardware that uses interfaces built exclusively on these standards. The EPCglobal architecture is described in an open and non-commercial manner. All interfaces between EPCglobal network elements are defined as open standards and developed primarily by the community associated with the EPCglobal Standards Development Process. The EPCglobal architecture is designed to work with all existing industry structures and standards. All standards development work is done through EPC working groups that operate at both a business and technical level (Szymonik, Zarządzanie bezpieczeństwem, 2016).

We distinguish three basic groups of standards (Figure 5.3): EPC physical object exchange, EPC data exchange, EPC infrastructure (Szymonik, Zarządzanie zapasami, 2013).

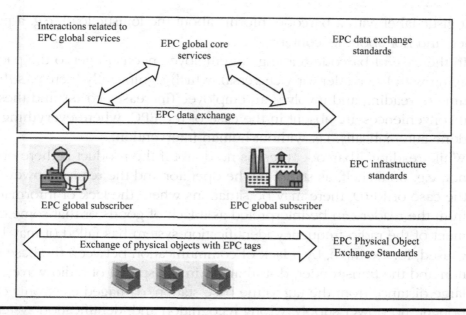

Figure 5.3 EPC global architecture. Source: Compiled based on EPCglobal – The EPCglobal Architecture Framework, Final Version of July 1, 2005; February 1, 2020.

The EPC specification in the GS1 Standard distinguishes four types of events (Hałas, 2012):

- First – Object Event (object identification) – refers to observing a certain group of EPCs; it says nothing about the relationships between objects.
- Second – Aggregation Event (data aggregation) – refers to observing a group of EPCs, e.g. products assigned to a pallet, or changes or events concerning such a group, e.g. loading or unloading.
- Third – Quantity Event (quantity identification) – refers to observing a certain group of EPCs representing one class of objects, e.g. ten cans of soft drink, and changes occurring in this group (quantity change).
- Fourth – Transaction Event (transaction identification) – refers to the assignment of observation to a business transaction or a change in such an assignment, e.g. delivery of goods to a transport company, receipt of goods into a warehouse in a distribution center.

Analyzing the usefulness of currently used barcodes and RFID, one can come to the following conclusions:

- The amount of information that can be obtained online about the logistic load is much greater when using EPC, as we can put the data in the tag itself as well as in the information system, while, for example, a

logistic label with a barcode informs about the logistic load, e.g. a pallet, and not about its contents.

■ In the case of barcode reading, an employee needs to get to the packaging with the reader (or vice versa), which significantly increases the
time of reading and involves an employee (increases costs), and these
inconveniences are absent in the case of the EPC, where everything is
done automatically, i.e. without human intervention.

■ While reading a barcode, there is no doubt if the product is there or
not, e.g. on a shelf, as stated by the operator and the reader; however, in
the case of RFID, there may be situations where the lack of information
from the reader can be interpreted as a lack of goods or that some element of the radio-frequency identification system has failed (it may be
caused, for example, by a lack of communication between the base station and the transponder, disturbances in the spread of radio waves, too
large distance from the tag to the base station, damaged electronic component, no power supply, wrong recognition and identification system).

■ EPC protects against counterfeit products (the information in the base
station allows coding of data about the product) and facilitates identification and tracking throughout the global supply chain of a single piece
of packaging, e.g. for traceability purposes.

■ EPC makes it possible to read multiple labels simultaneously, which is
not possible with barcodes.

■ EPC improves, e.g. baggage management at airports compared to barcodes, which have 70–80% readability (EPC baggage readability is
99.3%).

■ RFID eliminates checkout queues if good and reliable radio-frequency
identification systems (omnidirectional base station antennas) are used.

■ Barcodes will be used in logistics for a long time because of their
reliability (if a transponder is placed directly on metal packages, for
instance, its operating range is zero), universality and relatively low
costs of introduction and exploitation.

The presented analysis shows the advantages of barcodes and indicates that
there is no escape from RFID in logistics. The latter technology provides
better and cheaper solutions, and the RFID benefits are indisputable (e.g.
speed, reading without human intervention, protection against counterfeit
products). Currently, the best solution in the case of valuable "consignments"
that arrive "on time" is the simultaneous use of a label containing an RFID
tag and printed product code.

5.2.3 *Optical Character Recognition*

Analyzing printed and handwritten text identification systems, it is easy to see that they are developing with advances in electronics and IT. There are three types of text recognition technologies: OCR, ICR and OMR.

Optical character recognition (OCR) is a technology that allows the conversion of scanned text into digital form (Berchmans & Kumar, 2014). OCR is developing in two directions. On the one hand, better and better text recognition methods are being developed, including handwritten texts. Intelligent character recognition (ICR) deals with the latter. On the other hand, special fonts are being created to facilitate reading, i.e. OCR-A and OCR-B. Programs that work on images sent from scanners and digital cameras are used for character recognition. Special fonts are usually used when there is a need for frequent, fast and easy reading of information. The OCR systems employ barcode, typewriter, magnetic type, block type.

ICR stands for intelligent character recognition. The main task of this system is to recognize handwritten alphanumeric characters, i.e. it recognizes handwriting. It uses neural network mechanisms.

OMR stands for optical mark recognition. It refers to recognizing characters other than alphanumeric, such as checkboxes or barcodes (Pérez-Benedito et al., 2014). The OMR readers significantly facilitate the analysis of a large number of standardized forms and allow controlling the correctness of their completion. This system requires specially prepared forms and scanners that read selected types of markings placed in specific areas of the form. The OMR software recognizes the presence or absence of marks in specific places on the form and processes this signal into a computer record considering the location of these marks. The technology is useful for data collection provided that the data are relatively simple (e.g. yes or no answers or multiple choice closed-ended questions) and the forms are well prepared. OMR is not designed to deal with large amounts of text. In such situations, OCR or ICR are more useful.

OCR, ICR and OMR systems are used in different fields. Therefore, their effectiveness must be tested according to different criteria. For example, if the percentage of correctly read and analyzed data is the basic criterion, OMR systems are the most effective (up to 99.9%); OCR systems are less effective, and ICR systems have the highest percentage of misinterpretations. The latter two systems (OCR and ICR) can also achieve about 99% success rate, but only under very strict, almost "laboratory" conditions and after manual editing of errors (Szymonik, Informatyka, 2015).

5.2.4 *Voice Communication*

Voice systems are prevalent in warehouses (ranging from small food ware-houses to large pharmaceutical or tool warehouses) where picking is often performed. The main carriers of information in voice systems are voice messages sent between the operator and the WMS. Tasks to be performed are generated by the warehouse management system and transmitted via a radio network to the voice terminal (attached to the belt), where speech recognition software operates. The operator receives voice commands from the system and by voice confirms their execution, according to the designed scenario.

5.2.5 *Biometric Methods*

Biometrics are mathematical and statistical methods for studying the regulari-ties that guide variation in populations of living organisms. Biometrics is also the recognition of individuals based on their specific physical and behavioral characteristics. These characteristics include fingerprints, the shape of the face or hand, the iris of the eye, handwriting, speech, gait and even the vein pattern of the wrist.

Biometrics is used primarily as access control to protected premises or identification of users using specific devices (e.g. computer), data, informa-tion. More and more often, biometric systems support searching for a spe-cific individual and recording working time.

Along with various technologies, reliable systems are being created, enabling people to be identified based on their characteristic features. They carry out the verification or identification of a person in a fully automated manner. Specialized computer-aided apparatus automatically collects data essential for recognition, processes it and compares with a pattern from the database.

In practice, there are many types of biometric systems, which include (Zaworski, 2015):

■ Fingerprint recognition – this type of system consists of a scanner that collects data for analysis and software that records characteristic data of the fingerprint in a specific format. This information is entered in the database as a pattern and compared with new fingerprints entered by the scanner each time a user wants to access the system. The user will be recognized even if the finger is cut or dirty. Most systems enter more than one finger into the database as a security measure in case the system fails to recognize the user for some reason. At present, fingerprint recognition is the most widely used biometric technology.

■ Face recognition – the shape of the face, all its elements (nose, eyes, mouth etc.) and mutual relations between them (distance, proportions etc.) create a very unique structure for biometric systems. The principle of operation of the system is analogous to fingerprint recognition. The camera records the image of the face, and then the software selects detailed information, which it compares with the pattern registered in the database. Two technologies are used in the face recognition process. The first compares the sizes of individual facial features and the relationships between them. For example, nose length and pupil spacing. The second method compares the most characteristic data from the image transmitted from the camera (for example, the size of the nose) with the face pattern stored in the database. The face recognition system is reliable, but due to the high cost of the hardware and the complexity of configuring the system, it is not widespread.

■ Iris recognition – the iris of the eye includes a very large number of points characteristic and unique for each person. For biometric systems, it is an almost ideal data source. The camera scans the image of the user's iris and sends a sample for analysis. The program compares the sent data with the stored pattern and, based on the result, identifies the user.

■ Retina recognition – it is probably the most advanced and secure biometric system. The image of the retina, which is located at the back of the eye, is very difficult to capture. When a user is entered into the system, they must direct their gaze to a specific point and hold it in that state for a few seconds before the camera registers the iris image correctly. The only thing that is recorded is the pattern of blood vessels. This pattern is unique to each person, so identification is very accurate. Retina and iris recognition systems offer the highest system security due to the unique data sources and the quality of reading devices (specialized cameras for scanning the eye) (Choraś, 2012).

■ Hand geometry – in this system, a user puts the hand on a reader in the position recommended by a device manufacturer. The reader registers a three-dimensional image of the person's fingers and palm. The image is stored in the database as a pattern. Hand geometry recognition systems are one of the most accurate and widely used biometric systems. Such a system was used during the 1996 Olympics for security checks in the entire Olympic Village (Ayurzana et al., 2013).

- ■ Finger geometry – this system is similar to the previous one. The reader registers a three-dimensional image of one or two fingers (Malassiotis et al., 2006).
- ■ Palm recognition – this system is very similar to the fingerprint recognition system. In this case, the lines on the inside of the palm are captured by the scanner (Zhang & Hu, 2010).
- ■ Voice recognition – in this method, the sound of the user's voice is recorded, including the language habits (accent, intonation etc.) and any other speech defects that may facilitate identification. The biggest problem with this solution is the ease with which the system can be fooled by a voice recorded on tape. More advanced solutions require the user to say longer and more difficult phrases than just name and surname. It is also often required to say something different each time the user logs into the system. This process significantly increases the verification time and affects the efficiency of the entire system. Another disadvantage of this solution is that the system is susceptible to any changes in the user's voice caused, for example, by a cold or strain of the vocal cords. Another disadvantage is that the system is significantly affected by all the sounds. The advantage is the relatively low deployment cost for many users, as the system is compatible with such devices as telephones or very simple microphones. Therefore, these devices are already installed, or the cost of their purchase is low (Gupta et al., 2014).
- ■ Signature recognition – it is the most easily accepted system by all users. This is due to our habits and customs. For a long time, a handwritten signature on all kinds of documents has served as a form of identity verification. This system goes far beyond simple signature analysis. In addition to the shape of the signature and its content, it also checks the pressure of the pen, the speed of writing, the places where the pen is lifted. All of this is recorded using a specially designed pen and tablet. After processing, the data is saved in the database as a benchmark for comparison. The main problem with this system is that our signature changes over time. The database requires constant updating or storing a sufficiently large number of specimen signatures (Deore & Handore, 2015).

Biometric systems, in practice, can be used in the following areas of our life: health care, where the identification of patients is made through the introduction of a chip card (the use of biometric characteristics is considered for cardholder authentication); critical infrastructure protection, including access to buildings and systems; creating new levels of security for consumers in the banking sector and different services based on fast and efficient customer authentication at the point of use.

5.3 Electronic Data Interchange

The reasons for using electronic data interchange (EDI) include (Rutkowski, 2001): the growing interest in logistics, especially issues related to shortening lead times; the globalization of commercial transactions, forcing an agreement on a worldwide standard for documents; the development of computer technology and reducing the costs of its use.

Electronic data interchange is the electronic transmission of standard formatted data between the IT systems of trading partners with minimal human intervention (Hałas, 2012). Modern telecommunication offers various possibilities of EDI messages transmission using public telecommunication networks, through private networks providing additional services, so-called value-added network (VAN) or the internet. The EDI systems consist of components linked in a logical network (Figure 5.4). The common language in EDI is standards, a set of data and codes used to create messages that can be understood by the interested parties in the computer network. The standard messages include four basic groups (Hałas, 2012).

Today, the most popular EDI standards are ANSI X12 and UN/EDIFACT (United Nations/Electronic Data Interchange for Administration, Commerce and Transport), approved by the US Federal Government and United

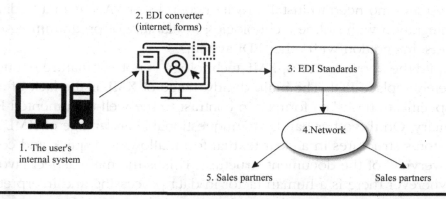

Figure 5.4 EDI standards. Source: Compiled based on *Kody kreskowe*, IliM, Poznań 2000, p. 227.

Nations. ANSI X12 is the main standard in the USA and UN/EDIFACT in other countries. Currently, all organizations responsible for EDI standardization have decided to migrate to EDIFACT. EDIFACT messages (documents) enable sending information necessary for business transactions. These messages can be divided into three groups (Hałas, 2012):

- commercial messages (price catalogue, order, invoice), which enable the exchange of information between the seller and the buyer;
- transport messages (transport order, delivery note) used to organize the delivery of goods;
- financial messages (transfer, account activity) used for making payments and informing about money flows.

In recent years, there has been an intensive development of the standard of electronic documents created using XML (Extensible Markup Language). This universal meta-language enables saving data and its structure. This functionality is available thanks to tags and their attributes, in which specific values are stored. In this respect, the structure of an XML document is similar to the markup system used in HTML. Since the definition of the XML 1.0 standard in 1998, there has been a steady increase in its popularity, mainly in web applications and data exchange applications between systems.

Conceptually, XML is very similar to EDI, and in a way, it is an extension of it. Its versatility enables both data circulation within the system of one company and many companies. The main advantages of XML include (Szymonik, Informatyka, 2015): flexibility – it is easier to make changes in the message structure; independence from the hardware platform and operating system – no need to install private networks or VAN as in a traditional EDI; integration with online technologies; availability of programming tools; low costs; integration with other EDI systems.

Despite the above features, XML technology is not yet mature enough to completely replace EDI. The main disadvantage of XML is the lack of a uniform specification of data formats in contrast to the well-documented EDI vocabulary. On the other hand, the unquestionable advantage of XML is that it stores structures in a clear textual form, allowing a quick and convenient overview of the document structure. This is the main aspect favoring XML wherever there is a human factor in data processing and interpretation. It is imperative in systems of interactive data exchange between the user and the network.

5.4 Traceability in Logistics

Traceability or Track, Trace and Control (TTC) systems enable: tracking (tracing) the path of a product from its manufacturing from raw materials to the moment it reaches the final customer in the supply chain, both upstream and downstream, and recording parameters identifying these goods and any location covered by the stream. TTC systems are applied, among others, in the food industry, pharmaceutical and cosmetics sectors. Using traceability in these areas has been enforced by the EU Commission regulations and national laws.

Traceability allows the precise identification of the material stream processes on the suppliers' and recipients' market, provided that all participants apply the same rules and standards, e.g. GS1 standards and European Union requirements.

The basic GS1 standards include Global Trade Item Number (GTIN), Serial Shipping Container Code (SSCC), Global Location Number (GLN), description of standards (barcodes, EPC, eCom messages and others).

These standards define and ensure that (Hałas, 2012): all tracked goods or shipments are identifiable by the same identifiers; the identifier remains on the goods/shipments throughout the entire tracking process; all locations (modal points) are identified by a GLN throughout the supply chain; data about the products and their physical flow is collected and shared according to agreed rules between trading partners (e.g. by GDSN, EDI messages, EPC IS). A model of how a traceability system works, in the supply chain, in practice is shown in Figure 5.5.

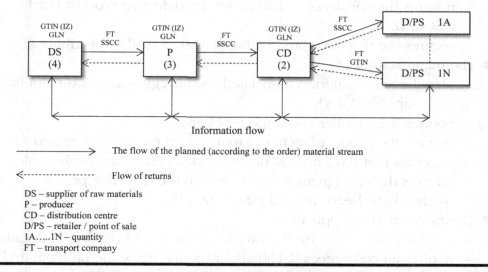

Figure 5.5   **A model of *traceability* system in the supply chain. Source: Own elaboration.**

The basic elements of the model are retailers – points of sale (1A...1N), distribution center (2), manufacturer (3), supplier of raw materials (4), transport companies that deliver raw materials and products to customers, information system that ensures the flow of information between links of the supply chain.

If the supply chain model functions smoothly, the flow of the material stream follows the orders that are placed sequentially by the retailers/ points of sale (1A...1N) with the distribution center (2), the center places an order with a manufacturer (3) and the manufacturer with the raw material supplier (4). In case of difficulties with the quality of products, specially developed procedures are followed, allowing quick action to eliminate any disturbances. Thanks to the applied standards and appropriate information technologies, in case of delivery of a defective product to the final consumer, the following actions are taken (Sokołowski, 2014):

■ The retailer – point of sale (1A):
  – identifies the defective product name, product number (GTIN), supplier (GLN), production lot number (IZ 10);
  – notifies the product distributor (2);
  – secures all products from the identified batch against further sale.
■ The distribution center (2):
  – identifies all products (GTIN) from the defective production lot that it currently has (MA 10);
  – notifies the supplier about the problem with the batch (GLN);
  – informs the consignee (GLN) about the defective product batch (SSCC, IZ 10);
  – secures the defective product batch against further distribution.
■ The manufacturer (3):
  – identifies raw materials associated with irregularities and identifies their supplier (GLN);
  – notifies the supplier about the problem;
  – secures the product batches manufactured from the identified raw materials that have not yet been shipped before any further sale;
  – informs the consignees (GLN) to whom the defective product batches have been shipped (SSCC, IZ 10).
■ The raw material supplier (4):
  – analyzes the reason for the problem – finds and confirms the cause;
  – notifies all consignees (GLN) about the nature of the problem and discloses the batch number of the raw materials (IZ 10);

- identifies all goods shipped from those delivery batches (SSCC);
- secures the remaining raw materials from those batches against further use.
■ The manufacturer (3) – based on historical data:
- traces defective product batches manufactured in the past;
- identifies SSCCs of boxes and pallets containing batches to be recalled;
- identifies the consignees (distribution center 3) of the defective products (GLN) and provides them with information regarding the products to be returned (SSCC, GTIN, IZ 10).
■ The distribution center – based on additional data received from the manufacturer (3):
- identifies boxes and pallets (GTIN, SSCC) to be returned;
- removes and returns defective products from the distribution center (GTIN, SSCC);
- provides retailers and points of sale (1A...1N) with SSCCs and/or GTINs and batch numbers of the shipped items to be removed;
■ The retailer – point of sale (1A...1N):
- retailers identify suspect items (using GTIN, IZ 10) and return them to the supplier – distribution center (2).

Traceability is also a system for automatic tracking of the production batch (Figure 5.6).

Tracking systems are also increasingly used in manufacturing companies, the OEM sector, the automotive industry (e.g. identification of parts/components used in the automotive sector – operated by GS1 Germany), the financial sector (e.g. identification of global transactions – operated by GS1 US, i.e. in the USA), the catering industry (improvement of food safety), health care (e.g. patient handling; fixed asset records).

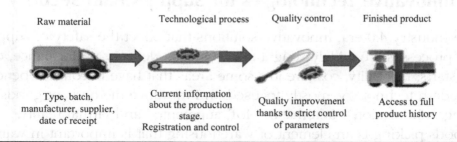

Figure 5.6   Traceability in batch tracking. Source: Compiled based on A. Szymonik, *Informatyka dla potrzeb logistyka (i),* **Difin, Warsaw 2015, p. 129.**

Using barcodes or RFID, the system registers all the operations performed on a given batch or product, which makes it possible to (Szymonik, Informatyka, 2015): reconstruct the product genealogy (who, when, with which machine, from what raw material, with what process parameters made it), control the process correctness (whether all the operations were performed in the right order and time interval), find numbers of all batches for which irregularities are suspected.

In manufacturing companies, traceability is done through manufacturing execution systems (MES) (Chao & Li, 2006). These systems use appropriate technologies, software, automation elements and data collected directly from production sites. The entire process takes place in real-time, which enables its transfer to the business area (Banaszak et al., 2011).

Thanks to the system functionality, it is possible to obtain immediate feedback on the level of production execution, make the right decisions and react on an ongoing basis to irregularities occurring during the production process. The production process data allow key efficiency indicators in production to be analyzed and an accurate picture of the production capacity utilization to be found.

Examples of MES functionalities include (Banaszak et al., 2011): flow tracking, production genealogy, real-time tracking and visualization of work in progress, tracking actual working time and productivity of machines and people, tracking downtime, recording the causes of downtime, planning the execution of production orders and controlling their implementation at the operational level, updating stock levels of materials, semi-finished and finished products, collecting information about production quality, generating automatic reports, analyzing the collected information, production cost accounting.

5.5 Innovative Technologies for Supply Chain Security

In the Industry 4.0 era, innovative solutions that affect the safety of supply chain processes are widely sought after. Quality, delivery performance, cycle time, starts, flexibility, cost are just some areas that have become dependent on modern technology, mostly focused on innovative methods of goods picking, robotization – automation, IoT, augmented and virtual reality.

Goods picking is an element of warehousing that is important in warehouse costs, maintaining the continuity of logistics processes and service level. Picking rate analysis is a tool to assess coordination within the supply chain. Based on the order picking accuracy, cooperating companies determine the range of acceptable quality of service, which consists of separating loading units into sets of individual or collective packages and putting them together following the customer's order.

Many modern solutions are applied to ensure efficient and effective execution of processes related to order picking. They include methods from the pick-by category used in warehouses and logistics centers. Examples are given below:

■ Pick-by-light systems are designed for indoor use. They can be used wherever there is manual picking and sorting of items. This applies to both dispatch and production warehouses (Skarbecki, 2021). The pick-by-light notification light on the picking conveyor indicates the order of picking and sets the path for the preparation of the products to be picked.

■ Pick-by-voice involves the use of voice technology and the warehouse IT system to handle order picking, often an additional module to the WMS. A person picking goods in the warehouse is equipped with a headset (headphones with a microphone). Based on the order, the system provides the employee with an optimized list of items and goods to pick, according to which the employee is guided around the warehouse. The employee is directed by voice to the appropriate place in the warehouse. The employee confirms the completion of each step into the microphone by providing control digits from location codes and product codes. Every picking step is verified by the system, including information about the number of products remaining after picking in each location. This permanent inventory allows errors to be identified before they occur or before shipments leave the warehouse (Pick-by-voice, 2021).

■ Pick-by-scan – orders from the ERP or WMS are sent to mobile devices (scanners) with which warehouse workers scan the article that is in the process of picking, take the desired quantity that appears on the device display, confirm and move to the next location in the warehouse, which is indicated by the system via a mobile device (Co rozumiemy pod pojęciem komisjonowania?, 2021).

■ Pick-by-point involves illuminating a storage slot with a beam of light based on information contained in an active order for preparation. When the order is activated, the storage location is marked with a light point. Information about the number of items to be picked and their characteristics is transmitted via wireless headphones (Złoch, 2021).

■ Pick-by-radar is a method that inspects surfaces and areas in front of racks or rows of pallets using a light curtain. With specialized software for image analysis, it is possible to precisely control access to storage slots by employees behind this surface. The system works on the poka-yoke principle, i.e. prevention of defects caused by errors and mistakes made by the operator due to lack of concentration (inattention). All parameters of access to individual slots are precisely recorded. Immediately after the activation of order, three surfaces are activated in front of the shelves: the retrieved (green), forbidden (red) and virtual button (blue). The employee can only reach into the slot behind the green area. After reaching into the forbidden area, an error is registered, and an alarm is triggered. The sizes and positions of the light curtain control areas are freely configurable (Złoch, 2021).

■ Pick-by-frame is based on a standard multi-compartment cart to which a self-supporting frame equipped with digital LED displays is docked and radio-coupled (Wi-Fi) to a central IT system. In this method, the picking cart waits in place while only the picking frame is used, which can be used simultaneously for picking another order. The employee in charge of picking takes the indicated quantity of goods that have been shown on the central display and places them in the locations indicated on the cart by the LED notification light located under the picking slots. The worker is then responsible for confirming each operation through a scanner or speech identifier. All the time, the process of the entire order picking is projected on the frame (Pick-by-Frame, 2021; Szymonik, Chudzik, Nowoczesna, 2020).

5.5.1 Artificial Intelligence in Supply Chains

Modern solutions are important for the security of supply chain processes. One of them is artificial intelligence (AI). It is most often defined as the ability of machines to exhibit human skills such as reasoning, learning, planning and creativity. It enables technical systems to perceive their environment, deal with what they perceive and solve problems by working towards a specific goal. A computer receives data (already prepared or collected through its sensors, scanners, cameras etc.), processes them and reacts. AI systems can adapt their behavior to some extent by analyzing the effects of previous actions and acting autonomously (Sztuczna inteligencja: co to jest i jakie ma zastosowania?, 2021).

AI provides tremendous opportunities to increase efficiency and eliminate errors associated with logistics and warehousing processes while maintaining the highest safety standards at every stage of the supply chain. Undoubtedly, artificial intelligence was introduced to develop and create "thinking machines" that can imitate, learn and replace human intelligence. It should be emphasized that the application of artificial intelligence in logistics is in its infancy. Nevertheless, it should be stressed that this field is rapidly developing, as evidenced by the practical solutions introduced. Below are some examples of AI applications.

First. Wide application and use of analytics and big data, which allow the improvement of (Nowik, 2021):

■ the use of resources and their deployment, reducing time, as well as waste disposal and returns;
■ the quality of customer service;
■ the synchronization between the links in the supply chain (all the data collected, once correctly interpreted, can serve as a source of detection of disruptions, risks and undesirable actions, contribute to their elimination and allow such events to be prevented);
■ the integration of companies participating in the supply chain (data may be collected from each process, at each stage of execution with regard to company operations or the whole supply chain on a global scale);
■ the collection of information for traffic, environmental and social risk analysis.

Second. Artificial intelligence has helped to introduce automation of warehouse processes that affect:

■ organizing and coordinating warehouse robots;
■ shortening process flows;
■ standardizing and stabilizing quality;
■ reducing warehousing cost per sales unit;
■ reducing the risk of errors in the picking process.

Third. AI contributes to optimizing the flow of the material stream in internal and external transport. The software can:

■ analyze the collected data that help plan how equipment (robots, automatic and semi-automatic systems) will be used in warehouse processes;

■ manage the transport fleet in terms of traffic volume or road conditions analysis (routes and travel times of carriers are optimized).

Fourth. Artificial intelligence facilitates managing information that is used to coordinate the flow of material stream and security of operations within the supply chain. Good, safe, reliable information facilitates (Sztuczna inteligencja: co to jest i jakie ma zastosowania? 2021):

■ automatic stock management – software monitors stocks in the warehouse on an ongoing basis and independently makes decisions about, e.g. the need for restocking due to the risk of shortage of goods;
■ traceability, i.e. the ability to track and locate products throughout the entire chain, which includes procurement, production and distribution, in real-time (e.g. immediate response to the recall of a defective product);
■ contact with customers through chatbots – these computer programs:
■ act as virtual assistants who, thanks to artificial intelligence, can hold conversations with people in natural language;
■ can recognize the meaning of the questions asked and give the correct answer.

5.5.2 Machine Vision in Supply Chains

Machine vision (MV) is a technology that uses cooperating electronic devices to perform an automatic visual analysis of the environment (allows machines to see). Images, or visual data, are captured and analyzed with a camera, analogue-to-digital conversion and digital signal processing, and then transferred to a PC where specialized software can process, analyze and measure various characteristics for decision-making.

Machine vision is a multidisciplinary field that borrows technologies from optics, electronics, mechanics, computer science and artificial intelligence research.

Machine vision is also involved in logistics processes carried out within the supply chain and affects their safety. The main tasks of these devices and systems include (Szymonik, Logistyka, produkcji..., 2010):

■ supporting the widely understood control and identification of the product in terms of its identity, physical parameters (quality and quantity);
■ participating in the control process of the flow of the material stream in the area of supply, production and distribution;

- transmitting information in ADC system used in logistic processes;
- blocking from access all goods considered to be defective and dangerous;
- sending notifications to all suppliers from which materials have been received about suspected defectiveness.

Machine vision is a future-proof tool for manufacturing and logistics processes, as evidenced by the many benefits of using this solution. Machine vision is applied primarily in solutions that require high product reliability and continuity of the automated production line through timely delivery of components to the manufacturing system, among other things. High reliability can be achieved by using this technology. In many cases, it is more reliable than humans because it can work 24 hours, is not subject to negative psychophysical factors etc. (Vernon, 1991).

Machine vision has found a place where traditional methods of automatic identification (i.e. barcodes, magnetic tracks, radio waves – RFID, character recognition) cannot be applied due to, for instance:

- poor reading quality due to a large accumulation of labels tags in a small space;
- interference or even attenuation of radio transmission due to placing tags on substances such as metal.

Another aspect favoring machine vision systems in supply chains is the care of high product quality. Automatic visual control allows for its free execution in the case of large-scale production (distribution) that involves multiple lots and repetitiveness, where a man often fails. The limitation here is, of course, the complexity of the task and the required capacity of the production system, which is extremely important when checking the product online (carried out during the product manufacturing process) and controlling the flow in production and logistics processes (Vernon, 1991).

In practice, in the supply chain, machine vision is also used for (Sztuczna inteligencja zmienia oblicze logistyki 2021):

- Supply chain planning (SCP) as part of supply chain management (SCM) systems. Extensive use is made of accumulated experience (i.e. databases) and knowledge that:
  - enables accurate forecasting of demand and delivery dates;
  - allows the availability of products for incoming inquiries and orders from customers to be determined in real-time (this enables

negotiating with the customer more effectively, immediately informing the customer about the date of availability of the product or
offering a substitute).

■ For efficient, effective, secure stock management for supply chain
needs, machine vision enables:

– analysis of huge amounts of data generated in warehouse management systems relating to the number of orders, returns and stock
levels (this allows customer preference patterns, information on what
goods are ordered most often and when, or which products are
mostly bought together to be determined and identified);

– picking of goods using pick-by systems and automated guided vehicles (AGVs), which can "learn" to move around the warehouse and
automatically adapt to changes in their environment, thus increasing
work safety;

– automation of warehouse processes that are fast, reliable and safe.
Undoubtedly, an example of using artificial intelligence and machine
learning should be shown here. The directions of logistics development can be perfectly seen in the example of Puma, which, together
with Magazino, Gigaton and ITG, opened the first fully automated
warehouse in the German town of Schwaig. Transport of goods in
the innovative warehouse is carried out by a new intelligent robot
TORU, developed to work in this type of facility, shown in Figure 5.7.

TORU is a highly intelligent machine that has been equipped
with a large number of sensors and cameras with which it makes
its own decisions and manages warehouse processes. It is an
example of an artificial intelligence robot that learns new behaviors

Figure 5.7   TORU at work in a warehouse. Source: Compiled based on Z. Piątek,
Robot w magazynie Puma, **https://przemysl-40.pl/, March 5, 2021.**

every day, based on which it optimizes warehouse operations daily. Its experience is based on daily analysis of warehouse topology, performed daily warehouse operations and cooperation with a human, who partly still participates in planning work in the described warehouse. Certainly, the main advantage of this robot is the learning itself, but what is most important in achieving high work efficiency is the ability to work 7 days a week, 24 hours a day, with higher efficiency than before (Powstaje pierwszy na świecie inteligentny magazyn, 2020).

– The application of intelligent vehicles in road transport will help to solve the problem of shortage of professional drivers on the labor market, reduce transport costs, shorten the time of goods delivery, reduce the negative impact of company operations on the environment and increase road safety. Road transport is already becoming automated with the increasing use of Internet of things devices. Autonomous vehicles can also form truck platooning, further enhancing the benefits. Companies such as DAF, Daimler, Iveco, MAN, Scania and Volvo are working on intelligent truck technology.

Chapter 6

Reverse Logistics in Supply Chains: Environmental Protection

6.1 The Essence of Reverse Logistics in Supply Chains

Reverse logistics essentially involves actions that minimize negative impacts on the environment. The safety of these actions is closely related to creating a resilient system by identifying processes, analysis and effective decision-making affecting the efficient and effective functioning of a circular economy.

In logistics, one can distinguish two types of supply chains. **The first** is most often identified with networks of producers, service providers, which create products and services provided to final consumers. The participants of such supply chain include mining companies, manufacturing and service companies, while the objects include raw materials, semi-finished products, parts, components supplied to production lines, service recipients, which form the finished product for the final consumer. **The second** is related to waste flows along the supply chain. The participants include companies collecting waste, transporting, storing (depositing), processing (recovering, neutralizing, incinerating), selling (intermediating) waste (e.g. markets). The objects include waste, i.e. substances or objects that the holder disposes of, intends to dispose of, or is obligated to dispose of. What fundamentally distinguishes this supply chain from the previous one is the reverse direction of the material flow. The processes carried out in the second supply chain are called reverse logistics, which is also referred to as backwards supply chain, aftermarket supply chain, aftermarket logistics or retrogistics.

DOI: 10.4324/9781003286110-6

The interest in reverse logistics in the supply chain is due to (Figure 6.1):

- global concern for the environment, which in many cases is degraded by business, economic activities;
- depleting non-renewable resources (fossil fuels, coal, oil, gas, metal ores and other elements), which forces waste reuse (recycling);
- development of technology, which allows ecological and reusable goods to be manufactured;
- customer requirements, who want to use a simplified system of returning goods (including those purchased electronically) to the manufacturer from points of sale for repair (not only warranty), recycling or disposal for the sake of environmental protection.

Based on the literature, it can be said that reverse logistics includes all processes of managing waste flows (including products of full value and damaged, but recognized by their owners as waste), as well as information (related to these flows), from their points of generation (appearance in the logistics system) to their destination for reuse, recovery of value (through repair, recycling or treatment) or proper disposal and long-term storage in such a way that these flows are economically efficient and minimize negative impacts on the human environment (Kisperska-Moroń & Krzyżaniak, 2009). With reference to the above findings, reverse logistics can be defined as an integrated supply chain system, which (Korzeń, 2001):

- is based on the concept of managing the recirculation of waste material streams in an economy and the flows of information coupled with them;

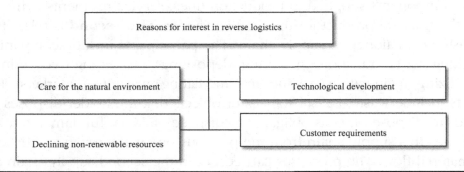

Figure 6.1   Factors of interest in reverse logistics. Source: Own elaboration.

■ ensures readiness and capacity for effective collection, segregation, processing and reuse of waste according to accepted technical and process principles, meeting normative and legal requirements for environmental protection;
■ makes it possible to take technical and organizational decisions to reduce (minimize) the adverse effects on the environment that accompany the supply, processing, production, distribution and service processes in logistic supply chains.

Critical waste management processes, which in phase view support reverse logistics within the supply chain, are the following functions (Figure 6.2) (Ustawa z dnia 14 grudnia, 2012):

■ separate collection, whereby a given waste stream consists only of waste possessing the same properties and characteristics to facilitate specific treatment;
■ storage (preliminary by the producer, temporary storage by the waste collector, principal storage by the waste treatment operator);
■ transport of waste is carried out in accordance with requirements concerning the protection of the environment and human safety, in

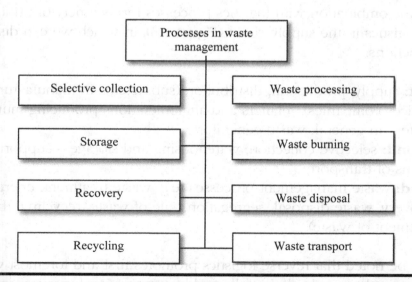

Figure 6.2 Types of waste management processes in the supply chain. Source: Own elaboration.

particular in a way that considers chemical and physical properties of waste as well as hazards that waste may cause;

■ recovery, the primary outcome of which is that the waste serves a useful purpose by replacing other materials that would otherwise be used to perform a function, or as a result of which the waste is prepared to perform such a function in a given plant or the economy in general;

■ energy recovery, the thermal treatment of waste for energy recovery;

■ waste collection, the accumulation of waste before transport to a treatment site, through sorting that does not result in a change of classification;

■ sale of waste, in a legal transaction between an authorized entity and a purchaser;

■ recycling, recovery, which consists of reprocessing substances or materials contained in waste in a production process to obtain a substance or material of primary purpose;

■ treatment, i.e. recovery or disposal;

■ incineration of waste by oxidation in specially built incineration plants;

■ waste disposal – means a process that is not recovery even if the secondary consequence of such a process is the recovery of substances or energy.

Ecology in combination with logistics processes forms a network (model) of reverse logistics in the supply chain (Figure 6.3), in which we can distinguish three functions:

■ **first:** supply, production, distribution (subsystems in manufacturing and services companies), retailers and agglomerations producing municipal waste – in general, waste generators;

■ **second:** selective collection, warehousing and storage – supported by means of transport;

■ **third:** waste management processes (e.g. waste treatment, energy recovery, waste disposal, segregation, sale of waste, recycling, thermal treatment of waste).

It should be noted that reverse logistics promotes first and foremost waste prevention in the supply chain, followed by preparation for reuse, recycling, other recovery processes and disposal.

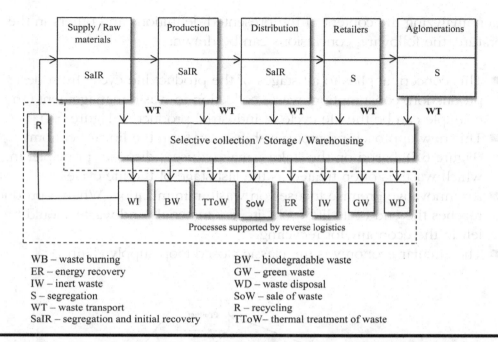

Figure 6.3 Reverse logistics network (model) of a supply chain. Source: Own elaboration.

6.2 Circular Economy

The circular economy is gaining more and more importance and practical application in economic systems, including the supply chain. In Europe, its popularization is related, among other things, to the European Union requirements.

There is no clear definition of a circular economy. Some definitions are given below.

- A circular economy is a production and consumption model that involves sharing, borrowing, reusing, repairing, renewing and recycling existing materials and products for as long as possible. In this way, the life cycle of the products is extended (Gospodarka o obiegu zamkniętym, 2021).
- A circular economy is an economic concept in which products, materials and raw materials should remain in the economy if possible, and the generation of waste should be minimized as much as possible (Gospodarka o obiegu zamkniętym, 2021).

When analyzing the content of the presented definitions and others in the literature, the following conclusions can be drawn:

■ This concept applies to all stages of the product life cycle: from design, production, consumption, waste collection to waste management (an example can be the life cycle of industrial products – Figure 6.4).
■ This new approach promotes a shift away from the linear economy (Figure 6.5), based on the "take – make – use – dispose" principle, in which waste is often treated as the last stage of the life cycle.
■ An innovative premise focuses on waste minimization. When a product reaches the end of its life cycle, its raw materials and waste should be left in the economy for recycling.
■ The circular economy is the classic closed-loop supply chain.

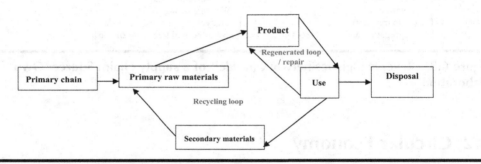

Figure 6.4 An industrial product life cycle model. Source: Compiled based on W. Stahel, "The product-life factor. An inquiry into the nature of sustainable societies. The role of the private sector", 1982.

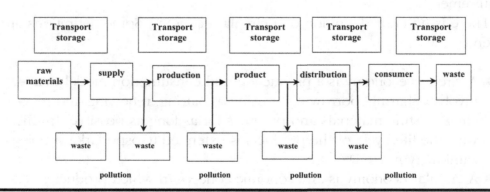

Figure 6.5 The linear model of the economy. Source: Compiled based on B. Tundys, "Green supply chain in a circular economy – assumptions, relations, implications", scientific work of the University of Economics in Wrocław, 2015, p. 299.

A circular economy is an industrial system intentionally designed to renew or regenerate. It replaces the current concept by shifting towards renewable energy, remediation and the elimination of toxic chemicals that hinder reuse and aims to eliminate waste through better design of materials, products and systems. Such an economy is based on several principles (Szymonik et al., 2021):

■ First, it is based on an economy that aims to design waste. Waste that does not exist is designed and optimized for the disassembly and reuse cycle. These closely related component and product cycles define the circular economy and differentiate it from disposal and even recycling, which loses large amounts of energy and labor.

■ Second, the cycle makes a strict distinction between the consumable and durable components of the product. Unlike today, consumables in a circular economy are largely made of organic components that are not only non-toxic but can even be safely returned to the biosphere – directly or in a cascade of subsequent uses. On the other hand, permanent components such as engines or computers are made from raw materials unsuitable for the biosphere, such as metals and most plastics, but are designed for reuse.

■ Third, the energy needed to drive this cycle should be inherently renewable, also to reduce resource dependency and make the system more resilient, for example, to oil shocks.

In the case of technical components, the circular economy largely replaces the concept of a consumer with that of a user. This requires a new contract between companies and their customers based on product performance. Unlike an economy built on the principle of a functional service model, where producers and retailers increasingly retain ownership of their products and act as service providers, whenever possible, selling the use of the product rather than its consumption. The model is presented in Figure 6.6, where the final consumer becomes the owner of only some of the products and uses the rest. Such a change directly impacts the development of effective and efficient economic systems and allows the proliferation of practical business models. This enables the manufacturing of more durable products with a longer life cycle, facilitating their dismantling, refurbishment and development, constituting a closed-loop supply chain.

Referring to the circular economy model presented by the Ellen MacArthur Foundation (Figure 6.6), it can be noticed that it is a closed-loop

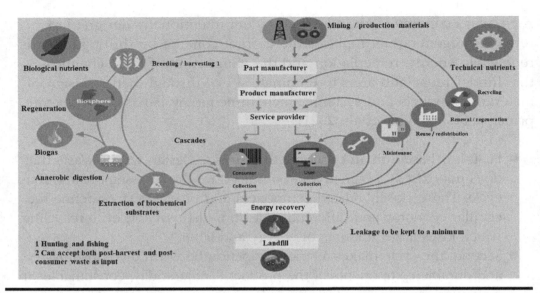

Figure 6.6   A circular economy model. Source: Compiled based on Ellen MacArthur Foundation, *Towards the circular economy*, 2013.

system that allows the added value of products to be maintained and waste to be eliminated for as long as possible. Raw materials are conserved within the economy, and products are used repeatedly, creating new value and productivity. The opposite is the linear economy where used products are not reused.

The transition to a circular economy requires changes in virtually every link in the value chain and thus also in the supply chain. To this end, restructuring must be carried out from the product design stage, and new business models are needed as well as close cooperation at every step of the supply chain. Such modifications require a systems approach, new ways of transforming waste into raw materials, the application of innovations and a change in mentality and approach to the use of products by consumers. There is also a need to implement technological, social and organizational innovations and new political and financial instruments.

The shift towards a circular economy can bring lasting benefits in terms of a more innovative, resilient and efficient economy. The main advantages of the transition to a circular economy are as follows (Dlaczego gospodarka, 2021):

■ Significant material savings and reduced exposure to price volatility: based on detailed modeling at the product level, the Ellen MacArthur Foundation estimated that in the industries with the moderate product life cycle, the circular economy introduces under an "advanced" scenario across Europe up to USD 630 billion per year. And in the case of fast-moving consumer goods, net material savings could reach USD 700 billion per year at a global level (data for 2016).

■ Increased potential for innovation and job creation: the circular concept as a "rethinking tool" has proven to be a powerful new thought framework capable of generating creative solutions and stimulating innovation. The impact of a more circular industrial model on the structure of the vitality of labor markets requires further study, but initial results indicate that the impact will be positive.

■ Increased resilience of living systems and the economy: worldwide land degradation costs an estimated USD 40 billion annually, not considering the hidden costs of higher soil fertilization, biodiversity loss, and the loss of unique landscapes. Better land productivity, less waste in the food chain and the return of nutrients to the soil will improve the value of land and soil as a resource (data for 2016).

6.3 Cleaner Production and Minimal Waste

"Cleaner production" is an environmental management strategy for production and services along the entire supply chain to prevent pollution and minimize the use of natural resources while reducing the company costs (Nowak, 2001).

Cleaner production is achieved through technical and organizational activities aimed at eliminating or reducing short- and long-term harmful effects of the production process and the product on people and the natural environment. Cleaner production refers to both the manufacturing processes and the ecological characteristics of a product throughout the life cycle along the supply chain. In relation to the production processes, this means eliminating harmful raw materials and emissions and rationalizing labor, material and energy consumption (Adamczyk, 2004).

Cleaner production is defined (understood) in various ways, but all terms include common measures (features) along the supply chain, which boil down to (Szymonik, Ekologistyka, 2018):

■ minimizing the amount of waste (pollutants) discharged into the environment;
■ limiting waste of raw materials, energy and human labor in the production system;

- reducing the quantity and toxicity of solid, liquid and gaseous waste generated in industrial processes, services and trade, simultaneously achieving economic benefits;
- limiting the negative impact of a product (service) on the environment – from its production to disposal;
- introducing reused raw materials and renewable energy;
- replacing non-renewable with renewable resources and harmful technologies with ones safer for the environment;
- manufacturing products in the "cleaner production" system, which should be:
  - non-toxic;
  - energy-efficient;
  - produced using renewable materials that are constantly replenished in a way that preserves the vitality of the ecosystem and the community they come from;
  - made of non-renewable but recycled materials that can be disposed of in a non-toxic and energy-efficient manner;
  - durable and reusable;
  - easy to disassemble, repair or reuse after renovation;
  - packed in a minimum and product-specific way, using recycled or recyclable or reusable materials.

Systemic analysis of the product life cycle must consider the near and far environment, considering internal and external factors related to the processes carried out in the supply chain. The answers regarding the further fate of products that have become waste, i.e. substances or objects that the owner discards, are helpful in such an analysis. Relevant questions include:

- What kind of waste do we deal with: municipal, medical, inert, hazardous, biodegradable, veterinary, green, accident-related, oils?
- How is waste management carried out in the area of: collection, transport, processing, disposal, selling?
- How is the waste storage carried out, considering its collection, temporary storage and collection by the waste treatment operator?
- What methods are used to prepare waste for reuse so that it can be used again without additional technological operations?
- What techniques are used for waste recovery to rationally reuse it for further production processes, recycling, energy recovery, incineration?
- What are the ways of preventing the generation of waste?

Cleaner production can be divided into two types of actions:

■ the first, consisting of the improvement of techniques and technologies for manufacturing products that do not harm the environment (with neutral or minimal negative impact);
■ the second, consisting of managing what is left:
  – after production in the manufacturing company (production waste, unnecessary machines and devices, consumables etc.);
  – at the customer (e.g. consumer, recipient, company) who first purchased (acquired) the product for manufacturing and then disposed of it because it is redundant (it has lost its use value).

When analyzing the division, it can be concluded that the first is related to production engineering in a broad (disciplinary) concept, and the second to waste, and strictly to waste management, in which reverse logistics plays a fundamental role.

6.3.1 Waste Minimization

The scope of ecology activities in logistics along the supply chain is relatively wide and includes:

■ waste minimization (waste prevention) along the entire supply chain ("cradle to grave");
■ educating society on sustainable development.

Waste prevention along the entire supply chain is the action applied to an object, material, substance before it becomes waste. It includes processes that reduce (Ustawa z dnia 14 grudnia, 2012):

■ the amount of waste, including by reusing or extending the life cycle of the product;
■ the negative impact of generated waste on the environment and human health;
■ the amount of heat and electric energy, water, gas consumed;
■ the content of harmful substances in the product and material.

Waste minimization is a continuous process that requires systematic action and self-discipline. It covers processes that start in the upper part of the supply chain (e.g. raw material mines) and end in its lower part (e.g. waste producers, waste sellers), including links, which include, among others, manufacturing, transport and services companies.

System analysis carried out to minimize waste in various stages of product life may lead to the reduction of the amount and harmfulness of waste and thus have a positive impact on the environment, despite the fact that the number of products manufactured in new technologies is increasing.

As practice shows, reducing waste in the supply chain, both at the junction of the chain and the level of its individual links, is possible when we reduce unplanned events that may occur at the stage of production, transport, storage and sales. Such situations include many elements (Figure 6.7). They include (Lewandowska & Januszewski, 2013):

■ lack of commitment from top management:
  – in product development;
  – in identifying market opportunities;
  – the cooperation of individual departments of the company and control over the production plan.
■ overproduction – mismatch between supply and demand;
■ deficiencies resulting from mistakes made by employees and deliveries of damaged raw materials and materials that affect the quality of manufactured goods (they are the cause of discards, e.g. bad food production procedure, for example, waste in a bakery supplying bread, among others, to a fast-food chain – 250 tons per week and 1,000 tons per month) (Molga, 2021);
■ unnecessary stocks that may increase the risk of damaging products;
■ undesirable external factors on goods during transport and storage:
  – uncontrolled changes in temperature (e.g. some solids lose their shape, properties and consistency, creams and ointments delaminate, and as a result, the disintegration of products, freezing and sublimation of solutions cause an increase in volume, which causes the containers to break);
  – negative effects of humidity (e.g. corrosion of metals, oxidation of electronic systems, bending of electronic components, tearing and deformation of printed circuit boards, peeling of layers, cracking air bubbles on the boards and defectiveness of soldered connections during high-temperature flow soldering or the lamination process) (Jaworowska, 2020);
  – chemical agents (e.g. uncontrolled chemical reactions, leaks);
  – biological factors (e.g. the influence of fungi, mold and bacteria).

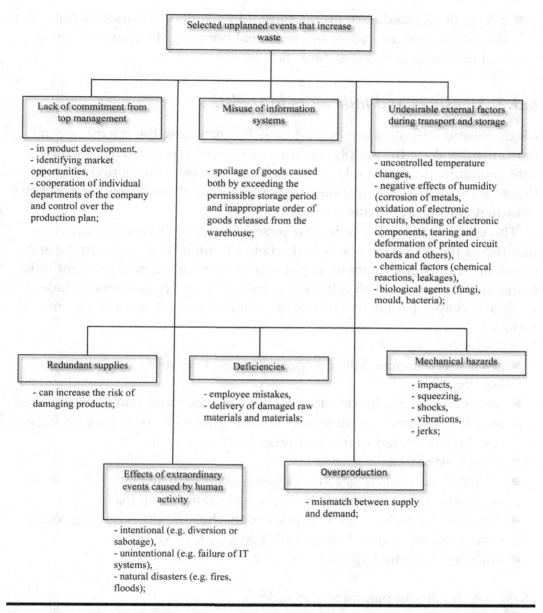

Figure 6.7   Selected unplanned events that increase waste. Source: Own elaboration.

- mechanical hazards (impacts, squeezing, shocks, vibrations, jerks) causing damage to the goods;
- improper use of information systems (e.g. goods spoilage caused both by exceeding the permissible storage period and inadequate order of goods released from the warehouse);

■ effects of extraordinary events caused by intentional human actions (e.g. diversions or sabotage) or unintentional ones (e.g. IT system failures) and natural disasters (e.g. fires, floods).

6.3.2 Measures and Indicators in Logistics

Measures and indicators are helpful tools for managing the environmental performance along the supply chain in waste containment. They help measure economic processes related to waste generation, considering the near (waste source) and far (consumers) environment and providing the necessary information to describe this process.

The essence of the measure in reverse logistics boils down to activities that reflect the events and facts in the field of minimizing waste in the supply chain and its environment, expressed in appropriate measurement units (allowing comparison with other phenomena). These parameters include the input and output parameters of any economic system. The input parameters include:

■ raw materials, materials, components used to manufacture products [e.g. kg, t];
■ consumables (e.g. lubricants, oils, inks, toners, spare parts for machines and devices used during repairs and maintenance, as well as packaging not directly related to finished products) [e.g. t, pcs];
■ energy, water, gas [e.g. m^3];
■ auxiliary materials (e.g. tools, cleaning agents, agents giving the manufactured products a specific feature, appearance) [e.g. PLN];
■ fuel used for technological, transport and heating purposes (e.g. coal, coke, briquettes, diesel oil, petrol, gas) [e.g. t, PLN];
■ other (e.g. cleaning agents) [e.g. PLN].

However, the output parameters include:

■ the amount of solid and liquid waste [e.g. kg, t, m^3];
■ number of complaints [e.g. pcs];
■ emission of air pollutants [e.g. kg CO_2/GJ];
■ sewage [e.g. m^3].

Chapter 7

Safety of the Information Flow in the Supply Chain

7.1 The Essence of Information Security

Managing the security of processes in the supply chain is not possible without ensuring a continuous flow of information on operations (Zaskórski, 2015). This flow impacts the effectiveness of the processes carried out as part of the physical movement of the material stream in the local, national, international and global areas.

The concept of information security (more and more often referred to as cybersecurity) can be understood as all methods, measures and procedures aimed at preventing the destruction, loss, copying and modification of the content of information (Pałęga, 2014). Security in the context of information resources and processes is understood by seven attributes (Ejdys et al., 2008):

1. Availability – this means unlimited use of information in the information process by authorized users. Therefore, information should be available to authorized persons at a specific place and time. Violation of availability may result from actions of an unauthorized user, errors made by the person involved in the implementation of the information process and failure, transmission disruption, software errors. Loss of availability may result from random events and deliberate actions.
2. Confidentiality – information is unavailable to all unauthorized entities. One way to ensure confidentiality is through data encryption. Loss of confidentiality can result from both inadequate security and a deliberate

DOI: 10.4324/9781003286110-7

attack. Information processes in which information disclosure would be costly are assigned a sufficiently high level of security.

3. Integrity – information cannot be changed or destroyed by unauthorized persons. Integrity may be compromised by an unauthorized user, errors or negligence of persons responsible for the information process. Loss of integrity can result from errors in information processing, disruptions, viruses, software bugs.
4. Reliability – consistency, intended behavior.
5. Authenticity – a property that ensures the identity of information as declared; authenticity results from checking whether someone or something is who or what they claim to be.
6. Secrecy – the level of data protection.
7. Accountability – a property that ensures that the activity of an entity can be assigned unequivocally only to that entity.

The security of the information process is ensured if it is possible to collect, process, store and transmit information efficiently and confidentially, using security measures, which should be understood as technological security and organizational measures that can be applied to computers, programs, data, processes and their users to ensure the protection of the company's interests and individual confidentiality (Sienkiewicz, 2008).

Nowadays, more and more attention is paid to cybersecurity for several reasons, which include the following five facts (TOP 5 faktów, 2021):

7.1.1 First Fact

According to Cybersecurity Ventures, global cybercrime costs will increase by as much as 15% over the next five years, reaching USD 10.5 trillion annually by 2025. Cybercrime causes more financial damage than natural disasters in a year. Costs include damage, damaged data, stolen money, intellectual property theft, loss of overall productivity, interception of personal and financial data, embezzlement, fraud, business disruptions, loss of reputation; after an attack (forensic investigation, restoration and removal of compromised data, systems).

7.1.2 Second Fact

In 2004, the value of the global cybersecurity market amounted to USD 3.5 billion, in 2007 over USD 120 billion. In 13 years, the number increased 35 times. Spending on security products is sure to exceed USD 1 trillion over five years (2017–2021).

7.1.3 Third Fact

Every IT department employee should be involved in protecting and defending applications, devices, infrastructure and people. According to Cybersecurity Ventures, there would be approximately 3.5 million vacancies in cybersecurity departments worldwide in 2021. This is based on previous Cisco (US-based IT company) estimates that one million jobs would be created in 2014. The unemployment rate associated with this sector was 0% in 2021 but only for experienced, skilled workers.

7.1.4 Fourth Fact

It was estimated that in 2021 the damage caused by ransomware would reach USD 20 billion (in 2015 – USD 325 million). From 2019 to 2021, the number of ransomware attacks in the medical industry would increase fourfold. Cybersecurity Ventures predicted that in 2021 companies would be attacked every 11 seconds compared to 2019 – 14 seconds. It is the fastest-growing type of crime.

7.1.5 Fifth Fact

In 2017, there were 3.8 billion internet users, which was 51% of the seven billion population. Cybersecurity Ventures estimated that there would be 6 billion internet users in 2022 (75% of the projected world population of 8 billion) and over 7.5 billion by 2030.

7.2 Threats

With the free flow of information and the wide availability of many resources, people using IT networks must understand all possible threats that should be treated as potential incidents that damage the subject of security (Kaczmarek & Ćwiek, 2009).

Hacking into systems occurs for many reasons, most often to obtain confidential data (usually for material benefits), gain recognition in one's community or disrupt the server's operation in the network using denial-of-service attack

(DoS attack) (Katkar & Kulkarni, 2013). The activities are carried out systematically when trying to penetrate the system, usually by consecutive steps. These steps include: identifying the system, entering the system, exploiting the system's weak points, gaining access to resources, taking over the system or extracting information of interest to the hacker, obliterating any traces of intrusion and leaving gaps in the system to facilitate another hacking.

These threats can take many forms, but all result in a loss of privacy and possibly the destruction of information and resources that can lead to material loss. Increasingly, information is made public about the devastation that results from data theft. Below are examples from the third quarter of 2020 (Siwek, 2021):

■ In January 2020, the Manor Independent School District in Texas (a public school district based in Manor, Texas (US)) lost USD 2.3 million after cybercriminals launched a successful phishing campaign;
■ In February, more than 440 million internal records were disclosed due to software security flaws and made their way online from cosmetic giant Estée Lauder;
■ In March, Marriott (a hotel chain) had the worst luck – as a result of a cyberattack, there was a data leak that affected 5.2 million hotel guests;
■ In May, there was an attack on Blackbaud, a cloud service provider that allowed hackers to hijack customers' systems – the company paid a ransom to prevent data leak online;
■ In June 2020, the University of California paid hackers a ransom of USD 1.14 million to save COVID-19 research;
■ In July, users of the popular Couchsurfing platform feared for their data, as 17 million records were found on an underground forum;
■ In September, the whole world followed with bated breath the ransomware attack on a German hospital, where a malware infection necessitated redirecting patients to other hospitals, with one of them dying.

The factors contributing to the emergence of threats to information security include (Szymonik, Informatyzacja, 2005): dispersion of ICT resources over a large area, unlicensed computer hardware, pirated (system and application) software, inappropriate measures to protect information (software and technical devices), hardware and software that has not been checked for the presence of the so-called bugs (hardware and software from reputable suppliers or ones recommended by certification bodies should be used), the reluctance of users and developers to apply information protection measures.

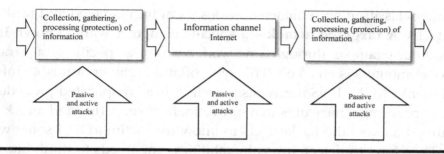

Figure 7.1   A simplified information diagram with places exposed to active and passive attacks. Source: Own elaboration.

Attacks on IT networks are carried out in various places (Figure 7.1). They relate to the collection, processing, storage, transmission and sharing of information and data. It is impossible to describe every network attack, as there is a whole range, and they come in different forms. The action strategy is variable and depends on the hacker's skills, the type of attacked target and its weaknesses.

Threats to the information system in terms of source of origin can be divided into (Szymonik, Technologie, 2010): random (e.g. temperature, humidity, pollution, power system disruptions, natural disasters, war, operator errors, administrator errors, defective system configuration, neglect, structure defects, hardware defects); intentional (conscious and deliberate).

One of the basic types of attacks is to search for a specific IP using a network scanner and then, once the "victim" is targeted, use the entire range of hacking tools. In general, the attack can be divided into passive and active. **A passive attack** involves intercepting specific data packets that flow through the network. Usually, sniffers and their advanced modifications automatically "translate" packets. Such attacks are very difficult to detect. Theoretically, it is possible, but it is hard to predict the time of sniffing the network and effectively defend it. Sniffer detection programs delay the flow of information a bit, but for the mass user, it is almost imperceptible. On the other hand, a person who would like to check if every mouse click is sniffed could feel a great discomfort at work. **An active attack** is a direct breach of the system security by exploiting vulnerabilities in the operating system or some running program, e.g. a mechanism for sharing files and folders. In addition, the user often does not use any password, which is an incentive for the hacker and sheer carelessness. This type of attack often employs Trojan horses, planted unnoticed in a victim's computer, opening almost unlimited access to it.

Another classification of attacks divides them into targeted and random attacks. **A targeted attack** – a specific computer with a known IP (obtained, for example, through a network scan) or a specific group (network) of computers is attacked. This type of attack gathers valuable information thanks to the DNS mechanism itself. It is a complicated procedure, and basic preventive measures may prove ineffective. A directed attack is not planned ad hoc; the hacker gets to know the victim to find some weak points. Therefore, to detect any vulnerabilities, one needs to think like a hacker and check any unsecured system areas one by one. It is also important not to download software from an unknown source because one never knows what is "attached" to an installation – executable (exe) file. **A random attack** is used most often by hackers because the only (main) selection criterion is to scan the network and look for an IP (computer) that is poorly secured.

In computer networks, attacks can be divided into three categories (Vademecum teleinformatyka, 2004): network, operating system and application attacks. **Network attacks** affect the communication infrastructure and can target network devices such as routers, switches and network-layer protocols on the server (layer 3). The target of a network attack is usually to obtain permissions that allow manipulating configuration settings that affect the routing of communication traffic. Layer 3 or lower attacks – often DoS attacks – affect network software modules of the server. In this case, the goal is to crash the server or at least slow it down significantly. A new version of DoS is a distributed denial-of-service (DDoS) attack, in which many agents distributed in the network launch such a DoS attack on a selected server. Agent modules are sent by hackers to computers they control – most often online – and activated at the opportune time to carry out a coordinated attack on a selected target, commit fraud, penetrate someone else's resources or take control over them (Szmit et al., 2005).

Operating system attacks take advantage of a wide range of bugs and vulnerabilities in commonly used operating systems. The most common is the attack on the superuser account (root in Unix systems or administrator in Microsoft Windows). Such a privileged user has the right to perform all operations in the system – has access to all files (including system files) and devices, create new users and grant them permissions. Most methods of obtaining superuser privileges use the so-called buffer overflow effect. It allows a hacker to insert a code into another program running on the computer and execute it in the context of that program's permissions. Typically, such a planted code creates an account for a new, privileged user. This allows the hacker to legally enter the system by logging in as that new user.

Application attacks – with internet development came wide use of applications such as web servers, e-mail and DNS servers. These applications are an ideal target because – by definition – they are designed to wait for inbound communication from the internet constantly, and external users can access them from anywhere in the network. Web servers are usually the first choice. An attack on a web server uses properly prepared HTTP requests considered legitimate from the firewall's perspective but prepared to exploit the server's weak points and gain access to confidential information stored in databases or execute their own program in the attacked web server.

Other attacks are related to the Common Gateway Interface (CGI). It is the basic means of executing web applications. After receiving the CGI request, the web server calls the appropriate program, passing the received parameters to it. Design errors often made in developing such programs, especially in the scope of data scope control, create opportunities for attacks. DNS servers are another case in point; after taking over such a server, it is easy to manipulate the internet address database, directing confidential information to the replaced physical addresses.

It is impossible to describe all network attacks because of their various forms and methods used. They can be carried out in multiple ways, depending on the target type and its weaknesses. The main types of attacks:

■ Buffer overflow (Vademecum teleinformatyka, 2002) is a popular method of attacking internet servers. It is possible when the application server software contains logical errors that can be used by an attacker to send data strings with sizes exceeding the input buffer. This can be used to obtain privileges to server resources and execute custom programs on the server. The search for hosts vulnerable to this type of attack is usually done with port scanning, making it possible to find computers on which a given service is running and exploit weaknesses (vulnerabilities) in the operating system's security.

■ Viruses, worms and Trojan horses form a specific group of programs that maliciously share, change or delete data from an infected computer. They are usually small, making them difficult to detect, but their code contains functions and commands that can harm the owner of the infected computer – from spying and intercepting personal data to deleting files from the disk. They are divided into three primary groups: viruses, worms and Trojans (Trojan horses) (Szymonik, Technologie,

2010). Viruses are programs that reproduce and spread to other computers. They infect files or boot sectors of data media. They transfer unnoticed on floppy disks, disks, through computer networks (including peer-to-peer), by e-mail or by simply downloading files from the internet. They put their copies in different places on the disk and work in different ways (Szymonik, Technologie, 2010). A worm is a program whose main purpose is to spread via a computer network. Once transferred, the worm continues to spread (if possible, it uses an e-mail address book to send a copy of itself to people from the book, for instance) and can perform tasks specified by its creator. Trojan horses are malicious programs that cannot copy themselves automatically. They are created to gain remote access to target computers. After installing the Trojan horse, the hacker can use the computer remotely and perform virtually any operation. The possible operations depend on the properties of the Trojan horse and the user permissions configured on the victim's computer. They often include modifying files, stealing data (personal details, credit cards, passwords etc.), keystroke logging, installing other software (including malicious ones) (Szymonik, Technologie, 2010).

■ Malicious software (malware) includes applications and scripts intended to execute a malicious, harmful or criminal activity. "Malware" is a single term for all kinds of malicious code, such as viruses, worms, Trojans, spyware. There are many different types of malware and how it works and spreads. Depending on the method of spreading, infection and the effects it causes, malware is divided into more dangerous and less dangerous. Malicious programs often have a mixed form – they combine several different functions (so-called hybrid), e.g. they can spread like a worm and contain Trojan functions and infect in various ways. Malware includes many types of malicious code, such as viruses, worms, spyware, adware, Trojan, rootkit, backdoor, keylogger (Szmit et al., 2008).

■ Botnets are computer networks composed of machines infected with a malicious backdoor that allows cybercriminals to control infected computers remotely (this may mean controlling a single machine, some computers making up the network or the entire network) (Feily et al., 2009). Botnets have tremendous computing power. They are a powerful cyberweapon and an effective tool to earn money illegally. The botnet owner can control the computers that make up the network from anywhere in the world – another city, country or even continent. The internet is structured in such a way that it is possible to control a botnet anonymously. Computers infected with the bot can be controlled either directly or indirectly. In the case of indirect control, the cybercriminal establishes a connection with the infected machine and manages it using the commands built into the bot program. In direct control, the bot connects to the control center or other machines on the network, sends a request and then executes the return command. The owner of an infected machine usually does not even suspect that cybercriminals are using the computer. This is why computers infected with a bot and secretly controlled by cybercriminals are also called zombies. Networks made up of infected machines are referred to as zombie networks. Most zombie machines are home user PCs (Szmit et al., 2008).

■ IP address spoofing (Vademecum teleinformatyka, 2002) involves an unauthorized person impersonating trusted IP addresses to pass through a security system based solely on computer IP addresses. Most firewalls detect packets with a fake return address and prevent them from being forwarded (Bi et al., 2009).

■ Easy passwords (Bi et al., 2009) – password crackers can try thousands of password combinations in a minute. As a result, they can exploit poorly chosen passwords to hijack a user's account or, worse, an administrator's. In order to protect against this, a policy of enforcing password changes and using "difficult" passwords (i.e. phrases with special characters, instead of single words) is applied. Passwords also apply to routers, switches and other network infrastructure equipment.

■ Session hijacking (Bi et al., 2009) – by guessing the IP sequence number, a hacker takes over the existing connection between the two computers and plays the role of one side of the connection. As a result, a legitimate user is disconnected, and the hacker "inherits" the ability to access data in the current session. Such a possibility is created by improper randomization (a procedure of randomly assigning entities to the test or control group so that the main characteristics of both groups are the same) of sequence numbers in the TCP/IP protocol stack of the operating system (Yongle & Jun Zhang, 2013).

■ Network snooping is a type of attack considered by many to be the most sophisticated method. Various types of network analyzers are employed to conduct it, thanks to which a potential hacker selects the attack method that will be the most effective in a given case. Often, network snooping comes down to analyzing protocols or tracking network traffic – the hacker looks for the weakest point of a given network or server in terms of the security and then uses this weak point through a specific intrusion technique, e.g. sniffing (network eavesdropping). Thus, network snooping is a weapon that prepares for another successful attack. A variation of network snooping is a probe, which consists of interviewing and accessing an object and examining its characteristics. This activity is so dangerous that it remains practically imperceptible as it is carried out through legitimate forms of access. In this way, sensitive information is collected and exposed, but this action is not picked by standard security systems. To prepare for an attack, a skilled thief usually needs a one-time examination of the system to initially assess the methods of an effective system attack (Krawaczyński & Zelek, 2021).

■ Backdoor is an application that allows its creator multiple unauthorized access to a remote system after obtaining administrator rights (or assigning appropriate permissions to a "malicious application", if needed) (Alminshid & Omar, 2013). These include, for example, user accounts with administrator privileges. One way to get a backdoor into the system is to create an account or process that allows other programs to run with superuser privileges. The number of possible backdoors for each platform is practically unlimited. Replacing one of the services with a specific program or using a substitution with superuser privileges will allow taking control of the system (Alminshid & Omar, 2013).

■ Denial-of-service (DoS) attack (Vademecum teleinformatyka, 2002; Fu, 2011) is one of the most effective ways to disable a network server. The main purpose of such an attack is to partially block access to selected services, e.g. internet or e-mail access, or disable the server altogether. In extreme cases, the system freezes completely, which requires the system to be restored by the administrator's physical intervention, i.e. a "reset". This attack consists in sending a huge number of queries to a network server in a short time. The server tries to answer each query, while the hacker constantly sends new ones without waiting for a reply from the server. This leads to a situation where the server is simply "flooded" with queries and cannot keep up with the responses. As a result, the system load increases, and when the number of queries exceeds the computing capacity of the server, it is blocked.

■ Living-off-the-land (LotL) attacks take advantage of standard applications and resources contained in every Windows computer. LotL cleverly combines popular Windows tools and applications such as PowerShell or BitLocker with a malicious script to infect. Such a successful, combined operation is followed by a final stage, which, depending on hackers' intentions, allows them to spy on and steal sensitive data or encrypt it to extort a ransom. For such attack patterns to be detectable, it is necessary to monitor the behavior of any suspicious processes to timely identify and thwart the attack (Trendy IT security, 2021).

■ Social engineering (Mouton et al., 2014) in ICT security is a set of methods to obtain classified information by a cybercriminal. Hackers often take advantage of the ignorance or credulity of information system users to defeat security measures that are resistant to all forms of attack. At the same time, they search for the weakest point of the security system, which is humans.

Online scammers often pretend to be other people to extract valuable data from their victims. For example, a hacker may pretend to be a bank administrator and send victims a link to a website, which is confusingly similar to their bank's website. Thanks to the mastery of social engineering, the scammer knows that the average user never checks if the bank's website is marked with a padlock, symbolizing a secure connection. As a result, careless customers leave their data to the online thief, which can be used to clear out their bank accounts. The action described in the above example is known as "phishing".

A variation of this group is ransomware, which is software and an attack method that blocks access to data or the entire computer system. The goal is to make its victim pay a ransom to unlock or decrypt data. Hence the name – ransom and software combined. Today, it is one of the greatest threats facing users and companies online. In 2019, a ransomware attack happened every 14 seconds on average, and in 2020, every 11 seconds. During an hour-long reading of this document, criminals will have time to attack over 250 companies. Global losses amounted to USD 20 billion, compared to only USD 325 million in 2015 (Raport Cyberbezpieczeństwo, 2021).

Cloud computing is gaining more and more attention in information security. The reason is the experience of working remotely and the need to ensure the availability of company resources. Companies already spend one-third of their IT investments on the cloud. The undeniable trend in 2021 is developing a multicloud practice, i.e. using many heterogeneous cloud service providers. This, in turn, increases the demand for solutions securing data in the cloud and guaranteeing business continuity (Raport Cyberbezpieczeństwo, 2021).

Mobile devices such as smartphones and tablets play an increasingly important role in supply chains. For example, many banking transactions are performed online with two-factor authentication. As a result, they have yet again become attractive to cybercriminals, who mainly use adware to spy on users and steal data.

A disturbing trend in the mobile sector is stalkerware, i.e. malicious software that can interfere with the victim's personal life. Stalkerware records the data entered into the device and sends them to a third party provided during installation. It works without the victim knowing that information is collected; as such, it is an invasion of privacy and is considered unwanted (Co to jest Stalkerware i jak wpływa na telefony z systemem Android, 2021).

Big corporations spend enormous sums of money to ensure their IT security. The costs include the purchase of specialized infrastructure (e.g. a firewall) and the employment of the best administrators who take care of constant software updates. However, all the security expenses can go to waste if all employees are not trained to defend themselves against social engineering.

The use of social engineering is a criminal offense under Polish law. Impersonating another person and taking over classified information is punishable by imprisonment. Public institutions and companies must introduce authentication systems for people who contact company employees electronically. It is necessary to constantly improve the ICT security qualifications of all employees who have access to classified information (Szymonik & Nowak, 2018).

7.3 Information Security Management System

An information security management system can be defined as a set of coordinated actions (planning, organizing, motivating, controlling, coordinating, deciding) concerning the information resources of the subject of security (finance, personnel, information technology, telecommunications, procedures, databases: data, models, knowledge, documents) to achieve the objectives (i.e. the desired level of information security, confidentiality, integrity, availability, accountability, authenticity, reliability) efficiently and effectively (Schetina et al., 2002). Thus, information security management systems include management functions, information resources (assets), organizational structure, policies, rules, procedures and processes.

The protection of classified information should be provided within one well-thought-out information security management system (ISMS), adjusted to the culture and specificity of the operation of a specific subject of security. There are many ways to protect against lurking dangers and comply with legal requirements. In general, they can all be termed "information security management". To ensure processed information security, companies and offices are obliged to comply with laws, regulations and standards, and there are over 200 such documents in Poland.

ISO/IEC 27001 is an international standard, developed on October 14, 2005 based on the British standard BS 7799-2. It is a specification of information security management systems for compliance with which audits can be carried out, based on which certificates are issued.

PN-ISO/IEC 27001 employs the well-known "plan–do–check–act" (PDCA) model, which is applied to the entire structure of ISMS processes. The ISMS introduction is presented in Figure 7.2 and defined as follows (Szymonik, 2015c):

- **Plan** – work begins with defining the scope, strategy and policy of the information security management system, setting the course of action in information protection. After approval, a risk analysis is performed, which includes an inventory of assets, identifying threats and vulnerabilities and determining the effects they may bring for the company. The result of this stage is the documentation of the information security

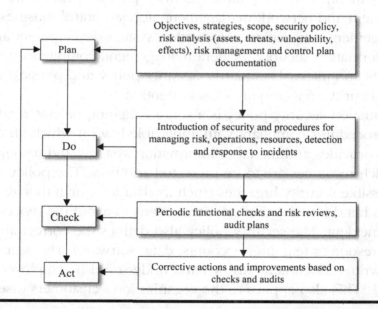

Figure 7.2   Processes of introducing and managing information security. Source: Compiled based on *ISO/IEC 27001* and J. Gryz, *Outline of the basics of safety theory*, AON, Warsaw 2010, p. 63.

management system, containing a risk treatment plan and a declaration of the use of risk control mechanisms.

- **Do** – at this stage, security measures and procedures are introduced to ensure the efficient operation of the information security management system, including risk management, operations management, resource management, detection of information security incidents and incident response. It also includes preparing and conducting a series of training for staff on introduced procedures and awareness of information security in the company.
- **Check** – as part of procedures related to the monitoring and reviewing of the information security management system, a plan of periodic functional checks and risk reviews is prepared, and an audit plan is developed based on an internal audit.
- **Act** – this stage of the PDCA cycle is fully supported by the company's internal structures, established to manage information security. Corrective actions and information security system improvements are introduced based on audit results, reviews and periodic checks.

ISO/IEC 27001 distinguishes 11 areas affecting information security in an organization. They include security policy, information security organization, asset management, human resources security, physical and environmental security, system and network management, access control, business continuity management, acquisition, information system development and maintenance, information security incident management, compliance with legal requirements and internal standards. Security policy and physical and environmental security areas require closer attention.

An information security policy is a set of coherent, precise regulations, rules and procedures compliant with applicable law on which an organization builds, provides and manages information systems and resources. It defines which resources are to be protected and how. The policy should indicate possible security breaches (such as data loss, unauthorized access), scenarios to handle such situations and actions to avoid the reoccurrence of a given incident. The security policy also defines the correct and incorrect use of resources (e.g. user accounts, data, software). The security policy must be a written document, known and understood by employees using IT resources. This also applies to the organization's customers (users of its resources).

During policy development, it is important to consider whether the organization will be able to bear the costs of implementing the policy. Increasing the level of security of an organization/system occurs most often at the expense of convenience and efficiency of operation. Therefore, based on the recommended models or standards in this field, it is vital to remember to adapt the solution to the specificity of the organization so as to give it features that facilitate its application in practice. The main task is to conduct a risk analysis and determine the acceptable risk level.

While creating an information security policy, it is crucial to bear in mind the company's goals. They include guaranteeing legal requirements for information protection, confidentiality, integrity, availability of processed information, security of strategic information, ensuring public trust and the company's prestige, security of the business continuity, cost reduction.

The information security policy should contain only a general description of the selected strategies and apply (Ciecińska et al., 2006): methods of achieving the optimal level of security, roles and responsibilities in creating security, management by quality systems, development of individual policies, security of information exchange, standardization and compliance with standards, information security in the internal and target environment of the company, response to incidents.

7.4 Physical Security

Physical security is intended to prevent unauthorized access to classified information. According to Liderman, the framework of physical security includes the following issues (Liderman, 2003): organization and access control systems, theft protection (anti-theft structures, alarm devices), systems and procedures ensuring continuous operation of network components, installation and maintenance of fire protection systems.

The system of physical security measures includes organizational solutions, equipment and devices for the protection of classified information and electronic auxiliary systems supporting the protection of classified information. Depending on the level of risks identified in the analysis in question, an appropriate combination of the following physical security measures is applied (Rozporządzenie Rady Ministrów, 2012):

■ **security personnel** – persons trained, supervised and, if necessary, with appropriate authorizations to access classified information, performing activities related to the physical protection of classified information, including access control to rooms or areas where classified information is processed, supervision of the video surveillance system as well as responding to alarms or emergency notifications;

■ **physical barriers** – measures protecting the boundaries of the place where classified information is processed, in particular fences, walls, gates, doors and windows;

■ **cabinets and locks** – used to store classified information or protect this information against unauthorized access;

■ **access control system** – including an electronic auxiliary system or organizational solution, used to guarantee access to the room or area where classified information is processed only by persons with appropriate authorizations;

■ **burglary and assault alarm system** – an electronic auxiliary system to carry out procedures for the protection of classified information and increase the level of security, which is ensured by physical barriers, and in rooms and buildings it replaces or supports security personnel;

■ **video surveillance system** – an electronic auxiliary system used for ongoing security monitoring or checking security incidents and alarms by security personnel;

■ **control system for people and objects** – including an electronic auxiliary system or an organizational solution consisting in requesting voluntary submission to checks or providing personal belongings for inspection, including items brought in or out – used to prevent attempts of unauthorized introduction into the protected area of things threatening the security of classified information or unauthorized removal of classified information from buildings or facilities.

The following protection zones are created (Rozporządzenie Rady Ministrow z 29 maja 2012 r. w sprawie środkow bezpieczeństwa fizycznego stosowanych do zabezpieczania informacji niejawnych, 2012):

■ protection zone I – a room or area in which classified information marked as "confidential" or more sensitive is processed in such a way that access to this room or area allows direct access to this information; the room or area meets the following requirements:
    – the highest classification level of the processed classified information clearly indicated in the protection plan;
    – clearly defined and secured borders;
    – the access control system is introduced, allowing access to persons with appropriate authorizations to access classified information to the extent necessary to perform work or service or assigned activities;

- entry is possible only from the protection zone.
■ protection zone II – a room or area in which classified information marked as "confidential" or more sensitive is processed in such a way that access to this room or area does not allow direct access to this information; the room or area meets the following requirements:
  - clearly defined and secured borders;
  - the access control system is introduced, allowing access to persons with appropriate authorizations to access classified information to the extent necessary to perform work or service or assigned activities;
  - entry is possible only from the protection zone.
■ protection zone III – a room or area that requires a clear definition of the boundaries within which it is possible to control persons and vehicles.
■ special protection zone – located within protection zone I or protection zone II, protected against eavesdropping, additionally meeting the following requirements:
  - keys and access codes to cabinets, rooms or areas in which classified information is processed may only be made available to those people who need to have the keys or know the codes to perform their official duties;
  - the codes are changed at least once a year, and in the case of any change in the composition of persons who know the code, there is a suspicion that an unauthorized person could learn the code when the lock was maintained or repaired.

Many products dedicated to the physical security of network components have appeared on the market. These include (Fizyczne zabezpieczenie sieci, 2021):

■ **LAN cable lock** (protection against disconnecting the RJ45 cable) – a device for mounting on patch cables with an RJ45 plug (patch cord) protects against attempts to disconnect the LAN cable from computers, servers, hubs or switches by an unauthorized person.
■ **Network port lock** (RJ45 port lock) – physically locks unused open LAN ports (RJ45) and:
  - can be used with any Ethernet port (RJ45);
  - prevents unauthorized network expansion by additional switch devices;

    – protects against plugging in a patch cord or inserting another foreign element in the network.

Many administrators and business owners consider empty and unused LAN ports normal, but they are perfect for an average hacker to infiltrate the entire system and network. The presented security components make it possible to stop unauthorized logging in, disconnecting from the network or uncontrolled network growth by additional switches.

Chapter 8

Supply Chain Safety Management Model

8.1 System Modeling in Supply Chain Management

Modeling is a special relationship between the original, i.e. the real object, and its image expressed in a specific language and form. Modeling is the process of mapping an object treated as an original into its image. The purpose of model development may be cognition, i.e. description, diagnosis, assessment, forecast or a decision concerning the real object (system) under study. The form of the model depends, for example, on its purpose (research goal) but also the adopted modeling language, qualifications and research competences.

The term "model" is most often used in two different ways to denote:

1) a theory that is structurally similar to another, which makes it possible to move from one theory to another by simply changing terminology – in this sense, the model is a means of cognition;
2) a system to which a certain theory applies for a simplified reflection of the reality under study – in this approach, the model is the subject of cognition.

The model is most often defined as:

- a system which, by reflecting or reproducing the object of examination, can replace it, so that its examination provides new information about this object;

DOI: 10.4324/9781003286110-8

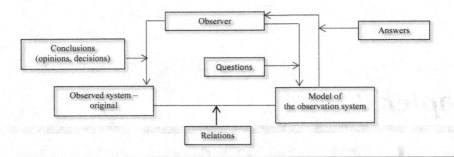

Figure 8.1 The role of the model in system observation. Source: Compiled based on A. Rokicka-Broniatowska (ed.), *Wstęp do informatyki gospodarczej,* **(ed.). A. Rokicka-Broniatowska, SGH, Warsaw 2006, p. 49.**

- replacement for the original, the adopted form of representation, used to explain and predict the behavior of the real system, the model must reflect reality in a manner adequate to the purpose of the research;
- some idealization or simplification of reality.

The very nature and degree of simplification depends on the knowledge, needs and awareness of the researcher and may change depending on the purpose of the research. Common to theory and model is the property of relating to reality perceived in a simplified, abstract form.

The model is an intermediary between the observer and the observed system (the original), and the quality of this projection is determined by (Figure 8.1) (Rokicka-Broniatowska, 2006): the degree of compliance with the objective of the observation; compliance with the observer's needs; the degree of correctness in the selection of the type of model used.

8.1.1 Principles for Describing Operating Systems

Defining the field of system research requires clarification:

- "extra-linguistic sphere", which is identified with the totality of real (empirical) systems;
- "linguistic sphere", which is identified with the entirety of conceptual systems;
- connection methods (transition, transformation, mapping) of the above-mentioned spheres.

The description of any real system, such as a supply chain, requires the determination of parameters describing the object from a specific point of view, i.e. *conceptualization*. A specific conceptualization is always matched by an observer who pursues the research goal (project, strategy, policy). When specifying the principles of system description, one should distinguish aspects characteristic of systems research. In the initial stage of system description, a significant role is played by the explication of primary concepts, translating the commonplace into exact mathematical concepts. It is often used in systems research.

The discussion on the correctness or adequacy of the description makes sense when considering the adopted research aspect and the properties of the language and description method used. The above remark helps to avoid many formal misunderstandings. To evaluate them, a metalanguage is needed, the object of which is a given language. The forms of representation of the examined systems are models used to describe, explain and predict the behavior of systems under various conditions.

Between the conceptual system adopted as a model of a given real system and the original (i.e. the real system), there must be at least a homomorphic relationship, i.e. an unambiguous two-part, antisymmetric relationship, expressing a greater or less similar (structural, functional) similarity between the model and the original. There are various classifications of the models used in the research (Table 8.1).

Three division criteria were adopted to classify the basic models used in systems research of an organization, including supply chains. **The first criterion** expresses the cognitive goal (modeling result) and allows us to distinguish the following:

■ phenomenal models (designating, explaining) aimed to obtain the desired explanation of the essence of the features (phenomena) of the system;

Table 8.1 Classification of Research Models

Layer \ Form	Descriptive (D) Models (M)	Formal (F) Models (M)	Mathematical (Mt) Models (M)
Phenomenal Models (P)	MDP	MFP	MMtP
Assessment Models (A)	MDA	MFA	MMtA
Decision Models (D)	MDD	MFD	MMtD

Source: Compiled based on J. Konieczny, *Podstawy eksploatacji urządzeń*, Warsaw 1975, p. 71.

- assessment models aimed to provide evaluations, i.e. statements expressing approval or disapproval of the state (past, current, future) of the system;
- decision models aimed to reach specific decisions necessary to ensure the state of the system required in terms of the adopted criterion.

In systems science of economic organizations, including the supply chain, all the above-mentioned types of models are used, with designating models (including diagnostic and prognostic) being the basic tool in the theory of real systems (organization), while assessment and decision models in system analysis and operating systems engineering.

Due to **the second criterion**, expressing the form of the message (modeling language), the following are distinguished:

- descriptive models expressed in natural language;
- formal models expressed in the language of logic, mainly mathematical logic;
- mathematic models expressed in the language of mathematics (e.g. set theory, algebra, functional analysis, probability).

The **third criterion** is related to the accepted aspect of systems research. The following three basic aspects can be distinguished:

- morphology (structure, make-up) of the system;
- functioning (behaviors, operations) of the system;
- development (evolution, changes) of the system.

Due to the object and method of mapping, the general scheme of the full cycle of systems modeling will be called system modeling. It is a creative process and constitutes such a sequence of activities which result in, for example, a mathematical evaluation (decision) model of the system, a new structure, a new model of processes implemented in the examined system etc. If the obtained model concerns only a selected aspect of research, it can be referred to as a partial (one-aspect) model, and if it concerns all of them, then it is a comprehensive (multi-aspect) model. It should be noted that the following aspects specify the presented scheme of system modeling: research methodology, correctness criterion, adequacy assessment, system concepts (Figure 8.2).

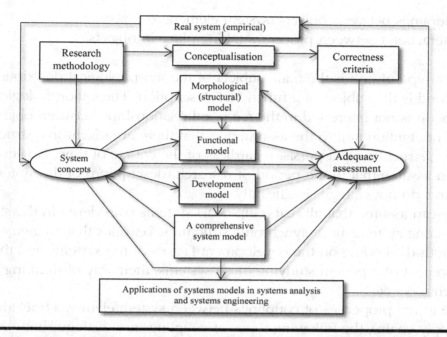

Figure 8.2   General scheme of system modeling. Source: Compiled based on P. Sienkiewicz, *Inżynieria systemów kierowania*, PWE, Warsaw 1988, p. 93.

The morphological description of the system is an expression of the structural approach in which categories such as element, composition, relations, structure and morphology are used. This description is used in solving tasks in which it is important to answer the following questions:

- What elements make up the system, and what are the differences between them?
- What type of links between the system components make up its structure(s)?
- What should be the most desirable components of the system being created in terms of the specified efficiency criterion?
- What should be the most desirable relationships between the elements of the system (structure) in terms of a specific criterion of effectiveness?
- How does the given system structure affect the functions performed?
- In what direction will the changes of the system structures go?

The morphological description primarily shows the desire to reproduce the internal organization of the system, the spatial distribution of elements and the ways of their interrelationships. Systems research distinguishes two types of internal links in the system:

- couplings between objects (system elements);
- interactions between processes taking place in objects.

The first type of link is the main subject of the morphological description; the second is the subject of a functional description. Thus, morphological description is not interested in the temporal relationships between objects. This is not tantamount to the assumption that there are diachronic structures, i.e. structures that persist regardless of the course of time. However, one can assume that in the period of research (description) of the system, its structures do not change significantly.

One can assume that all real (empirical) systems considered in the study of operating systems have synchronic structures, i.e. ones that change over time, both depending on the development factors of the systems and the development of a person studying these systems, their way of thinking, research tools etc.

Due to the properties of couplings between system elements (including the supply chain), the following types of couplings are distinguished:

- localization, that is, coupled elements must remain in mutual relations due to the represented systemic features;
- energy, i.e. there are connections between elements when one of them is the basis for the formation of the other;
- existent, i.e. coupled elements, the existence of which as elements of systems is determined by relations with other elements, at least non-destructively influencing them;
- coexistent, that is, the elements are coupled, between which there are relations corresponding to their needs (e.g. the relation of cooperation within the links of the supply chain).

For a complete description of the morphological system, the following is necessary:

- mapping, system structures in the form of a flat or topological graph;
- determination of the degree and order of a graph, cyclomatic number, full chromatic number etc.;
- demonstrating the graph consistency or determining the probability of graph consistency;
- determining the amount of structured information in the system;
- defining the type of structure.

The functional description is an expression of the functional approach (processual, event, dynamic) of the system, in which such categories as time, state, event, function, process etc., are used. This description is used when solving tasks in which it is important to answer the following questions:

- What functions and processes are implemented in the system?
- What is the system's behavior under the given conditions?
- What is the organization of processes (functions) by the system?
- What should be the most desirable course of processes in the system?
- Do the system structures correspond to the implemented processes in the sense of the adopted criterion of effectiveness?
- How do the features of the system components affect the efficiency of processes etc.?

The functional description expresses the desire to map the functions and processes of the system, the spatial-temporal organization of the system's functioning and its dynamics. Functional research aims to establish the causal relationships, states, functions and processes in individual interconnected elements or subsystems of a given system. The functional description characterizes the interactions between the processes taking place in the objects. The relationships expressing these interactions can be divided into:

- cooperation, i.e. links between objects (their features); they may be cooperative or conflicting;
- functional, ensuring the proper course of processes (performance of the function);
- energetic, expressing energetic (energy-material) interactions of objects;
- informational, expressing informational (information-decision) interactions.

The developmental description assumes that for each real system, three system features expressed by categories are of fundamental importance: (1) structure, (2) behavior, (3) development.

In the light of the conclusions drawn so far based on systems research, one can state that development somewhat includes the other two concepts. So one can assume that system development may refer to system structure development and/or process development. The developmental description of the system is an expression of a prognostic approach that uses concepts such as development, evolution, progress and growth. This description is used in solving tasks in which it is important to answer the following questions:

- In what direction will the changes in the system structure and/or changes in the dynamic structure of the system go?
- How do structural changes affect the processes and functions of the system?
- How do changes to processes and functions affect the structure of the system?
- How to control the development of the system so that changes in the structure and processes go in the desired direction etc.?

The developmental description is characterized primarily by the desire to map all the events causing changes and predict the structures and processes that will describe the system in the future.

All systems, whose structures, elements, processes and functions change over time due to growth, aging, expansion, evolution etc., are called development (*developing*) systems. The development of a system is described by the type of development dynamics. The following development dynamics are distinguished:

- progressive development of the evolutionary type, when the system gradually adopts features (states) more favorable than original features (states);
- retrograde development of the evolutionary type, when the system gradually adopts features (states) less favorable (less desirable) than original features (states);
- catastrophic, when there is a sharp decrease in the value of positive (beneficial) system features;
- explosive, when there is a sharp increase in the system and a transition to the dominance of certain positive system features;
- functional, when there are fluctuations in the values of basic system features around certain mean values (each change in the system causing its development has specific causes and effects).

The basis for describing a developmental system is the knowledge of its morphological and functional description. In the case of convergence (concurrence), the development of the system consists of striving for the disappearance of specialization in the system, i.e. as a result of development, all elements of the system implement elementary processes of the same type. In the case of divergence (discrepancy), the development of the system causes the opposite phenomenon, i.e. all elements of the system will implement processes of various types. Both the divergence and the convergence of systems are related to changes in functional information but in opposite directions.

It was found that, depending on the emergence of needs, the development of the system may concern (1) only the processes organizing the operation (control, directing, management), (2) only working processes (executive, energy-material), (3) both processes. The comparison of needs and development gives rise to two characteristic cases: (1) the case of the normal system developing in relation to the needs and (2) the case of the system not keeping up with the needs.

The concept of system development forecast (development model) is characteristic of development research. Most often, a forecast is the result of a scientifically based prediction of the course and state of possible (probable) events (things, facts, phenomena) expressed in the form of prognostic information. In the development description, the so-called system development forecasts will be used.

Quantitative development forecasts are determined based on mathematical development models and simulation models, while qualitative development forecasts are most often determined using heuristic techniques, among which expert assessment is still of fundamental importance. Conclusions about the type of system development can be made based on a simulation system development study. We believe that simulation studies of systems development will be of fundamental importance for development analysis and forecasting research in the near future.

In order to obtain a complete description of the development, it is necessary to: verify the structural model and the functional model; compile a list of possible causes and effects of system development; establish the basic features and characteristics of the development of the system; define development control possibilities; determine the development structure of the system; verify the development model by identifying important factors of comprehensive systems modeling – the degree of certainty of the forecast (Figure 8.3).

The location of the supply chain as an essential part of business indicates the multiplicity of relations and feedback loops between the elements of individual links in the supply chain. It is, therefore, necessary to use a mapping technique called modeling, which is a universal way of expressing

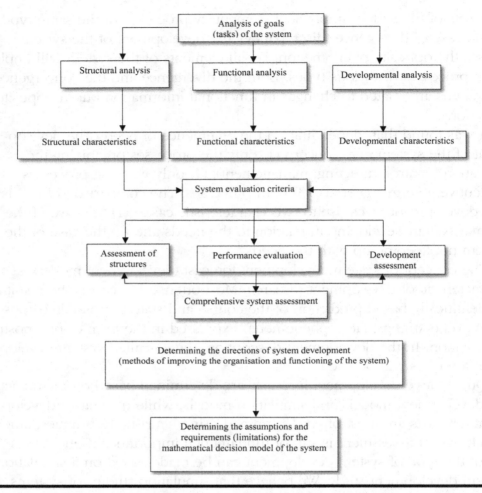

Figure 8.3   Important factors in complex systems modeling. Source: Own elaboration.

"what we are doing or will be doing, as well as what was done in the past and what exists now" (Dumnicki et al., 1998). This applies to advanced modeling methods and techniques that would allow the analysis of the dynamics (processes) and statics (structures) of the studied (modeled) logistics systems (networks).

8.1.2 Modeling of Supply Chains

Each supply chain carries out processes that undergo constant changes and transformations, and their end result sometimes does not have a predetermined and planned course due to the changing environment (threats) in which the material stream and information flow happen, which may mean non-linear nature of the relationship between the attributes (system features).

Therefore, it is not enough to provide a static description of the supply chain by presenting its internal (organizational, functional) structures. Additionally, dynamic changes in the analyzed supply chain and its environment, which significantly impact the course of processes, should be considered. Therefore, the supply chain mapping must be based on the connection of static and dynamic description, useful in the design of logistic simulation experiments, considering units subordinate to the Ministry of the Interior (Police, State Fire Service) and government and local administration. Thus, in general, the following can be distinguished in a supply chain model:

- the facility – the logistic processes, more precisely the flow of material and information stream;
- the user – the part of the reality surrounding the facility (e.g. production company, transport company, warehouse, logistics center, consumer);
- the surrounding (environment) – the facility and the user are related to other external elements (e.g. bank, government and local government institutions, natural environment) that influence (positively or negatively) their behavior;
- internal and external relations – the ability to ensure the functioning of the facility (logistic processes) and the user (e.g. a company) and "establishing" contacts with the environment (e.g. with the market of suppliers and recipients) and influencing the situations that arise there.

The facility, which is the supply chain, has many important properties, such as:

- the ability to establish stable relations (connections) with the environment (e.g. supplying the economic system with the necessary components, products according to the plan or reacting and neutralizing crises during floods, fire and other threats).
- the ability to "establish contacts" with the environment and influence the situations that arise there (e.g. market research and forecasting of demand and supply or researching the needs related to the neutralization of threats).
- the ability to link the supply chain with relations of activities related to the facility and the environment, thanks to which a given facility identifies specific phenomena that affect the effectiveness of its activities (e.g. meeting the basic needs of the injured, measuring customer satisfaction, the efficiency of logistics processes, including transport). Links with

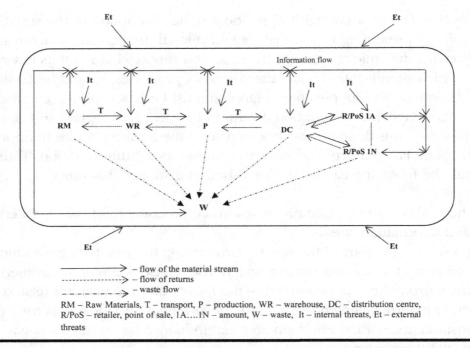

Figure 8.4   The structure of a supply chain – basic links. Source: Own elaboration.

the environment may result from internal reasons related to the facility (e.g. the number of the ordered components depends on the customers' demand for manufactured products), or they are the result of external causes that force or even establish these relationships (e.g. market collapse, financial crisis, competition, crises).

Facility description – the supply chain (Figure 8.4), in general, may refer to three of its aspects (Paszkowski, 1999):

- functioning (material processes), i.e. fulfilling the tasks provided for by the user (ensuring the place and time of the material stream being moved, i.e. delivering everything where there is a demand among the links in the supply chain);
- morphology (structure), i.e. internal structure, the composition of elements, connections between elements, properties of elements etc. (this applies to participants of the supply chain, which can include, inter alia, transport, production and service companies, warehouses, logistics centers);
- organization (information and decision processes) – including the movement of information, cooperation of control algorithms along the entire supply chain.

Considering the content of the tasks performed along the supply chain, one may be tempted to simplify it somewhat. The effectiveness and efficiency of the supply chain depend on the condition and susceptibility of individual links in logistic activities, each of which has features such as morphology, functionality, relationships, environment, organization of the information and decision process.

The overall assessment focuses on analyzing individual participants and describing their strengths and weaknesses for the whole, i.e. the supply chain. When creating a supply chain model, it is helpful to build models similar to the strongest link, leading and considered the best in the analyzed field (benchmark). Such an example may be a production company model useful for further analyses and assessments in the context of logistics processes. In such a model, one can distinguish logistic subsystems (facility): management (LSM), supply (LSS), production (LSP), distribution (LSD), recycling (LSR). The first one is the control subsystem, while the rest are executive subsystems. The functioning of the company's logistics system, which is an important link in the supply chain, would not be possible without considering the surrounding (environment) and links (relations), which include:

- external supply (e.g. supply market – SM);
- recipients of manufactured goods (e.g. recipient market – RM);
- companies dealing with secondary raw materials and waste disposal (e.g. the market of recycling and management of secondary raw materials – MRaMSRM);
- the impact of the subject of security's environment – SSE (near environment: e.g. strikes, blockades, natural disasters, competition, legal regulations, the state's economic condition, socio-political environment, the level of technology and technology; far environment: e.g. global economy, infrastructure, international institutions, economic alliances, global financial market, legal conditions, financial crises), which can be divided into those about which the user has information and those that are unknown, i.e. threats).

In such a system, there is a quantitative and qualitative transformation in the flow of the material stream in the subsystem of supply, production, distribution and utilization (Figure 8.5), considering activities in the upper and lower part of the supply chain.

An important function in the model of an enterprise that is a link in the supply chain is played by the management subsystem, which deals with

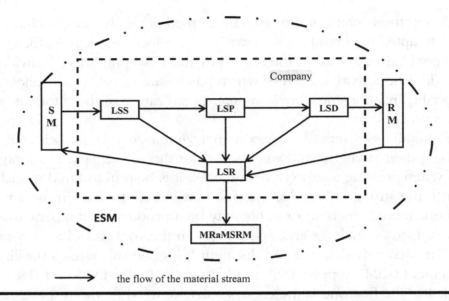

Figure 8.5   A logistic model of a production enterprise that is a link in the supply chain – material stream. Source: Own elaboration.

planning, coordinating and executing logistics (related to real processes). Thanks to the exchange of information between the logistic subsystems of the company (LSM, LSS, LSP, LSD, LSR), the supply and customer market and the subject of security's environment (SSE), it is possible to effectively and efficiently manage planning and execution logistics (Figure 8.6). Information streams concern:

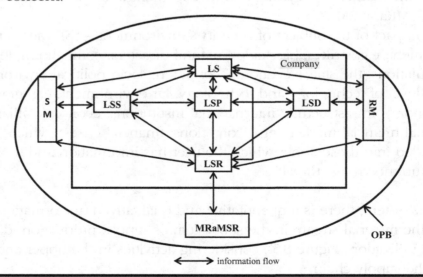

Figure 8.6   A logistic model of a production enterprise that is a link in the supply chain – information flow. Source: Own elaboration.

- logistics processes carried out by executive subsystems in conditions known and occurring unplanned, e.g. in connection with crises;
- monitoring of events positively and negatively influencing the implemented logistics processes;
- reports on the degree of implementation of logistic tasks;
- interaction between all logistics subsystems of the economic system;
- the relationship between the sales and supply markets as well as the near and far environment.

8.2 Analysis of Research Results

Currently, activities in the supply chain are interdisciplinary. This is due to its essence, which is now increasingly supported by modern technologies, in particular the new generation ICT (information & communication technologies). One of the key issues of effective and efficient operation of modern supply chains in a dynamically changing environment is ensuring the desired security level in conditions of disruptions and internal and external threats. The sensitivity (susceptibility) of supply chain structures to various threats may result in an organizational crisis, structural changes and even bankruptcy.

Research in the area of supply chain security, due to the extensive structural and functional connections and legal limitations of the links (systems) operating in it, is extremely complicated. This is due to the complexity and variety of these systems, which show (Świeboda, 2009):

- the multifunctionality resulting from the fact that safety rules necessitate sets of various requirements, which are grouped according to the area of the future, planned operation of the systems;
- the complexity of the structure of operating systems (activities within interconnected companies that are spread out in space);
- a large number of subsystems (supply, production, distribution, storage, transport) included in the supply chain, remaining in various relationships (relations, couplings) and a large number of multiple relationships with the near and far environment;
- the specificity and dynamics of processes in logistics systems and external random (stochastic) interactions (extortions);

- the large spatial range of systems, lack of unambiguous boundaries (international, global dimension);
- a distributed control system for information and decision processes (e.g. many decision-making centers, no clear scope of responsibilities etc.);
- developed, open and extensive ICT infrastructure in a state of continuous development.

The extensive and multidimensional structure of supply chains makes assessing its vulnerability difficult both quantitatively and qualitatively. The authors have made some assumptions and simplifications when assessing supply chain performance. The most important one is that the security potential of the whole supply chain W_{SC} (t) is a function of the vulnerability of its components, individual logistics systems $M_{ILS}(t)$.

$$W_{SC}\left(t\right) = f[M_{ILS}\left(t\right)] \tag{8.1}$$

Supply chain security capability is a dynamic, time-varying quantity, and its measurement can be made only at fixed moments under strictly determined conditions and constraints.

According to the functional criterion, the logistics potential of the enterprise (logistics system), which is a link in the industrial supply chain $P_{ISC}(t)$, can be divided into the logistics potential: supply $P_{LS}(t)$, production $P_{LP}(t)$, distribution $P_{LD}(t)$, waste $P_{LW}(t)$ and logistics management $P_{LM}(t)$ (Brzeziński, 2015):

$$P_{ISC}\left(t\right) = f\left[P_{LS}\left(t\right), P_{LP}\left(t\right), P_{LD}\left(t\right), P_{LW}\left(t\right), P_{LM}\left(t\right)\right] \tag{8.2}$$

In the context of basic supply chain processes, we can divide the supply chain security capability P_{SCS} (t) into: transport $P_T(t)$, storage $P_S(t)$ and management $P_M(t)$:

$$P_{SCS}\left(t\right) = f\left[P_T\left(t\right), P_S\left(t\right), P_M\left(t\right)\right] \tag{8.3}$$

The supply chain security potential presented in this way can be called general, while the degree of its utilization can be called the specific logistics security potential of P_{SLS}. It depends on the degree of its utilization under given conditions. Thus, it is the part of the overall potential that depends on the influence of external factors, thus:

$$P_{SLS} = K \times P_{SCS} \tag{8.4}$$

where: K denotes the total coefficient of the influence of external factors, which in turn is a certain function of the coefficients of influence of different conditions:

$$K = f\left(k_1,\ k_1, \dots\dots\dots\dots k_n\right) \qquad (8.5)$$

where: $k1$, $k2$,...kn denote individual coefficients of each external factor, e.g. threats.

When evaluating the security of the supply chain, it is useful to determine the matching factor (MF), in which we define its capabilities $M_{ILS}(t)$ and needs $W_{SC}(t)$, in terms of full satisfaction of customers, in a given time and space, considering the threats. It can be defined as:

$$MF = W_{SC}\left(t\right) / M_{ILS}\left(t\right) \qquad (8.6)$$

The matching coefficient in the security context can take values:

MF $= 1$ – a full matching W_{SC} (t) to $M_{ILS}(t)$ (a)
MF < 1 – the needs of W_{SC} (t) are smaller than those of $M_{ILS}(t)$ (b)
MF > 1 – the needs W_{SC} (t) are greater than $M_{ILS}(t)$ (c)

In situations b and c, there is a mismatch in emergency (crisis) situations between the needs and the capabilities of the supply chain. The former generates losses resulting from the overestimation of resources related to the maintenance of the increased security potential in the supply chain, and the latter causes that orders are not delivered in the appropriate quantity and time to the recipient, for example.

In order to determine the security potential of the supply chain, a diagnosis and analysis of the operation of organizational-functional, technical and legal conditions in its individual links, logistics systems (companies, institutions) were made in terms of application and use of opportunities provided by current solutions:

■ legal in terms of compliance and observance of crisis management procedures;
■ compliance with national and European standards;
■ functioning in organizational structures of units responsible for the security of supply chains;
■ modern management of the organization to ensure the required level of security escalating towards increasing supply chain security.

This approach results from the position that the security potential of the whole supply chain W_{SC} (t) is a function of the vulnerability of its logistics system components $M_{ILS}(t)$.

The components (companies, institutions) that affect the supply chain security potential were assessed by surveying views and opinions by indirect and direct methods using a questionnaire, which contained 18 items, including 16 closed- and 2 open-ended questions. The questionnaires were sent to 168 different companies, of which 92 provided responses, including 4 micro-, 24 small-, 29 medium and 35 large-sized companies. In addition, five interviews were conducted with experts, logisticians of large private and public companies based on the material collected in the questionnaire to verify the research results.

The purpose of the questions was to obtain answers to problems related to legal, organizational, technical bases, procedures, monitoring, management systems in situations of threats that may arise in the supply chain.

As part of the research, five in-depth interviews based on the items contained in the questionnaire were designed and conducted, which were extended to include additional issues related to logistics security. In the survey, an important issue was determining the relationship between the responses and the characteristics of the surveyed companies. The assessment was made using, in particular, Pearson's contingency coefficient, the chi-square test of independence. The study of the relationship with the above-mentioned mathematical model made it possible to infer the problems occurring in given groups, i.e. links in the supply chain. The results also indicate irregularities in the functioning of the tested systems and allow verification of working hypotheses.

Below are selected results of substantive research on logistics systems of companies (institutions), which are supply chain links.

Question 1: Has the legal basis for crisis management been implemented in the security management of logistics systems?

The adaptation of the legal basis of crisis management contributes to ensuring the coordination of flows of material resources, information, people in situations of undesirable events, consequently becoming a factor in increasing the level of security. In total, out of 92 surveyed companies, 63 cases (which is 68% of the sample) have implemented the legal basis of crisis management in logistics systems security management, while for 32% (29 companies), the problem remains unresolved (Table 8.2).

The share of companies broken down by their size is presented in Figure 8.7.

Table 8.2   Distribution of Responses to the Question: Has the Legal Basis for Crisis Management Been Implemented in the Security Management of Logistics Systems?

		N=92	
Question	Answer	n	%
Has the legal basis for crisis management been implemented?	Yes	63	68
	No	29	32
Total		92	100

Source: Own elaboration.

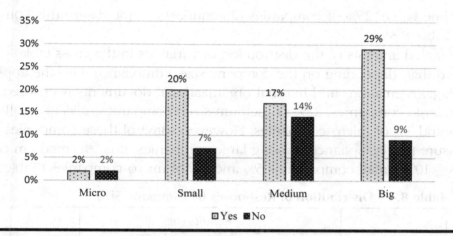

Figure 8.7   The share of companies that have implemented the legal basis of crisis management in the area of logistics system security management by company size. Source: Own elaboration.

The analysis of the distribution of variables in the cross table revealed that, depending on the company size, compliance with the current legal regulations and internal organizational documents is ensured by 29% of large companies, 17% of medium-sized companies, 20% of small companies and 2% of micro-companies. However, not all companies ensure operational compliance. Among large companies, it is 9%, medium companies – 10%, small companies – 5% and micro-companies – 1% (Figure 8.7).

Question 2: Is the entity's functioning compliant with the applicable legal regulations and internal organizational documents supporting crisis management?

Among the surveyed companies, ¾, i.e. 75% (69 entities) ensure compliance of the entity's operations with the applicable legal regulations and internal organizational documents supporting crisis management, at the

Table 8.3 Distribution of Responses to the Question about Ensuring Compliance of the Entity's Operations with the Applicable Legal Regulations and Internal Organizational Documents Supporting Crisis Management

Question	Answer	N=92 n	%
Has the compliance of the entity's operation with the applicable regulations been ensured?	Yes	69	75
	No	23	25
Total		92	100

Source: Own elaboration.

same time ¼, i.e. 25% of companies (23 entities) do not ensure this compliance (Table 8.3).

A detailed analysis of the distribution of variables in the cross table revealed that, depending on the company size, compliance with the applicable legal regulations and internal organizational documents is ensured by 29% of large companies, 22% of medium-sized companies, 21% of small companies and 3% of micro-companies. However, some of these companies do not ensure this compliance. Among large companies, it is 9%, medium companies – 10%, small companies – 5% and 1% of micro-companies (Table 8.4).

Table 8.4 Distribution of Responses by Company Size

Company Size	Results Yes	Shares (%)	No	Shares (%)	Total
Micro	3	3	1	1	4
Small	19	21	5	5	24
Medium	20	22	9	10	29
Large	27	29	8	9	35
Total	69	75	23	25	100

Source: Own elaboration.

Question 3: Is the structure of costs (losses) of protection against the effects of security threats (disturbances) in the crisis management system identified and analyzed?

In the total number of responses to the question about the confirmation of activities, including identification and analysis of the cost structure of protection against the effects of threats and their balancing in the crisis management system, 53 companies, which constitute 58% of the surveyed

**Table 8.5   Distribution of Answers to the Question about the Cost Structure
(Losses) of Protection against the Effects of Security Threats (Disturbances) in the
Crisis Management System**

Question	Answer	N=92	
		n	%
Is the structure of security costs against threats identified and analyzed?	Yes	53	58
	No	39	42
Total		92	100

Source: Own elaboration.

companies, chose the affirmative answer. On the other hand, 39 companies
(42%) do not carry out such activities and do not recognize costs or balance
them (Table 8.5).

Depending on the company size, the cost structure analysis is carried out
in 21% of large companies, 18% of small companies, 16% of medium-sized
companies and 2% of micro-companies. A high percentage of companies
do not analyze the structure of security costs. Among large companies, it is
17%, small companies – 18%, medium-sized companies – 15% and micro-
sized companies – 2%. The summary is presented in Figure 8.8.

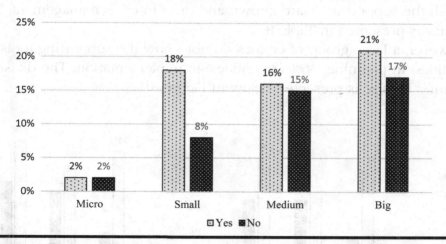

**Figure 8.8   Companies that analyze the costs of protection against the effects of
security threats (disruptions) in the crisis management system by company size.
Source: Own elaboration.**

Question 4: Do companies know about tools supporting crisis management in planning (designing) logistics systems or the implementation
(deployment) of logistics systems?

Table 8.6 Distribution of Answers to the Question about Tools Supporting Crisis Management

Question	Answer	In Planning (Designing) Logistics Systems		In the Implementation (Deployment) of Logistics Systems	
		n	%	n	%
Are there any tools supporting crisis management known to the company?	Yes	60	65	59	64
	No	32	35	33	36
Total		92	100	92	100

Source: Own elaboration.

The knowledge of tools supporting crisis management, which should include the planning (design) stage of logistics systems, and the implementation, i.e. system deployment, determine the success in protecting against the effects of threats. In the surveyed sample, the percentage of responses regarding the knowledge of tools supporting crisis management covering the planning and the implementation stage is similar and amounts to 65% of companies (60 entities) in planning, and 64% (59 entities) in implementation, in which the support tools are known and used in crisis management. The summary is presented in Table 8.6.

However, a large group of entities do not know the supporting tools: 35% (32 entities) in planning, 36% (33 entities) in implementation. The division of companies by size is presented below in Figure 8.9.

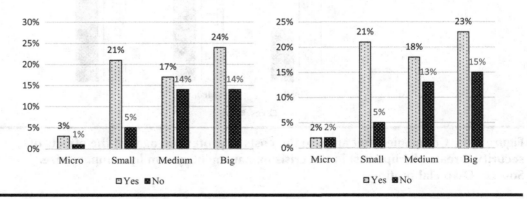

Figure 8.9 Companies declaring knowledge of tools supporting crisis management for the design and implementation stage of logistics systems by company size. Source: Own elaboration.

Depending on the company size, the greatest knowledge of tools supporting crisis management at the design stage is in 22 large companies, which constitutes 24% of the research sample, 19 in small companies (21%), 16 medium-sized companies (17%) and 3 micro-companies which accounts for 3% of the surveyed entities. Lack of knowledge of the tools for the planning stage was shown by 14% of large and medium-sized companies, 5% of small companies and 1% of micro-companies (Figure 8.9). In the case of knowledge of tools supporting crisis management in the implementation of logistics systems, the distribution of responses depending on the company size is as follows: 23% of large companies, 23% of small companies, 18% of medium-sized companies and 2% of micro-companies (Figure 8.9). It is noteworthy that a large percentage of companies do not know the tools in the group of large (15%) and medium-sized (13%) companies and a small percentage (5%) in the group of small companies.

Question 5: Does the development strategy of the company/institution include activities ensuring the security of planned and implemented logistic processes?

Research confirms that many companies include activities that guarantee planned and implemented logistics processes in their strategies. This situation results from the pressure exerted by other entities on cooperating companies which, having such an approach, are treated as reliable and serious, guaranteeing high quality, safety and responsibility of the conducted activity. As a result, 76% of the companies in the surveyed group declare that their strategy includes activities that ensure the security of planned and implemented logistics processes, while a significant percentage (24%) of the surveyed entities do not have them (Table 8.7).

Table 8.7   Distribution of Answers to the Question about Ensuring the Security of Logistics Processes

Question	Answer	N=92	
		n	%
Does the company's development strategy include activities ensuring the security of logistics processes?	Yes	70	76
	No	22	24
Total		92	100

Source: Own elaboration.

The in-depth interviews (experts from large production and service companies) show that the strategy for the protection against the effects of threats includes:

- ways to protect the company's brand and reputation;
- ways of identifying, managing and monitoring current and future threats affecting the functioning of the company;
- actions in the event of unplanned events (threats) that paralyze the achievement of the company's goals;
- ways to minimize the impact of incidents;
- measures to minimize downtime during incidents and shorten recovery time;
- ways to improve actions, plans and procedures in case of emergencies;
- ways to quickly locate the product on the market and in the supply chain to guarantee its immediate recall if it poses a threat to the safety of life and health.

An in-depth analysis of the answers on the relationship between activities ensuring the security of planned and implemented logistics processes in the strategies and the size of companies leads to the conclusion that 28% of large companies (26 entities) confirmed the use of such provisions in the strategy. The same applied to 23% of medium and small companies (21 entities each) and 2% of micro-companies (2 entities). Depending on the size, the companies that did not include actions ensuring the safety of logistics processes in their strategy were represented by 9 large companies (10%), 8 medium-sized companies (9%), 3 small companies (3%) and 2 micro-companies (2%). The summary is presented in Figure 8.10.

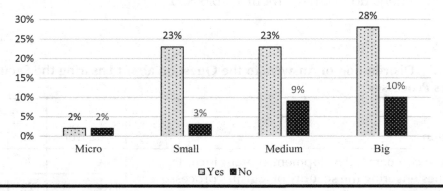

Figure 8.10 Companies that declare taking actions to ensure the security of planned and implemented logistic processes in the company's strategy by company size. Source: Own elaboration.

Question 6: Are there any procedures for managing the risk of loss of business continuity of the company/institution?

Effective increase of security of logistics companies causes more and more companies to implement procedures for loss of business continuity in addition to risk analysis of threats. The benefits of developing such procedures include:

- reducing to minimum disruptions and adverse events in the company or institution, thanks to procedures for effective response to crises;
- ensuring the possibility of restoring the company's or institution's ability to operate uninterruptedly or to resume operation in a specified time and at a specified level in crises;
- increasing the credibility of the company in contacts with customers and contractors, in the eyes of investors and shareholders;
- increasing competitive advantage thanks to ensuring business continuity regardless of adverse situations.

The concept of ensuring business continuity is a compromise between the level of protection against adverse events (crises) and the costs of this protection. It is about identifying potential (possible and probable) threats and the probability of their occurrence. The consequences are estimated considering the suspension time of production or service processes. A special role is given to the resources, the availability of which must be ensured in a crisis; it is a necessary condition for maintaining business continuity or undertaking main (key) processes as soon as possible from the interruption. This is shown in Table 8.8 and Figure 8.11. The developed business continuity risk management procedures function in 63 entities, which constitutes 68% of the surveyed group. In 29 companies, i.e. 32%, business continuity procedures were not implemented (Table 8.8).

Table 8.8 Distribution of Answers to the Question Regarding the Loss of Business Continuity

Question	Answer	N=92	
		n	*%*
Are there any business continuity risk management procedures in the company/institution?	Yes	63	68
	No	29	32
Total		92	100

Source: Own elaboration.

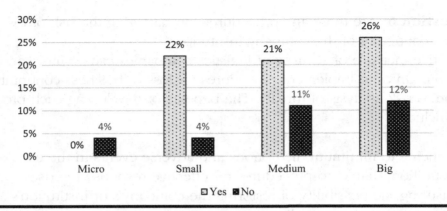

Figure 8.11 Companies that declare that they have business continuity risk management procedures by company size. Source: Own elaboration.

In the analyses examining the distribution of variables in the cross table, depending on the company size, it should be stated that the most implementations are in large companies – 24 entities, which is 26% of affirmative responses, and in small companies – 20, which constitute 22%, in medium companies – 19, which is 21% of responses confirming the implementation of procedures. The lack of implementation of the procedures was declared by 11 large companies (12%), 10 medium-sized companies (11%), 4 small and micro-companies, which represents 4% of negative answers each (Figure 8.11).

Question 7: What is the form of the safety monitoring of the operation of the logistics system (physical and visual tracking, measures of the logistics system safety effectiveness)?

In an open-ended question, the study participants were asked to describe the activities undertaken as part of the observation (monitoring) of the criteria selected to track the effectiveness of the logistics security system. Out of 92 surveyed entities, 62 companies, which constitute 67% of the total answers, provided short descriptions of the monitoring forms, but 30 entities did not reply (33%) (Table 8.9).

It turned out that 24% of small companies (compared to 2% with no information) and 24% of large companies and 17% of medium-sized companies provided the most information on the monitoring carried out and measures of logistics system security. In the group of large and medium-sized companies, 14% each did not provide information about their monitoring systems. There are 4 micro-companies in the research group, of which 2 provided data (Table 8.10).

Table 8.9   Distribution of Answers to the Question Regarding the Security Control of the Logistics System Operation

Question	Answer	N=92	
		n	%
What is the form of the safety monitoring of the logistics system operation (physical and visual tracking, measures of the logistics system safety effectiveness)?	Yes	62	67
	No	30	33
Total		92	100

Source: Own elaboration.

Table 8.10   Distribution of Answers by Company Size

Company Size	N=92				Total
	Yes	Shares %	No	Shares %	
Micro	2	2	2	2	4
Small	22	24	2	2	24
Medium	16	17	13	14	29
Big	22	24	13	14	35
Total	62	67	30	33	92

Source: Own elaboration.

Question 8: Was the structure of the company/institution examined in terms of susceptibility to internal and/or external threats (disruptions) to the functioning of the logistics system?

Effective company management requires a good knowledge of the vulnerability to various types of threats, both internal and external, that could disrupt the functioning of the logistics system. Among the 92 companies surveyed, 64 entities (70%) gave an affirmative answer, confirming that they know the vulnerabilities (sensitivity) of their structures to both internal and external threats, which may affect the functioning of the logistics system. The problem remains unresolved for 28 entities, i.e. 30% of companies. The results are summarized in Table 8.11.

Analysis of the distribution of affirmative responses, depending on the division by company size, is very similar to each other and is as follows: the susceptibility of structures is known to 22 small companies (24%), 20 large companies (22%) and 19 medium-sized companies (21%). The percentage of companies that do not know the vulnerability of structures is 16% for large

Table 8.11 Distribution of Answers to the Question about the Company's Structure in Terms of Vulnerability to Internal and/or External Threats

Question	Answer	N=92	
		n	%
Was the structure of the company/institution examined in terms of susceptibility to internal and/or external threats (disruptions) to the functioning of the logistics system?	Yes	64	70
	No	28	30
Total		92	100

Source: Own elaboration.

companies, 11% for medium companies, 2% for small companies and 1% for micro-companies. It is noteworthy that among large companies, as much as 75% do not know the vulnerability of their structures to threats. The situation is similar in the case of medium-sized companies, where 52% of the surveyed entities do not know the vulnerability of their structures. This finding suggests that these companies do not carry out any risk analyses, including business continuity management. Small companies, in which only a negligible percentage (2%) have no knowledge of the vulnerability of their structures to threats, should be singled out as a positive example. Figure 8.12 presents the results.

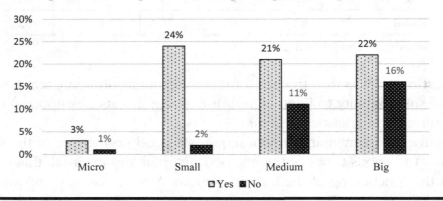

Figure 8.12 Answers to the question about the knowledge of the company/institution structures susceptibility to internal and/or external threats to the functioning of the logistics system by company size. Source: Own elaboration.

Question 9: What is the degree of independence (autonomy) of the safety management of the logistics system in the company? The following options were considered: full independence, co-management of security with other entities, management by an external entity.

Out of 92 responses, 34 entities declare full independence in managing the security of the logistics system, which constitutes 37% of responses,

Table 8.12 Distribution of Answers to the Question Regarding the Degree of Independence in Managing the Security of the Logistics System

Question	N=92	
What is the degree of independence in managing the security of the logistics system?	*n*	*%*
Full independence	34	37
Co-management with other entities	53	58
An external entity	5	5
Total	92	100

Source: Own elaboration.

while co-management with other entities was reported by 53 companies, which constitutes 58% of the respondents. Management by an external entity was indicated 5 companies, i.e. 5% of responses. The list of data is presented in Table 8.12. Co-management with other entities was most frequent, while management outsourcing was the least numerous.

Full independence of logistics system security management was reported by 15% of medium-sized companies (14 entities of the research sample), 13% of large companies (12 entities), 5% of small companies (5 entities) and 3% of micro-companies (3 entities). It is noteworthy that there was no management by an external entity in the case of small companies and micro-companies (option c). Therefore, the logistics system security management based on an external entity applies only to medium-sized companies (3 entities, which constitute 3%) and large companies (2 entities, i.e. 2% of the surveyed companies). Table 8.13 shows the breakdown by company size.

Table 8.13 Distribution of Answers by Company Size

Company Size	N=92						Total
	a	*%*	*b*	*%*	*c*	*%*	
Micro	3	3	1	1	0	0	4
Small	5	5	19	21	0	0	24
Medium	14	15	12	13	3	3	29
Big	12	13	21	23	2	2	35
Total	34	37	53	58	5	5	92

Source: Own elaboration.

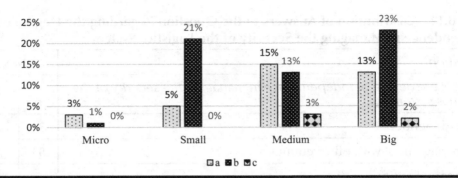

Figure 8.13 The option of managing the security of the logistics system by company size. Source: Own elaboration.

Option "b", in which the security management of the logistics system is based on co-management with other entities, was reported by all companies regardless of size. This solution was most frequent in large companies: 23% (21 entities), 21% in small companies (19 entities), 13% of medium-sized companies (12 entities), 1% in micro-companies (1 entity in the sampled group). The summary is presented in Figure 8.13.

Question 10: Is there a unit (person) responsible for the security of the logistics system in the structure of the management system of the company?

The efficiency of managing the security of the logistics system depends, among other things, on introducing institutional solutions in companies, which include, e.g. appointing units or persons responsible for it. In practice, it comes down to whether there are units or persons responsible for the continuity of security in the existing structure of the company (which means activities in the field of organization, operation, decision-making, monitoring). The functioning of the units responsible for system security affects the quality of the security system, although it is not the only quality factor of the system.

Such solutions exist in companies and institutions, and in the case of research, as many as 66 entities (72%) indicate the existence of such solutions. There is also a large group of entities in which such a unit has not been established. It is 26 entities, which constitutes 28% of the research group. Table 8.14 presents the question results. This means that these entities are not responsible for certain processes that supervise the security system.

The analysis of the distribution of variables reveals a very even distribution of the reported choice. Depending on the company size, the security unit was present in the company structures: in 25% of large companies (23 entities), 24% of small companies (22 entities), 20% of medium-sized

Table 8.14   Distribution of Answers for the Question Concerning the Functioning of the Unit Responsible for the Logistics System Security

Question	Answer	N=92	
		n	*%*
Is there a unit (person) responsible for the security of the logistics system in the structure of the management system of the Company?	Yes	66	72
	No	26	28
Total		92	100

Source: Own elaboration.

Table 8.15   Distribution of Answers by Company Size

Company Size	N=92				Total
	Yes	%	No	%	
Micro	3	3	1	1	4
Small	22	24	2	2	24
Medium	18	20	11	12	29
Big	23	25	12	13	35
Total	66	72	26	28	92

Source: Own elaboration.

companies (18 entities) and 3% of micro-companies (3 entities in the studied group). Entities that do not have a unit or person responsible for managing the security of logistics systems include large companies – 12 entities (13%), medium-sized companies – 11 entities (12%), small companies – 2 entities (2%), and micro-companies – 1 entity (1%). The summary is presented in Table 8.15.

Question 11: How does the management of own resources (material, human, financial, information) take place to ensure the required level of security of the logistics system operation: autonomously – is an integral part of the company's management or is it carried out by a specialized external entity?

The first method of resource management, which is an integral part of the company's management, is the most popular. It is used by 86% of the surveyed companies. The second way in which companies outsource resource management to specialized third parties is done in 12% of companies. In the case of 2% of companies (2 surveyed entities), resource

Table 8.16 Distribution of Answers to the Question on Managing Own Resources

	N=92	
The Method of Managing Own Resources	n	%
Autonomous	79	86
An external entity	11	12
Among the surveyed companies, two entities declared both the first and the second method of resource management	2	2
Total	92	100

Source: Own elaboration.

management involved both variants. The obtained answers are presented in Table 8.16.

The autonomous method of managing own resources is the basic procedure for 30% of large companies (18 entities of the studied group). In the group of large companies, the second method, based on a specialized external entity, is also used in 7% (6 companies in the studied group). This group includes 1% of companies (1 entity) where resource management uses both variants. The mixed variant is used in the group of small companies. And 1% of the surveyed companies were identified as such (1 entity of the surveyed group). Variant "a", i.e. autonomous resource management, is the only management method reported by micro-companies and constitutes 4% of all surveyed companies. In small companies, variant "a" is the basis for resource management for 24% of entities (22 companies), and in medium-sized companies, it is 27 entities (25 companies) (Figure 8.14).

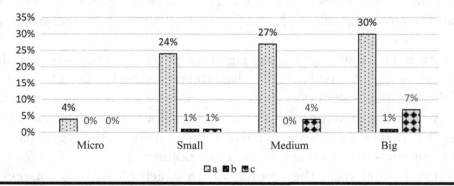

Figure 8.14 Answers to the question about the way of managing the company's resources by company size. Source: Own elaboration.

Question 12: Have the procedures of cooperation with the external environment been implemented to manage the security of the logistics system effectively?

The conditions in which modern logistics systems achieve their goals, especially regarding security management, force them to enter into relationships based on cooperation. Thanks to efficient and effective cooperation, i.e. successful and economical, entities can achieve goals, including security goals, the fulfillment of which would be impossible on their own, or it would be necessary to allocate much more efforts and resources. Collaboration allows the crossing of the boundaries of systems and, more and more often, even the boundaries of sectors. The guarantee of cooperation of various separate organizations and institutions for the agreed (security) goals may be realized by sharing information and knowledge between cooperating entities, the basis for implementing procedures regulating cooperation. In the group of 92 surveyed logistics entities, 65% of companies have implemented procedures of cooperation with the environment, compared to 35% of companies that have not – Table 8.17.

Thanks to in-depth interviews, information was obtained about activities, most often long-term ones, undertaken to eliminate the negative effects of the functioning of logistics systems. These activities include:

- periodic security audits (physical, ICT, fire protection, technical devices) by specialized companies;
- systematic training of personnel by external specialists in starting and implementing procedures in the event of unplanned situations;
- physical protection by professional companies such as specialized security and protection services in the field of protection of persons

Table 8.17 Distribution of Answers to the Question Regarding the Implementation of the Procedure of Cooperation with the External Environment to Effectively Manage the Security of the Logistics System

Question	Answer	N=92	
		n	*%*
Have the procedures of cooperation with the external environment been implemented to manage the security of the logistics system effectively?	Yes	60	65
	No	32	35
Total		92	100

Source: Own elaboration.

Table 8.18 The Frequency of Responses to the Question about Confirming the Implementation of Procedures by Company Size

Company Size	N=92			
	Yes	Shares %	No	Shares %
Micro	0	0	4	4
Small	22	24	2	2
Medium	18	20	11	12
Big	20	22	15	16
Total	60	66	32	34

Source: Own elaboration.

and property – they are obliged to cooperate with the police, state fire service and the municipal police;

■ preparation of backup logistics infrastructure (e.g. storage, transport, water, gas, electricity);

■ stocks held by other economic operators.

Depending on the company size, the number of implementations of procedures is similar in the distinguished company types. The largest number is in small companies – 24%, with a very small percentage of the lack of implementations – 2%. Another group includes large companies – 22%, in which there is also a large group of companies that do not have these implementations – 16%. Similarly, 20% of medium-sized companies have them compared to 12% that do not. The identified micro-companies do not have procedures for cooperation with the environment (Table 8.18).

Question 13: Do the developed procedures and separated resources ensure the acceptable (by the company and applicable formal and legal requirements) level of security comply with the applicable national and European standards?

Out of the total number of answers, 79% of companies have developed procedures and separated resources that meet the acceptable level of security and comply with applicable national and foreign standards. And 21% of the companies reported that they did not ensure such compliance (Table 8.19).

There are slight differences among companies categorized by size in the percentage of entities ensuring compliance of procedures and separated resources and an acceptable level of security with the applicable national and European

Table 8.19 Distribution of Answers to the Question Regarding Compliance with the Applicable National and European Standards

Question	Answer	N=92	
		n	%
Do the developed procedures and separated resources ensure an acceptable level of security comply with the applicable national and European standards?	Yes	73	79
	No	19	21
Total		92	100

Source: Own elaboration.

Table 8.20 Distribution of Answers to the Question about the Compliance of Internal Procedures with National and European Standards by Company Size

Company Size	N=92			
	Yes	Share %	No	Share %
Micro	4	4	0	0
Small	23	25	1	1
Medium	22	24	7	8
Big	24	26	11	12
Total	73	79	19	21

Source: Own elaboration.

standards. In the surveyed entities, 26% of large companies, 25% of small companies and 24% of medium-sized companies ensure compliance. Compliance is not provided by 12% of large companies, 8% of medium-sized companies and 1% of small companies. There are no micro-companies that do not ensure compliance of internal procedures with the standards (Table 8.20).

Question 14: What are the examples of practical and specific solutions (organizational, technical and others) for ensuring the security of logistics systems in the company?

Out of 92 surveyed companies, examples of practical and specific solutions for ensuring the security of logistics systems were provided by 59% of companies. And 41% gave a negative answer (one can only assume that the reason was probably the lack of such experiences or ignorance) (Table 8.21). Only 24% of small companies and 21% of large companies, 12% of medium-sized companies and 2% of micro-companies provided examples of such solutions (Figure 8.15).

Table 8.21   Distribution of Answers to the Question Regarding Examples of Security of Logistics Systems

		N=92	
Question	*Answer*	*n*	*%*
Are there practical examples of solutions for ensuring the security of logistic systems in the company?	Yes	54	59
	No	38	41
Total		92	100

Source: Own elaboration.

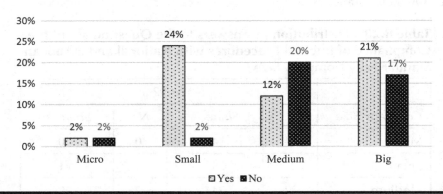

Figure 8.15   Answers on examples of the security of logistics systems by company size. Source: Own elaboration.

The group of companies that did not share their knowledge on applied practices included 20% of medium-sized companies, 17% of large companies and 2% of small and micro-companies. In the segment of medium-sized companies, the percentage of companies that did not provide examples exceeds the percentage of companies that provided examples of solutions (Figure 8.15).

Question 15: Is there training in the management of the security of logistics systems? If so, is it carried out by internal specialists or with the help of specialized external companies?

Training should be treated as a long-term investment that will increase efficiency in several system areas (organization, institution, logistics), e.g. reduced costs related to security, increased level of security, increased awareness. Currently, training, apart from traditional forms, is supplemented with tools that, for example, enable simulations, which is of great importance for the practice in crisis management. In companies, the safety of logistics systems impacts efficiency and effectiveness. Appreciating the importance of raising qualifications and competences in safety, companies conduct training. The forms of training depend on many factors (e.g.

Table 8.22 Distribution of Answers to the Question about Training in the Security of Logistics Systems

Question		N=92	
How are the training courses related to the security management of logistics systems conducted in the company?	Answer	n	%
Internal training	Yes	55	60
	No	37	40
Using specialized external companies	Yes	40	43
	No	52	57

Source: Own elaboration.

financial, personal, purpose). The management staff decides about the form of training, which formulates the goals to be achieved by the entity. In the total number of surveyed entities, 60% of companies chose option "a" – internal training, and 43% stated that they use option "b" of training, i.e. use the help of specialized external companies (Table 8.22).

Among large companies, option "a" is more popular, i.e. conducting training on one's own. And 21% of large companies choose this option, while 14% choose "b" – training by specialized external companies. The situation is similar in the case of medium-sized companies. Option "a" was reported by 17% of companies, and 9% indicated the second option. Option "a" was reported twice as often as "b". In the group of small companies, the number of answers "a" and "b" was comparable: option "a" accounts for 20% and "b" for 21% of answers. Micro-companies constitute a small group in the studied population of companies. They chose "a" most often. The summary is presented in Table 8.23.

Table 8.23 Distribution of Answers by Company Size

Company size	N=92 (option "a")				N=92 (option "b")			
	Yes	%	No	%	Yes	%	No	%
Micro	2	2	2	2	0	0	4	4
Small	18	20	6	7	19	21	5	5
Medium	16	17	13	14	8	9	21	23
Big	19	21	16	17	13	14	22	24
Total	55	60	37	40	40	43	52	57

Source: Own elaboration.

8.2.1 Conclusions

The study results showed that there are shortcomings (weaknesses) in the functioning logistics system links of the supply chain, including:

■ more than 30% of companies do not have implemented a legal basis in the area of security management of logistics systems;
■ 25% of companies do not ensure compliance of its operations with applicable legal regulations and internal organizational documents supporting crisis management;
■ more than 40% of companies do not identify the cost (loss) structure of securing against the effects of security threats (disturbances) in the crisis management system, including 17% of large and 15% of medium companies;
■ 32% of companies do not have procedures for business continuity risk management (Table 8.8), including 12% of large and 11% of medium companies;
■ in 30% of the structure of the company in terms of vulnerability to internal and/or external threats (disruptions) to the functioning of the logistics system is unknown, including 16% of large and 11% of small companies;
■ in 28% of companies, there is no person responsible for the organization and functioning of the logistics system security, including 13% of large and 12% of small companies;
■ 35% of companies do not have procedures for interaction with the external environment to manage the security of the logistics system effectively.

It should be kept in mind that the security potential of the whole supply chain is a function of the vulnerability (weaknesses) of its component, individual logistics systems, to threats. The presented shortcomings resulting from the research encourage the development of a model that would facilitate the management of security in the supply chain.

8.3 Proposed Model for Supply Chain Security Management

The purpose of supply chain security management modeling (SChSMM) is to construct a model to learn about the dependencies in a real-world entity in which the movement of a material stream and accompanying information takes place. The supply chain security management model and the experiments conducted with it allow learning about these dependencies, i.e. achieving the modeling objective.

The goals for which supply chain security management models are built include:

■ cognitive goals, such as identification of logistics subsystems, determination of relationships between quantities occurring in the studied SChSMM and determination of the course of variation of these quantities resulting from the scale of threats, which may also be the subject (goal) of research;
■ practical (utilitarian) goals, which concern, for example:
  – development and implementation of supply chain security management procedures considering the system itself and its near and far environment;
  – search for optimal solutions, e.g. selection of procedures, resources ensuring an acceptable level of security, choice of IT solutions;
  – analysis and assessment of the option of functioning of the legal and organizational conditions supporting supply chain security management;
  – method of threat monitoring (indirect, direct, with or without the use of state-of-the-art technical solutions);
  – identification and balancing of costs incurred to protect against the effects of unplanned actions;
  – technical and organizational equipment (capability) for supply chain security management;
  – selection of security management capabilities depending on the threats to the implemented logistics processes.

The multiplicity of issues in SChSMM causes different models to be built based on pre-planned and thought-out procedures for specific stages. During these activities, the following should be considered:

■ Various stages should be treated systemically (components are not isolated, they are connected by relationships with each other and the environment).
■ Constraints that exist or will exist during the modeling period should be considered (e.g. availability of monitoring data, size of finances,

measurement capabilities, availability of procedures and calculation algorithms, preparation of future users).
■ SChSMM constructing allows cyclic repetition of activities, which facilitates returning to the appropriate stage of model construction in the event of non-compliance of the results with the assumed (accepted, formulated criteria, e.g. with acceptable levels or delivery times).

Supply chain security management modeling should be completed by obtaining a specific result, i.e. achieving the assumed, planned goal. Thus, the modeling objectives should be defined and subordinated to specific logistics systems and possible threats in the first stage.

The selection of the model category and the definition of its structure is the stage of transformation, from the point of view of modeling objectives, the data and knowledge about the selected logistics system and threats into a set of dependent and non-antagonistic, incompatible, logical relations.

The choice of SChSMM categories is dictated by:

■ the degree of compliance with the modeled supply chain security management in the security domain, consistent with its acceptable security level;
■ ergonomics and functionality of use;
■ the resources available.

The presented considerations force a trade-off between the given constraints. This allows an optimum SChSMM to be chosen, which should provide a balance between the resources involved and the potential losses because of the appearance of undesirable actions. It may turn out that more resources are involved than can be lost due to unplanned actions connected with crises, for example. Modeling is a process of arriving at statements according to the scheme of hypothetical-deductive reasoning. In this sense, a model can be treated as a developed hypothesis. The procedure for constructing a logistics system security management system model is shown in Figure 8.16.

It consists of six stages. It is worth emphasizing that at each stage, modeling is to provide only as much information as is needed at a given moment, leaving out irrelevant details. These stages are interrelated; they cannot be treated independently. In the event of inconsistency with the experimental data, they require modifying the assumptions or parameters in the right direction until an acceptable solution for a specific purpose is found.

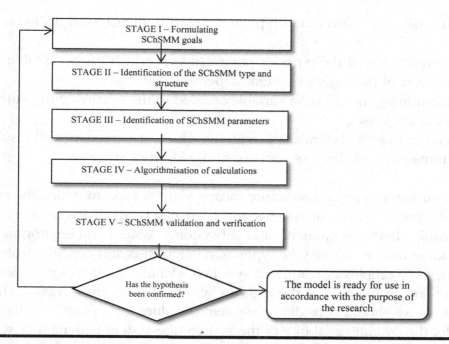

Figure 8.16   The procedure of constructing SChSMM (mathematical modeling scheme), where: SChSMM – supply chain security management model. Source: Own elaboration.

Stage I – formulation of SChSMM goals, including:

■ definition of objectives (Figure 8.17):
  – main (P);
  – specific (e.g. P1, P2, P3);
  – applications (e.g. P4, P5, P6, P7, P8, Pn).
■ identifying and defining initial information about the test object;
■ determination of mapping accuracy.

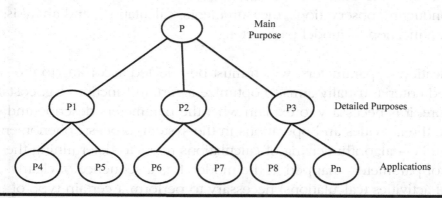

Figure 8.17   Hierarchy of objectives (Stage I). Source: Own elaboration.

Stage II – determination of the type and structure of SChSMM, including:

- determination of the types of parameters on which the acceptable security level of the logistics system depends;
- determining the decision variables related to the occurring unplanned situations, crises;
- determining the boundary conditions which, if exceeded, will result in an unacceptable level of security of the logistics system.

Determining the type and structure means identification in which the system is fragmented into subsystems and elements, which helps recognize the relationships between elements and subsystems, system and environment, at the same time recognize the types of relationships and describe features (arguments) (complexity feature of systems), identify the number of element connections. In the case of the logistics system, it concerns a socio-technical system, so we should consider the system of values and needs. We also consider the overall variability of the system (the system is dynamic), which can refer to the possibility of changes in the system structure and changes of processes in the system (or subsystems) within the original structure.

Another feature is determining the system's stability, as the ability to maintain the state (identity) in the face of disturbances and internal forces and possible and probable adverse events often leading to crises. It is also necessary to determine the ability to adapt the system by identifying regulatory couplings that counteract the negative effects caused by the environment.

Stage III – identification of SChSMM parameters, including:

- plan of observation, measurement, calculation and analysis;
- conducting observations, measurements, calculations and analysis;
- identification of model parameters.

Identification of parameters, which must be selected according to the assumed criteria, usually aims to optimize a certain function (e.g. costs). Therefore, it is necessary to explain what the parameters describe and characterize the activities and operations in the system, process, phenomenon.

Stage IV – algorithmicizing of calculations refers to determining the values of parameters mapped in the model. It is a sequence of clearly defined activities (calculations) necessary to perform a certain type of tasks previously defined and diagnosed. In the case of system modeling, it is the creation (description, execution) of a system from the initial to the final stage.

Stage V – validation and verification are processes that inspect the requirements and objectives. They include activities (operations, actions) that should be conducted in all modeling stages (it is worth remembering that both these activities occur at many different times and may appear in many stages of system creation). The differences between verification and validation primarily concern the perspective of the checks (i.e. whether it is technological and typical of the teams building the system or concerns the perspective of end-users who are not required to understand the technical side of the system they will be using). To summarize:

- Validation should answer the questions: is a correct model built? Is the model a faithful representation of reality from the perspective of its intended use?
- Verification should answer the questions: is the model built correctly? Is the implementation of the model consistent with the description and specification of its developer?

In general, verification and validation tools can be divided into four categories (Karkula, 20120):

1) informal – model verification and validation is done without formal mathematical tools;
2) formal – solutions from this group involve testing the correctness of the model using mathematical tools;
3) static – used to validate the conceptual model and the correctness of the translation to the computer model, they include data flow analysis, syntax and semantics analysis of the model;
4) dynamic – require "running" the model and analyzing its dynamic behavior; this group of methods is particularly important for validating logistic processes and systems models.

The validation and verification of the simulation model are not unitary processes and do not constitute a clearly separated stage – they should be treated as a continuous process occurring during the modeling cycle. The model validation and verification are integrally related to each of the previous stages of constructing a logistics system security management model. Therefore, it should occur not only after completing the whole procedure but also in all model construction stages. When verifying the model, an important element is to determine the criteria on the basis of which it will be possible to assess whether the conditions for compliance are met or not. A positive assessment ends the process of building the SChSMM, while a negative one causes a return to the earlier stages of model building.

The purpose of the research model is to gain knowledge by identifying the elements, the relationships that connect the elements of the selected systems of different research areas and learn about their impact on the security management of logistics systems. The infinite number of factors affecting facilities (systems, subsystems) makes it impossible to build a model considering all possible internal and external influences. Therefore, in a model, the number of "connections" is limited to those that significantly influence the behavior of the facility (system) for the purposes of the analysis.

The presented model is iconic, i.e. a graphic representation of the analyzed research areas. Such an approach allows us to make sense of all the observed elements and facilitates understanding of the internal organization of the research areas. The ability to imagine a certain structure of the conducted research is the basic step in solving the examined problem. The constructed research model presents the existing relationships and relations between individual elements: research areas, set of methods and research tools, and the effects of the conducted research.

When modeling, the following should be kept in mind:

■ Simplifying the SChSMM may not achieve the expected results.
■ Complexity will make the model impossible to implement in practice.

Modeling can be defined as an expression attempt through a special graphical notation of the most important features of the developed system and its environment.

The identified research areas discussed and analyzed in supply chain security management include:

■ supply chain structure (participants);
■ threats (intentional and unintentional human actions, environmental impacts – climate) in the supply chain links;
■ computer-aided decision-making;
■ national and international standards in supply chain security;
■ information technologies supporting information flow;
■ security in transport and storage management;

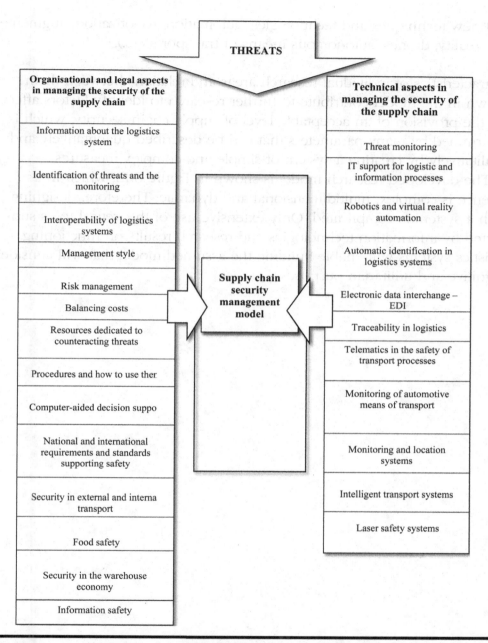

Figure 8.18 Supply chain security management model. Source: Own elaboration.

■ new techniques and technologies (automation, robotization, augmented reality, drones, autonomous means of transports etc.).

Characteristics of individual research areas and relations between them shown in the model contribute to further research to identify factors affecting the provision of an acceptable level of supply chain security, which is determined by many parameters that can be described quantitatively and qualitatively by creating a system of simple and complex measures.

The developed research model is shown in Figure 8.18, which in its essence is complex, multidimensional and dynamic. Therefore, designing such a system is complicated. Only extensive use of theoretical tools supported by information technologies and research results on functioning logistics systems will enable building the assumed model that will consider cognitive and utilitarian purposes.

Conclusions

The subject of the book *Supply Chain Security: How to Support Safety and Reduce Risk in Your Supply Chain Process* and its content is up-to-date and useful in practice and theory for several important reasons. They are described below.

Firstly

The presented material is the result of a critical domestic and foreign literature analysis as well as empirical research on the safety and risk of logistics processes implemented in supply chains. The presented research is based primarily on management and quality sciences and safety sciences, automation, electronics and electrical engineering, technical information technology and telecommunications, and transport. Such an approach allows the current situation to be assessed and, based on the use of the latest theoretical knowledge, innovations in practice to be implemented to manage the flow of the material stream and accompanying information, including unforeseen threats.

Secondly

Due to globalization, innovative technological solutions in logistics processes and high requirements for availability, efficiency and quality, modern logistics chains constitute a complex, dynamic system in which producers and service providers cooperate to process and move goods from the raw material stage to the final consumer. Therefore, innovative technologies employed and improved for the needs of supply chains in Industry 4.0 deserve

DOI: 10.4324/9781003286110-9

attention in the context of its safety and the minimization of losses in logistics processes. They include IT systems, innovative methods of picking goods, robotization – automation – IoT, self-steering vehicles, cloud computing, augmented and virtual reality, artificial intelligence and machine vision.

Thirdly

The spectrum and complexity of operations carried out in supply chains causes an increase in the number and scale of potential disruptions affecting security, causing delayed supply and, in many cases, their complete interruption due to external factors such as natural and biological disasters (e.g. COVID-19), and political disputes (e.g. the trade war between the US and China, the migration crisis in Poland, Lithuania, Estonia), technological issues (e.g. cyber-attacks, data loss, damage to servers and transmission channels). As a result, it may make it impossible to achieve the basic goal of the supply chain, which is to deliver to the end customer the ordered goods of the required quantity and quality at the agreed time and place.

Fourthly

Unplanned situations always appear unexpectedly, but this does not mean that management has no influence on the surrounding reality. Continuous, systematic search and improvement of effective safety management systems for logistics processes after the emergence of threats allow the adverse effects that may arise during the flow of the material stream and accompanying information to be reduced and sometimes completely eliminated. This requires integrated management based on coordination, interoperability and mutual trust of all actors who are linked to suppliers and customers within a single supply chain. The managers, suppliers and customers should look for the best solutions to minimize the risks associated with supply chain disruptions and the costs associated with disruptions, and ensure sustainable growth and prosperity. The correct way to minimize all kinds of wastage in supply chains in the event of the emergence of threats is the improvement of activities contributing to the maintenance at the appropriate substantive level of the four phases, which include:

■ prevention, that is, actions anticipating, eliminating or reducing the possibility of unplanned situations;

■ preparation, in which the key element is the development of emergency plans, which describe who will do what and when, with what force and means, and on what legal basis (before, during and immediately after an unplanned event);

■ reacting when a real threat or event occurs;

■ restoration, the final stage in the cycle of the emergence of a breakdown in the flow of the material stream and accompanying information (rebuilding is continued until all systems return to a previous state or better than the previous one).

Fifthly

Effective and efficient safety and risk management requires systematic search and implementation of new tools and instruments, which include:

■ ongoing visualization of the supply chain by monitoring and analyzing the performance of individual elements of the supply chain;

■ identification of its weak points (threats) along with ordering the effects according to importance and consequences;

■ analysis of causes of supply chain interruptions and possible losses for the production, storage or transport of goods to recipients;

■ developing a risk mitigation strategy;

■ diversification of suppliers and optimization of the level of safety stocks to ensure constant production capacity;

■ constant cooperation and communication with partners through consultations with other participants in the supply chain and external entities;

■ proactively counteracting cyber threats.

Sixthly

The presented model of supply chain security management in the form of a graphical representation of the analyzed research areas is not without significance for the practice. This approach illustrates the risk in logistics processes, considering organizational, legal and technical aspects in managing supply chain security. This makes it easier to understand the internal organization of the research areas in connection with the external environment. The characteristics of individual research areas and the relationships between them, shown in the model, determine the direction of further research to identify factors influencing the assurance of an acceptable level of supply chain security.

References

Adamczyk, W. (2004). *Ekologia wyrobów: jakoś ć, cykl życia, projektowanie*, PWE, Warszawa.

Akgun, E.Z., Monios, J., Rye, T., Fonzone, A. (2019). Influences on urban freight transport policy choice by local authorities. *Transport Policy*, 75, 8–98.

Alminshid, K., Omar M.N. (2013). Detecting backdoor using stepping stone detection approach, [in:] Informatics and Applications (ICIA), Second International Conference.

AQAP 2000 (2003). *Polityka NATO dotycząca zintegrowanego systemowego podejścia do jakości w cyklu życia*, Ed. 1, June.

AQAP 2070 (2004). *Proces NATO dotyczący wzajemnej realizacji rządowego zapewnienia jakości GQA*, Ed. 1, January, C-4.

Aqlan, F.S., Lam, S. (2016). Supply chain optimization under risk and uncertainty: A case study for high-end server manufacturing, *Computers & Industrial Engineering*, 93, 78–87.

Automatyzacja połączona siecią - W jaki sposób możecie zoptymalizować tworzenie wartości dodanej poprzez automatyzację w łańcuchu dostaw (2021). Available at: https://www.lila-logistik.com/pl/automatyzacja, 09.05.2021.

Ayurzana, O., Pumbuurei, B., Hiesik, K. (2013). A study of hand-geometry recognition system, 8th International Forum on Strategic Technology (IFOST), 2.

Banaszak, Z., Kłos, S., Mleczko J. (2011). *Zintegrowane systemy zarządzania*, PWE, Warszawa.

Bartczak K. (2006). Technologie informatyczne i telekomunikacyjne jako podstawa tworzenia systemów telematycznych w transporcie, [ed.] *Współczesne procesy i zjawiska w transporcie*, Uniwersytet Szczeciński, Szczecin.

Bates J. (1989). Information as an economic good: A re-evaluation of theoretical approaches, (eds.) B. D. Ruben, L. A. Lievrouw, *Mediation, Information, and Communication. Information and Information, and Communication*, Transaction Publisher, New Brunswick, 3/1989, 379–394.

Berchmans, D., Kumar, S.S. (2014). Optical character recognition [ed.] an overview and an insight, Control, Instrumentation, Communication and Computational Technologies (ICCICCT), International Conference.

Beyer, M.A., Laney, D. (2012). *The Importance of "Big Data": A Definition*, Gartner Publication, 1–9.

Bezpieczeństwo teleinformatyczne. (2021). Available at: http://bip.abw.gov.pl/, 30.01.2021.

Bi, J., Liu, B., Wu, J., Shen Y. (2009). Preventing IP source address spoofing, [ed.] A two-level, state machine-based method, *Tsinghua Science and Technology*, 14, 4.

Biała Księga Plan utworzenia jednolitego europejskiego obszaru transportu: dążenie do osiągnięcia konkurencyjnego i zasobooszczędnego systemu transportu /* COM/2011/0144 końcowy */. Available at: http://ec.europa.eu/, 10.03.2021.

Biedrzycki, N. (2020). Co to jest blockchain: wszystko co trzeba o nim wiedzieć. Available at: https://norbertbiedrzycki.pl, 30.11.2020.

Big Data Challenges of Industry 4.0. (2020). Available at: http://www.datanami.com, 22.11.2020.

Big Data. Czym są i dlaczego mają znaczenie? (2021). Available at: https://www.sas .com/pl, 22.04.2021.

Biała Księga Bezpieczeństwa Narodowego Rzeczpospolitej Polskiej (2013). *Biuro Bezpieczeństwa Narodowego, Warszawa 2013, 71*, White Book of National Security of the Republic of Poland, Warsaw, 71.

Biuletyny informacyjne PSP za 2019 r. (2021). Available at: http://www.straz.gov.pl/, 26.02.2021.

Blog poświęcony e-commerce i promocji w Internecie. (2020). Available at: http:// thewebcherry.com, 20.12.2020.

Bolan, P. (2008). A review of the electronic product code standards for RFID technology, Proceedings of the 7th International Network Conference, University of Plymouth, Conference in Plymouth, UK, 8–10 July.

Bozarth, C., Handfield, R.B. (2007). *Wprowadzenie do zarządzania operacjami i łańcuchem dostaw*, Helion, Gliwice, Poland.

Brichler, U., Bütler, M. (2007). *Information economics*, Routledge, London.

Brilman, J. (2002). *Nowoczesne koncepcje i metody zarzadzania*, PWE, Warszawa.

Brookson, C., Cadzow, S., Eckmaier, R., Eschweiler, J., Gerber, B., Guarino, A., Rannenberg, K., Shamah, J., & Górniak, S. (2016). Definition of cybersecurity: Gaps and overlaps in standardization. https://www.enisa.europa.eu/publications/ definition-of-cybersecurity, 18.07.2020.

Brzeziński, M. (2015). *Inżynieria systemów logistycznych*, WAT, Warszawa.

Bundy, J., Pfarrer, M. D. (2015). A burden of responsibility: The role of social approval at the onset of a crisis. *Academy of Management Review*, 40, 345–369, doi.org/10.5465/amr.2013.0027

Business Strategy, (2021). Available at: https://businessjargons.com/business-strategy .html, 04.03.2021.

Cambrigde Dictionary. (2021). Available at: https://dictionary.cambridge.org/pl/ dictionary/english/conservatism, 04.04.2021.

Chao, I., Li, Q. (2006). Manufacturing execution systems (MES) assessment and investment decision study, [ed.] IEEE International Conference on Systems, Man and Cybernetics, SMC '06, 6.

Cheung, K.F., Bell, M.G.H. (2019). Attacker–defender model against quantal response adversaries for cyber security in logistics management: An introductory study. *European Journal of Operational Research*, 291(2), 471–481, doi.org /10.1016/j.ejor.2019.10.019.

Chmielarz, W., Turyna, J. (ed.) (2009). *Komputerowe systemy zarządzania*, Wydawnictwo Naukowe Wydziału Zarządzania Uniwersytetu Warszawskiego, Warszawa, 72.

Choraś, R. (2012). Retina recognition for biometrics [ed.] Seventh International Conference on Digital Information Management (ICDIM), doi.org/10.1109/ ICDIM.2012.6360109.

Chow, H. K.H., Choy, K.L., Lee, W.B., Chan, F. T.S. (2005). Design of a knowledge-based logistics strategy system, *Expert Systems with Applications*, 29(2), 272–290, doi.org/10.1016/j.eswa.2005.04.001.

Ciecińska, B., Łunarski, J., Perłowski, R., Stadnicka, K. (2006). *Systemy zarządzania bezpieczeństwem w przedsiębiorstwie*, Politechnika Rzeszowska, Rzeszów.

Ciesielski, M., Długosz, J. (ed.) (2010). *Strategie łańcuchów dostaw*, PWE, Warszawa.

Closs, D.J., McGarrell, E.F. (2004). Enhancing security throughout the supply chain, *Special Report Series*, IBM Center for the Business of Government. Available at: www.businessofgovernment.org

Co rozumiemy pod pojęciem komisjonowania? (2021).Available at: www.bito.com, 24.02.2021.

Co to jest Stalkerware i jak wpływa na telefony z systemem Android? (2021). Available at: https://pl.unedose.fr/article/what-is-stalkerware-and-how-does-it -affect-android-phones, 27.05.2021.

Collins Online English Dictionary. (2020). Available at: www.collinsdictionary.com/ dictionary/english/strategy, 22.11.2020.

Collins Online English Dictionary. (2021). Available at: www.collinsdictionary.com/ dictionary/english/trust, 12.10.2021.

Competitiveness report 2019 (2019). Available at: https://www.8-international.com/ /wp-content/uploads/2019/10/competitiveness-report-eight-advisory-2019.pdf, 04.10.2019.

Concise Statistical Yearbook of Poland 2020 (2020). Statistics Poland, Warsaw.

Coombs, W.T. (2015), *Ongoing Crisis Communication: Planning, Managing and Responding* (4th edn), Sage, Thousand Oaks, CA.

Culot, G., Nassimbeni, G., Orzes, G., Sartor, M. (2020). Behind the definition of industry 4.0: Analysis and open questions. *International Journal of Production Economics*, 226, 107617, doi.org/10.1016/j.ijpe.2020.107617.

Czym Jest Big data? Wykorzystanie Danych w Biznesie (2021). Available at: https:// blog.sagiton.pl, 28.05.2021.

Davenport, T., Barth, P., Bean, R. (2012). How 'Big Data' is different, *MIT Sloan Management Review*, 54(1), 23–45.

David, S.L., Chen, X., Bramel, J. (2004). *The Logic of Logistics: Theory, Algorithms, and Applications for Logistics and Supply Chain Management*. 2nd ed. New York: Springer.

Deniz, N. (2021). The roles of human 4.0 in the industry 4.0 phenomenon, *Logistics 4.0: Digital Transformation of Supply Chain Management*, Taylor & Francis Group, New York, 338–350.

Deore, M.D., Handore S.M. (2015). A survey on offline signature recognition and verification schemes, International Conference on Industrial Instrumentation and Control (ICIC).

Dlaczego gospodarka o obiegu zamkniętym jest istotna. (2021). Available at: http://cima.ibs.pw.edu.pl, 03.05.2021.

Doktryna Logistyczna Sił Zbrojnych Rzeczypospolitej Polskiej DD/4. (2004). Sztab Generalny, Warszawa.

Drewek, W. (2011). Monitorowanie ładunków niebezpiecznych w transporcie drogowym, *Logistyka*, 5, 513–522 .

Dubiel, Ł. (2021). Zarządzanie przepływami: podstawowe narzędzia wyszczuplonego wytwarzania. Available at: https://www.logistyczny.com/biblioteka/kaizen-lean/item/1447, 20.04.2021.

Dumnicki,R., Kasprzyk, A., Kozłowski, M. (1998). *Analiza i projektowanie obiektowe*, HELION, Gliwice.

Dworakowska, K., CSI. (2021). Available at: https://www.seaoo.com/blog/csi-2/, 22.04.2021.

Dziuba, D.T. (2007). *Metody ekonomiki sektora informacyjnego*, Difin, Warszawa.

ECR w praktyce. (2021). Available at: www.ecr.pl, 17.01.2021.

Edwards, P., Peters, M., Sharman, G. (2001). The effectiveness of information systems in supporting the extended supply chain. *Journal of Business Logistics*, 22(1), 1–27. doi.org/10.1002/j.2158-1592.2001.tb00157.x.

Ejdys, J., Lulewicz, A., Obolewicz, J. (2008). *Zarządzanie bezpieczeństwem w przedsiębiorstwie*, Politechnika Białostocka, Białystok.

Ellis, S. C., Raymond M. H., Jeff S. (2010). Buyer perceptions of supply disruption risk: A behavioral view and empirical assessment. *Journal of Operations Management* 28, 34–46. https://doi.org/10.1016/j.jom.2009.07.002.

Erikshammar, J., Wetterblad, J., Wallin, J., Herder, M., Svensson, T. (2013). *Vendor Managed Inventory: A Sawmills Potential Offering for Builders Merchants*, Luleå University of Technology, Luleå, 9–11.

ERTMS. (2021). Available at: https://www.utk.gov.pl/pl/interoperacyjnosc/ertms/14871, 23.03.2021.

Encyklopedia zarządzania (2020). Available at: http://mfiles.pl/, 02.08.2020

Fan, W., Bifet, A. (2012). Mining Big data: Current status, and forecast to the future, *ACM SIGKDD Explorations Newsletter*, SIGKDD Explorations, ACM, New York, 14(2), 1–5, doi.org/10.1145/2481244.2481246.

Feily, M., Shahrestani, A., Ramadass, S. (2009). A survey of botnet and botnet detection, [in:] Third International Conference on Emerging Security Information, Systems and Technologies, Athens/Glyfada, Greece, 2009. SECURWARE '09, doi.org/10.1109/SECURWARE.2009.48.

Fink, S. (1986). *Crisis Management: Planning for the Inevitable*, American Management Association, New York.

Fizyczne zabezpieczenie sieci. (2021). Available at: https://smartkeeper.pl/fizyczne
-zabezpieczenia-sieciowe/, 19.02.2021.

Forkiewicz, M. (2020), Przedsiębiorstwo ochrony w portach morskich. Available at:
http://www.ptzp.org.pl/, 01.12.2020.

Fu, Z. (2011). Mitigating distributed denial-of-service attacks, application-defense
and network-defense methods, Seventh European Conference on Computer
Network Defense (EC2ND), 59.

Gillet, S.E., Kapor, M. (1997). *The Self-Governing Internet: Coordination by Design*,
MIT Press, Cambridge, MA.

Gonzálvez-Gallegoa, N., Molina-Castillob, F.J., Soto-Acostaa, P., Varajaoc, J., Trigo,
A. (2015). Using integrated information systems in supply chain management,
Enterprise Information Systems, 9(2), 210–232, doi.org/10.1080/17517575.2013
.879209.

Gordon, I.H. (2001). *Relacje z klientem. Marketing partnerski*, PWE, Warszawa.

Gospodarka o obiegu zamkniętym. (2021). Available at: https://www.gov.pl,
02.05.2021.

Gospodarka o obiegu zamkniętym: definicja, znaczenie i korzyści (wideo). (2021).
Available at: https://www.europarl.europa.eu, 29.04.2021.

Greer, C., Burns, M., Wollman, D., Griffor, E. (2019). Cyber-physical systems
and internet of things. National Institute of Standards and Technology, US
Department of Commerce. Available at: https://nvlpubs.nist.gov/nistpubs/
SpecialPublications/NIST.SP.1900-202.pdf, 18.July 2020].

Grzeszak, J., Sarnowski, J., Supera-Markowska, M. (2019). *Drogi do przemysłu
4.0 Robotyzacja na świecie i lekcje dla Polski*, Polski Instytut Ekonomiczny,
Warszawa, 8.

Grudzewski, W.M., Hejduk, I.K., Sankowska, A., Wańtuchowicz, M. (2007).
Zarządzanie zaufaniem w organizacjach wirtualnych, Difin, Warszawa.

Gryz, J. (2013). *Kształtowanie strategicznego zarządzania bezpieczeństwem
narodowym*, [ed.] Strategia bezpieczeństwa narodowego Polski, PWE, Warszawa.

Gupta, A., Patel, N., Khan, S. (2014). Automatic speech recognition technique
for voice command, International Conference on Science Engineering and
Management Research (ICSEMR), Chennai, India, doi.org/10.1109/ICSEMR.
2014.7043641.

Gurtu, A., Johny, J. (2021). Supply chain risk management: Literature review, *Risk*,
9(16), doi.org/10.3390/risks9010016, 1–16.

Gustavsson, M., Johansson, A. M. (2006). *Consumer Trust in E-commerce*,
Kristiandstad University, Kristiandstad, 1–80.

Gwilliam, K.M., Geerlings, H. (1994). New technologies and their potential to
reduce the environmental impact of transportation, *Transportation Research
PartA: Policy and Practice*, 28(4), 307–319.

HACCAP. (2020). Available at: http://www.izz.waw.pl/, 12.12.2020.

Hakanen, M., Kossou, L., Takala, T. (2016). Building interpersonal trust in business
networks: Enablers and road-blocks, *Journal of Business Models*, 4(1), 45–62,
doi.org/10.5278/ojs.jbm.v4i1.1198.

Hałas, E. (2012). *Kody kreskowe i inne globalne standardy w biznesie*, ILiM, Poznań.

Halicka, K. (2010). Wykorzystanie systemów CRM w logistyce obsługi klienta, [ed.] Ekonomia *i* Zarządzanie, 4.

Hammervoll, T. (2009). Value-creation logic in supply chain relationships, *Journal of Business-to-Business Marketing*, 16, 220–241, doi.org/10.1080 /1051712080248457.

Hattangadi, V. (2019). The complete guide to offensive and defensive strategies. Available at: https://drvidyahattangadi.com/offensive-defensive-strategies, 11.11. 2019.

Hompel ten M., Kerner S. (2015). Logistik 4.0 Die Vision vom Internet der autonomen Dinge, *Informatik Spektrum*, 38(3), 176–182, doi.org/10.1007/s00287 -015-0876-y.

Hong-ying, S. (2009). The application of barcode technology in logistics and ware-house management, *Education Technology and Computer Science, ETCS '09*. First International Workshop on, 3.

Instrukcja o zasadach i organizacji przechowywania oraz konserwacji uzbro-jenia i sprzętu wojskowego DD/4.22.8 (2013). Inspektorat Wsparcia SZ RO, Bydgoszcz, 30.

Inteligentne Systemy Transportowe. (2021). Available at: https://neurosoft.pl/obszary -dzialania/inteligentne-systemy-transportowe/, 11.14.2021.

Internet rzeczy (IoT), (2021). Available at: https://wdx.pl/2020/11/24/internet-rzeczy-iot/, 04.2021.

IoT w polskiej gospodarce, Raport Grupy Roboczej do Spraw Internetu Rzeczy przy Ministerstwie Cyfryzacji. (2019), Ministerstwo Cyfryzacji, Warszawa.

ISO 45001:2018 – nowa norma dotycząca zarządzania BHP. (2020). Available at: https://www.iso.org.pl/, 12.12.2020.

ISO/IEC 27001, http://pl.wikipedia.org/wiki/GSCF, 10.04.2021.

ISO/IEC 27001 (2021). Available at: https://pl.wikipedia.org/wiki/ISO/IEC_27001, 24.04.2021.

ISPS – Międzynarodowy Kodeks Ochrony Statku i Obiektu Portowego. (2021). Available at: https://bbats.pl/, 17.05.2021.

Iwasiewicz, A. (1999). *Zarządzanie jakością*, Wyd. Naukowe PWN, Warszawa, Kraków.

Jaworowska, M., Korozja płytek drukowanych, https://elektronikab2b.pl, 06.07.2020.

Jażdżewska-Gutta, M. (2020). Zagadnienie bezpieczeństwa jako bariera funkc-jonowania międzynarodowych łańcuchów dostaw. Available at: http://bazhum .muzhp.pl, 20.12.2020.

Jaźwiński, I., Ważyńskia-Fiok, K. (1993). *Bezpieczeństwo systemów*, PWN, Warszawa.

Juttner, U., Peck, H., Christopher, M. (2003). Supply chain risk management: Outlining an agenda for future research, *International Journal of Logistics: Research and Applications*, 6(4), 197–210.

Kaczmarek, T. (2004). *Zarządzanie ryzykiem handlowym, finansowym, produk-cyjnym dla praktyków*, Ośrodek Doradztwa i Doskonalenia Kadr, Gdańsk, 16.

Kaczmarek T. (2003). *Zarządzanie zdywersyfikowanym ryzykiem w świetle badań interdyscyplinarnych*, WSZiM, Warszawa.

Kaczmarek, T. (2006). *Ryzyko i zarządzanie ryzykiem*, Difin, Warszawa.

Kaczmarek, T., Ćwiek, G. (2009). Ryzyko kryzysu a ciągłoś ć działania. *Business Continuity Management*, Difin, Warszawa.

Karkula, M. (2012). Weryfikacja i walidacja dynamicznych modeli symulacyjnych procesów logistycznych, *Logistyka*, 2, 717—726.

Katkar, V.D., Kulkarni, S.V. (2013). Experiments on detection of denial of service attacks using ensemble of classifiers, International Conference on Green Computing, Communication and Conservation of Energy (ICGCE). Available at: https://www.takmaghale.com/uploads/product/hzggga _149614635172992.pdf.

Kielesinska, A. (2014). Aspekty prawne bezpieczeństwa żywności w logistyce, *Logistyka*, 6, 134–154.

Kisperska-Moroń, D., Krzyżaniak, S. (2009). *Logistyka*, ILiM, Poznań.

Klatka, N. (1972). *Konflikt i gra*, Wyd. MON, Warszawa.

Klimczak, W. (2001). Model sytemu zapewnienia jakości wyrobów obronnych w Polsce, *rozprawa doktorska*, AON, Warszawa.

Kolibabski, K. (2021a). Ever given blokuje Kanał Sueski, przez który przechodzi 12 proc. handlu. Czego może zabraknąć w sklepach? Available at: https://next .gazeta.pl/next/, 01.04.2021.

Kołodziński, E. (2021b). Istota inżynierii systemów zarządzania bezpieczeństwem. Available at: http://www.uwm.edu.pl, 10.04.2021.

Kondariuk, J., Strategie zarzadzania popytem w SAP. (2021). Available at: https:// www.snp-poland.com/pl/poradnik/strategie-zarzadzania-popytem-w-sap/, 20.04.2021.

Konieczny, J. (1975). *Podstawy eksploatacji urządzeń* , WAT, Warszawa.

Konserwatyzm. (2021). Available at: http://www.wosna5.pl/, 03.04.2021.

Kopaliński, W. (2020). Słownik wyrazów obcych. Available at: http://www.slownik -online.pl/kopalinski/, 23.10.2020.

Korzeń Z. (2001). *Ekologistyka*, ILiM, Poznań.

Koślicki, K. (2021). *Co oznacza status upoważnionego przedsiębiorcy (AEO)?* Available at: http://www.podatki, 21.03.2021.

Koźmiński, A., Piotrkowski, W. (1996). *Zarządzanie. Teoria i praktyka*, Wydawnictwo Naukowe PWN, Warszawa.

Krajowy Plan Bezpieczeństwa 2019–2022 Załącznik do Krajowego Programu Bezpieczeństwa w Lotnictwie Cywilnym. (2019). Biuro Zarządzania Bezpieczeństwem w Lotnictwie Cywilnym Urząd Lotnictwa Cywilnego, Warszawa.

Krawaczyński, P., Zelek, D. (2021). Rodzaje i klasyfikacja włamań oraz ataków internetowych. Available at: https://nfsec.pl/ai/290, 27.01.2021.

Kudelska, I., Ponikierska, A. (2009). Analiza technik automatic data capture w organizacji przepływu materiałów przez magazyn, *Logistyka*, 2, 48–49.

Kulasa, K., Kryzhanivska, V. (2021). Procedura rozwoju nowego produktu. Available at: https://mfiles.pl/, 13.01.2021.

Kulińska, E. (2011). Metody analizy ryzyka w procesach logistycznych, *Logistyka*, 2, 385–409.

Kupczyk, M., Pruska, Ż., Hadaś, Ł, Cyplik, P. (2014). Czynniki i bariery integracji w łańcuchach dostaw, *Logistyka*, 3, 3535–3537.

Kwinta, W. (2021). Śmiertelne wypadki drogowe w Europie – zestawienie. Available at: https://inzynieria.com/drogi/rankingi/59291,smiertelne-wypadki-drogowe-w-europie-zestawienie, 08.2021.

Leończuk, D. (2012). Możliwości zastosowania technologii cloud computing w logistyce, *Logistyka*, 5, 627–634.

Lewandowska, J., Januszewski, F. (2013). Przyczyny i miejsca powstawania strat w łańcuchu dostaw, *Logistyka*, 5, 133–136.

Li, S., Da Xu, L., Zhao, S. (2015). The internet of things: A survey. *Information Systems Frontiers* 17 (2), 243–259, doi.org/10.1007/s10796-014-9492-7

Liderman, K. (2003). Podręcznik administratora bezpieczeństwa teleinformatycznego, *MIKOM*, 204.

Logistyka 4.0 – przewodnik. (2021). Available at: https://wdx.pl/2020/11/19/logistyka-4-0-przewodnik/, 01.05.2021.

Lotko, A. (2003). *Zarządzanie relacjami z klientem*, Politechnika Radomska, Radom.

Łubiński, M. (2021). Najbardziej zakorkowane miasta świata. Warszawa na 20. *Miejscu*. Available at: https://www.wyborkierowcow.pl, 06.03.2021.

Lysenko-Ryba, K. (2020). *Prokonsumencka polityka zwrotów*, Wyższa Szkoła Informatyki i Zarządzania z siedzibą w Rzeszowie, Rzeszów.

Majewski, J. (2002). *Informatyka dla logistyka*, ILiM, Poznań.

Malassiotis, S., Aifanti, N., Strintzis, M.G. (2006). Personal authentication using 3-D finger geometry, *IEEE Transactions on Information Forensics and Security*, 1(1), doi.org/10.1109/TIFS.2005.863508.

Malinowska, M., Rzeczycki, A. (2016). *Rozwiązania cloud computing w logistyce: stan obecny i tendencje rozwojowe*, PTiL, Szczecin, 4(36).

Mangan, J., Lalwani, C.C. (2016). *Global Logistics and Supply Chain Management*, John Wiley & Sons, New York.

McKinnon, A. (2016). Freight transport deceleration: Its possible contribution to the decarbonization of logistics. *Transport Reviews*, 36(4), 418–436, doi.org/10.1080/01441647.2015.1137992.

McQuaid, R. W. (2009). Theory of organizational partnerships: Partnership advantages, disadvantages and success factors, (ed.) S.P. Osborne, *The New Public Governance: Critical Perspectives and Future Directions*, Routledge, London, 125–146.

Mechelewski, T. (2020). Zintegrowane Zarządzanie Ryzykiem – COSO II – standard nie tylko popularny.... Available at: https://www.pbsg.pl/coso-ii-standard-nie-tylko-popularny/, 11.11.2020.

Mell, P., Grance, T. (2015). The NIST definition of cloud computing. Available at: http://csrc.nist.gov/publications/nist-pubs/800-145/SP800-145.pdf, 11.11.2015.

Mika, I., Godek, J. (2021). System SRM. Available at: https://mfiles.pl/pl/index.php/System_SRM, 15.04.2021.

Moduł identyfikacji kontenerów i pojemników typu dzwon (2021). Available at: https://www.eltegps.pl/, 24.03.2021.

Molga, T. (2021). Cmentarzysko fast foodu. Tu kończą życie produkty zbyt mało doskonałe. Available at: https://wiadomosci.wp.pl/, 22.08.2021.

Molková, T. (2009). Hodnocení kvality v dopravním a přepravním procesu, *DF JP*, Univerzity *Pardubice*, Czech Republic,15.

Mollenkopf, D., Russo, I., Franker, R. (2007). The returns management process in supply chain strategy, *International Journal of Physical Distribution & Logistics Management*, 37(7), 568–592, doi.org/10.1108/09600030710776482.

Mouton, F., Malan, M.M., Leenen, L., Venter, H.S. (2014). Social engineering attack framework, *Information Security for South Africa (ISSA)*, doi.org/10.1109/ISSA .2014.6950510.

Müller, J.M., Buliga, O., Voigt, K.I. (2018). Fortune favours the prepared: How SMEs approach business model innovations in Industry 4.0, *Technological Forecasting and Social Change*, 132, 2–17, doi.org/10.1016/j.techfore.2017.12.019.

Myles, G.D., Carnovale, C.S., Yeniyurt S. (2015). An analytical framework for supply network risk propagation: A Bayesian network approach. *European Journal of Operational Research*, 243(2), 618–627, doi.org/10.1016/j.ejor.2014.10.034.

Neumann, T. (2018). The importance of telematics in the transport system, *The International Journal on Marine Navigation and Safety of Sea Transportation*, 12(3), 617–623, doi.org/10.12716/1001.12.03.22.

Niedzielski, E. (1986). Próba systematyzacji procesów rozwoju systemów informaty- cznych, *Wiadomości Statystyczne*, 4, 20–23.

Niyato, D., Lu, X., Wang, P., Kim, D.I., Han, Z. (2015). Economics of internet of things (IoT): An information market approach, *IEEE Wireless Communications*, 23(4), 136–145 doi.org/10.1109/MWC.2016.755303.

Nogalski, B., Marcinkiewicz, H. (2004). *Zarządzanie antykryzysowe przedsiębiorstwem*, PWN, Warszawa.

Norma ISO 27001. (2021). Available at: http://www.mackowiakbs.pl/, 23.04.2021.

Nowacki, G., Olejnik, K., Walendzik, M. (2017). Ocena stanu bezpieczeństwa trans- portu drogowego w UE, *Autobusy*, 116.

Nowak Z. (2001). *Zarządzanie środowiskiem*, PŚ, Gliwice.

Nowik, M. (2021). *Big Data innowacją w logistyce i zarządzaniu łańcuchem dostaw.* Available at: http://dx.doi.org/10.18778/8142-085-3.10, 03.03.2021.

Obłój, K. (2000). *Strategia organizacji, W poszukiwaniu trwałej przewagi konkurencyjnej*, PWE, Warszawa, 232.

Ocena ryzyka na potrzeby zarządzania kryzysowego Raport o zagrożeniach bezpieczeństwa narodowego. (2013). Rządowe Centrum Bezpieczeństwa, Warszawa.

Odlaniecka-Poczobutt, M., Capota, W. (2009). Formy kooperacji z dostawcami w łańcuchu dostaw, [ed.] R. Borowiecki, A. Jaki, *Wyzwania dla zarządzania współczesnym przedsiębiorstwem*, UE, Kraków.

Okuniewski, M. (2021). Jaką metodę wybierzemy…metodę zarządzania ryzykiem? Available at: http://www.mkidn.gov.pl, 01.05.2021.

Oleander-Skowronek, M., Wydro, K.B. (2007). *Wartoś ć informacji*, Telekomunikacja i Techniki Komunikacyjne, Warszawa, 1–2.

Oxford Advanced Learner's Dictionary (collective publication). (2021). Oxford University Press, Oxford, 1276.

Pagano, A. M., Liotine, M. (2020). *Technology in Supply Chain Management and Logistics: Current Practice and Future Applications*, Elsevier, Cambridge, 13–14.

Pałęga, M. (2014). Bezpieczeństwo informacji w logistycznym systemie informatycznym klasy CRM, *Logistyka*, 3, 4931–4936.

Paszkowski, S. (1999). *Podstawy teorii systemów i analizy systemowej*, WAT, Warszawa.

Pérez-Benedito, J.L., Aragón, E.Q., Alriols, J.A., Medic, L. (2014). Optical mark recognition in student continuous assessment, *IEEE Revista Iberoamericana de Tecnologias del Aprendizaje*, 9(4), 133–138, doi.org/10.1109/RITA.2014.2363005.

Pick-by-voice (2021). *Nowoś ć Dascher dostępna w Polsce*. Available at: https://www.logistyka.net.pl/, 22.02.2021.

Pilkington M. (2016). *Blockchain Technology: Principles and Applications*, University of Burgundy, Dijon, 1–39.

Pisz, I. Łapuńka (2013), Systemy transportowe wspomagające realizację projektów logistycznych w branży transport spedycja logistyka, *Logistyka*, 5, 362 and next.

Pisz, I., Sęk, T., Zielecki, W. (2013). *Logistyka w przedsiębiorstwie*, PWE, Warszawa.

Pokora, P. (2021). Zarządzanie relacjami z dostawcami. Available at: https://grant-thornton.pl/publikacja/zarzadzanie-relacjami-z-dostawcami/, 12.01.2021.

Polska na 26. miejscu w rankingu Światowego Indeksu Bezpieczeństwa Żywnościowego 2018. (2021). Available at: https://www.portalspozywczy.pl, 12.12.2021.

Popławski, W., Sudolska, A., Zastepowski, M. (2008). *Współpraca przedsiębiorstw w Polsce w procesie budowania ich potencjału innowacyjnego*, Dom Organizatora, Toruń, 61–62.

Powstaje pierwszy na świecie inteligentny magazyn, obsługiwany przez robota (2020). Available at: www.wiadomoscihandlowe.pl, 22.11.2020.

Rabsztyn M. (2013). *Biuletyn informacyjny infrastruktury, Ministerstwo Transportu, Budownictwa i Gospodarki Morskiej*, Warszawa, 6.

Ramaa, A., Subramanya, K.N., Rangaswamy, T.M. (2012). Impact of warehouse management system in a supply chain, *International Journal of Computer Applications* (0975 – 8887), 54(1), 14–20.

Raport Cyberbezpieczeństwo: Trendy 2021. Przed jakimi wyzwaniami stanie biznes? (2021). Available at: https://aspolska.pl/raport-cyberbezpieczenstwo-trendy-2021-przed-jakimi-wyzwaniami-stanie-biznes/, 18.02.2021.

Raportu w sprawie bezpieczeństwa. (2020). UTK, Warszawa.

Richards, G. (2014). *Warehouse management: A complete guide to improving efficiency and minimizing costs in the modern warehouse*, Kogan Page Limited, London, Philadelphia, New Delhi, 36–57.

Roboty magazynowe w erze logistyki 4.0 (2021). Available at: https://www.mecalux.pl/, 08.05.2021.

Rokicka-Broniatowska, A. (2006). *Wstęp do informatyki gospodarczej*, SGH, Warszawa.

Rolbiecki, R. (2012). Infrastruktura transportowa a efektywnoś ć procesów logistycznych, *Logistyka*, 2, 36–39.

Romanowska, M., Trocki, M. (2002). *Przedsiębiorstwo partnerskie*, Difin, Warszawa, 80–81.

Rosenberg, J., Mateos, A. (2011). *Chmura obliczeniowa. Rozwiązania dla biznesu*, Helion, Gliwice.

Rozporządzenie ministra pracy i polityki socjalnej z 26 września 1997 r. w sprawie ogólnych przepisów bezpieczeństwa i higieny pracy (Dz.U. z 2003 r. Nr 169, poz. 1650 ze zm.).

Rozporządzenie Rady Ministrów z 29 maja 2012 r. w sprawie środków bezpieczeństwa fizycznego stosowanych do zabezpieczania informacji niejawnych.

Rutkowski, K. (2001). *Logistyka dystrybucji*, Difin, Warszawa.

Sadowski, A. (2010). *Ekonomiczne i ekologiczne aspekty stosowania logistyki zwrotnej w obszarze wykorzystania odpadów*, Wyd. UŁ, Łódź.

Schetina, E., Green, K., Carlson, J. (2002). *Bezpieczeństwo w sieci*, Helion, Gliwice.

Schroeck, M., Shockle, R, Smart, J. (2012). *Analytics: The Real-World Use of Big Data: How Innovative Enterprises Extract Value from Uncertain Data, Executive Report*, IBM Institute for Business Value and Said Business School at the University of Oxford, 12, 1–20.

Sethi, S. (2010). *Enhancing Supplier Relationship Management Using SAP® SRM*, Galileo Press, Bonn-Boston, 43–47.

Shaheen, S., Finson, R. (2013). *Intelligent Transportation Systems*, University of California, Berkeley, 12, doi.org/ 10.1016/B978-0-12-409548-9.01108-8.

Shannon, C. (1948). A mathematical theory of communication, *The Bell System Technical Journal*, 27 (6–9), 379–423, 623–656.

Shivajee, V., Singh, R.K., Rastogi, S. (2019). Manufacturing conversion cost reduction using quality control tools and digitalization of real-time data. *Journal of Cleaner Production*, 237, 117678, doi.org/10.1016/j.jclepro.2019.117678

Siambi, S., Okibo, B. W. (2014). Determinants of strategic supply chain management in enhancing organization performance: A study of eldoret water and sanitation company (ELDOWAS), *International Journal of Recent Research in Commerce Economics and Management*, 1(3), 53–59. Available at: www.paper-publications.org.

Sienkiewicz, P. (1988). *Inżynieria systemów kierowania*, PWE, Warszawa.

Sienkiewicz, P. (2005). *10 wykładów*, AON, Warszawa.

Sienkiewicz, P. (2007). Teoria i inżynieria bezpieczeństwa systemów, *Zeszyty Naukowe AON*, 1(66), 252—269.

Sienkiewicz, P. (2008). *Bezpieczeństwo informacji i usług w nowoczesnej instytucji i firmie*, AON, Warszawa.

Sienkiewicz, P. (2015). *25 wykładów*. AON, Warszawa.

Sienkiewicz, P. (2015). *Teoria i inżynieria systemów*, [in:] Inżynieria systemów bezpieczeństwa, PWE, Warszawa.

Sinha, A., Lahiri, R.N., Chowdhury, S., Chowdhury, S.P., Song, Y.H. (2007). Complete IT solution for Enterprise Asset Management (EAM) in Indian power utility business, 42nd International Universities Power Engineering Conference, UPEC 2007, Brighton, United Kingdom, doi.org/10.1109/upec.2007.4469024.

Sitkowski, L. (2009). Zarządzanie bezpieczeństwem dla łańcucha dostaw: ISO 28000, *Przemysł Środowisko Jakoś ć Zarządzanie*, 4(13), 28–29.

Siwek, Ł. (2021). Cyberprzestępczoś ć statystyki 2020. Available at: www.vida.pl/naj-grozniejsze-ataki-hakerskie-i-najwieksze-wycieki-danych-w-2020-r/, 15.02.2021.

Skarbecki, S. (2021). *Pick-by-light – kompletacja po nowemu*. Available at: https://www.logistyczny.com/biblioteka/w-magazynie/item/889-pick-by-light-komple-tacja-po-nowemu, 21.02.2021.

Skarżyński, A. (2000). Próba ogólnej systematyki sytuacji kryzysowych oraz wybranych towarzyszących im działań techniczno-organizacyjnych, *Materiały z XI Międzynarodowej Konferencji Naukowo-Technicznej Inżynierii Wojskowej, t. 1, Zarządzanie i organizacja działań w sytuacjach kryzysowych.* Ratownictwo i ochrona ludności, Warszawa.

Skowronek, C., Sarjusz-Wolski, Z. (2008). *Logistyka w przedsiębiorstwie*, PWE, Warszawa.

Slack, N., Lewis M. (2002). *Operations Strategy*, 3rd ed. Harlow: Prentice-Hall.

Słownik synonimów i antonimów. (2021). Available at http://megaslownik.pl/, 03.04.2021.

Sokołowski, G. (2014). *Traceability: bezpieczeństwo i śledzenie przepływu produk-tów w łańcuchach dostaw, w oparciu o standardy GS1 i wymagania UE*, ILiM, Poznań.

Sokołowski, G. (2020). Jak łańcuch dostaw wpływa na wartoś ć marki producentów? Available at: https://www.logistyka.net.pl, 27.12.2020.

Sokołowski, S.J. (1988). *Szkice prakseologiczne*, Warszawa., Instytut Wydawniczy Związków Zawodowych

Spekman, R. E., Davis E. W. (2004). Risky business: Expanding the discus-sion on risk and the extended enterprise. *International Journal of Physical Distribution & Logistics Management*, 34, 414–33, doi.org/10.1108/09600030410545454.

SQAS (Safety and Quality Assessment System), czyli System Badania i Oceny Bezpieczeństwa i Jakości. (2021). Available at: http://www.iso.org.pl, 04.12.2021.

Stahel W. (1982). The product-life factor, *An Inquiry Into the Nature of Sustainable Societies. The Role of the Private Sector.*

Statistical Yearbook of the Republic of Poland 2020 (2019). Statistics Poland, Warsaw.

Statystyka przewozów towarowych. (2021). Available at: https://utk.gov.pl/, 10.03.2021.

Stoner, J.A., Frejman, R., Gilbert, D. (2001), *Kierowanie*, PWE, Warszawa.

Strategia Bezpieczeństwa Narodowego Rzeczypospolitej Polskiej. (2014). Warszawa.

Strategia rozwoju transportu do 2020 roku (z perspektywą do 2030 roku). (2013). *Ministerstwo Transportu*, Budownictwa i Gospodarki Morskiej, Warszawa.

Synergius CRM (2020). Available at: https://synergiuscrm.pl, 20.09.2020.

System Zarządzania Bezpieczeństwem Informacji zgodny z ISO/ IEC 27001. (2021). Available at: http://www.iso.org.pl/iso-27001, 24.04.2021.

Szarf, D. (2021). 10+ narzędzi dla e-commerce wspierających sprzedaż online. Available at: https://brand24.pl, 09.05.2021.

Szczurek, T. (2006). Problematyka podejmowania decyzji w sytuacjach kryzy-sowych, *Świadczenia na rzecz obrony realizowane w sytuacjach kryzysowych*, AON, Warszawa.

Szkoda, J. (2004). *Sterowanie jakością procesów produkcyjnych. Teoria i praktyka, Wyd,* Uniwersytetu Warmińsko-Mazurskiego, Olsztyn.

Szmit, M., Gusta, M., Tomaszewski, M. (2005). *101 zabezpieczeń przed atakami w sieci komputerowej,* Helion, Gliwice, 155.

Szmit, M., Tomaszewski, T., Lesiak, D., Politowska, I. (2008). *13 najpopularniejszych sieciowych ataków na twój komputer,* Helion, Gliwice.

Szołtysek J. (2010). Typologia obszarów stosowania logistyki: propozycja rozwiązania, *Gospodarka Materiałowa i Logistyka,* 8, 2–6

Szołtysek, J. (2009). *Logistyka zwrotna,* ILiM, Poznań.

Sztompka, P. (2005). Kultura zaufania [in:] Socjologia, *Analiza społeczeństwa,* Znak, Warszawa, 321.

Sztuczna inteligencja: co to jest i jakie ma zastosowania? (2021). Available at: https://www.europarl.europa.eu/news/pl/, 22.03.2021.

Sztuczna inteligencja zmienia oblicze logistyki (2021). Available at: https://www.suus.com/suus-news/2494/sztuczna-inteligencja-zmienia-oblicze-logistyki, 22.03.2021.

Szulc, W. (2020). Elektroniczne metody monitorowania ruchomych środków transportowych. Available at: http://www.zabezpieczenia.com.pl/, 17.03.2020.

Szymonik, A. (2005). *Informatyzacja zarządzania logistycznego,* Bellona, Warszawa.

Szymonik, A. (ed.) (2010). *Logistyka produkcji Procesy Systemy Organizacja,* Difin, Warszawa, 192.

Szymonik, A. (2010). Technologie informatyczne w logistyce, Placet, Warszawa.

Szymonik, A. (2010). (2011). *Organizacja i funkcjonowanie systemów logistycznych, Difin, Warszawa 2011, Logistyka w bezpieczeństwie (wyd. 1 i 2),* Difin, Warszawa.

Szymonik, A. (2013a). *Ekonomika transportu dla potrzeb logistyka(i) Teoria i Praktyka,* Difin, Warszawa.

Szymonik, A. (2014c). *Zarządzanie zapasami i łańcuchem dostaw,* Difin, Warszawa.

Szymonik, A. (2014a). *International logistics,* Lodz University of Technology Press, Lodz.

Szymonik, A. (2014b). Zarządzanie ryzykiem systemach logistycznych, *Logistyka,* 6, 10534-10536.

Szymonik, A. (2015a). *Bezpieczeństwo systemu logistycznego w nowoczesnym zarządzaniu,* Difin, Warszawa.

Szymonik, A. (2015b). Bezpieczeństwo żywnościowe, *Logistyka,* 5.

Szymonik, A. (2015c). *Informatyka dla potrzeb logistyka (i),* Difin, Warszawa.

Szymonik, A. (2015d). *Zarządzanie dystrybucją,* WSOWL, Wrocław.

Szymonik, A. (2016b). *Inżynieria bezpieczeństwa systemów logistycznych,* Difin, Warszawa.

Szymonik, A. (2016c). *Logistyka w bezpieczeństwie i bezpieczeństwo w logistyce, Zarządzanie bezpieczeństwem gospodarczym w systemie bezpieczeństwa narodowego. Aspekty logistyczne,* Wydawnictwo Politechniki Łódzkiej, Łódź.

Szymonik, A. (2016d). *Zarzadzanie bezpieczeństwem gospodarczym w systemie bezpieczeństwa narodowego Aspekty logistyczne,* Wydawnictwo Politechniki Łódzkiej, Łódź.

Szymonik, A. (2018). *Ekologistyka Teoria i praktyka*, Difin, Warszawa.

Szymonik, A., Bielecki, M. (2015). *Bezpieczeństwo systemu logistycznego w nowoczesnym zarządzaniu*, Difin, Warszawa.

Szymonik, A., Chudzik D. (2018). Zapewnienie bezpieczeństwa żywnościowego w łańcuchu dostaw, XXI Konferencja Innowacje w Zarządzaniu i Inżynierii Produkcji, Zakopane.

Szymonik, A., Chudzik, D. (2020). *Nowoczesna koncepcja logistyki produkcji*, Difin, Warszawa.

Szymonik, A., Nowak, I. (2018). *Współczesna logistyka*, Difin, Warszawa.

Szymonik, A., Stanisławski, R., Błaszczyk, B. (2021). *Nowoczesna koncepcja ekologistyki*, Difin, Warszawa.

Świeboda, H. (2009). Zagrożenia informacyjne bezpieczeństwa RP. *Rozprawa doktorska*, AON Warszaw.

Świniarski, J. (1997). O naturze bezpieczeństwa, *Prolegomena do zagadnień ogólnych*, Wyd. ULMAK, Warszawa-Pruszków.

Tabakow, M., Korczak, J., Franczyk, B. (2014). Big data: definicje, wyzwania i technologie informatyczne, *Informatyka Ekonomiczna Business Informatics, Wydawnictwo Uniwersytetu Ekonomicznego we Wrocławiu Wrocław*, 1(31), 141.

Tasca, P., Tessone, C. (2019). Taxonomy of blockchain technologies. Principles of identification and classification, *Ledger*, 4, 1–39, doi.org/10.5195/ledger.2019.140.

Technologia 5G – czym jest? (2021). Available at: https://otvarta.pl/blog/technologia-5g-czym-jest, 04.05.2021.

Technologia 5G i korzyści dla logistyki. (2021). Available at: https://tsl-biznes.pl, 08.05.2021.0

Telematyka (2021). Available at: https://pl.wikipedia.org/wiki/Telematyka, 39.03.2021.

Teunissen, P.J.G., Montenbruck, O. (2017). *Springer Handbook of Global Navigation Satellite Systems*, Springer International Publishing, Switzerland, doi.org/10.1007/978-3-319-42928-1.

Traczyk, W. (2020). Smart factory: czyli fabryka przyszłości, www.elektrotechnikautomatyk.pl, 22.11.2020.

Trendy IT security w 2020 roku. (2021). Available at: https://nextserv.pl, 05.05.2021.

Tundys, B. (2015). *Zielony łańcuch dostaw w gospodarce o okrę żnym obiegu: założenia, relacje, implikacje*, Prace naukowe Uniwersytetu Ekonomicznego we Wrocławiu.

Upoważniony przedsiębiorca (AEO) jako odrębna instytucja prawa celnego. (2021). Available at: https://mojafirma.infor.pl, 29.04.2021.

Upoważniony przedsiębiorca (AEO - *Authorised Economic Operator*): zmiany po 1 maja 2016 r. (2012). Available at: http://www.finanse.mf.gov.pl, 22.04.2021.

Ustawa z dnia 14 grudnia (2012). *r. o odpadach*, Dziennik Ustaw Rzeczpospolitej Polskiej.

Ustawa z dnia 4 września. (2008). *r. o ochronie żeglugi i portów morskich*.

Vernon, D. (1991). *Machine Vision, Automated Visual Inspection and Robot Vision*, Prentice Hall International, Cambridge, 5.

Vademecum teleinformatyka II. (2004). IDG, Warszawa.

Verwijmeren, M. (2004). Software component architecture in supply chain management. *Computers in Industry*, 53, doi.org/10.1016/j.compind.2003.07.004.

Walas-Trębacz, J., Ziarko, J. (2011). *Podstawy zarządzania kryzysowego*, Krakowskie Towarzystwo Edukacyjne sp. z o.o. – Oficyna Wydawnicza AFM, Kraków.

Wanagos, M. (2010). Skargi i reklamacje: jak utrzymać klienta? *Zeszyty Naukowe Akademii Morskiej w Gdyni*, 65, 5–15.

Waśkiewicz, J., Kamińska, E. (2018). Średnie koszty jednostkowe w przewozach międzynarodowych realizowanych przez badane przedsiębiorstwa w relacjach z rynkami innych krajów UE oraz w relacjach z rynkami wschodnimi, *Transport samochodowy*, Wydawnictwo ITS, Warszawa, 3–7.

Waters, D. (2001). *Zarządzanie operacyjne Towary i usługi*, PWN, Warszawa.

What is the smart factory and its impact on manufacturing? (2019). Available at: www.ottomotors.com/blog/what-is-the-smart-factory-manufacturing, 21.11. 2019.

Wiener, N. (1985). *Cybernetics or control and communication in the animal and the machine* (2nd ed.), MIT Press, Cambridge, MA, 18.

Williams, Z., Lueg, J. E., LeMay, S. A. (2008). Supply chain security: An overview and research agenda, *The International Journal of Logistics Management*, 19(2), 254–281, doi.org/10.1108/09574090810895988.

Wirkus, M., Roszkowski, H., Dostatni, E., Gierulski. W. (2014). *Zarzadzanie projektem*, PWE, Warszawa.

Witkowski, J. (2010). *Zarządzanie łańcuchem dostaw. Koncepcje>Procedury>Doświadczenia*, PWE, Warszawa.

Wodnicka, M. (2021). Technologie blockchain przyszłością logistyki, Zeszyty naukowe Małopolskiej Wyższej Szkoły Ekonomicznej w Tarnowie, tom 1, Tarnów, 51.

Wołejszo, J. (2005). *Teoretyczne aspekty współdziałania, Współdziałanie systemów dowodzenia wojsk operacyjnych i wsparcia krajowego*, AON, Warszawa.

Wydajna chmura obliczeniowa w logistyce i transporcie: co warto wiedzieć? (2021). Available at: https://www.beyond.pl/, 22.04.2021.

Wydro, K.B. (2021). Telematyka: znaczenia i definicje terminu. Available at: http://yadda.icm.edu.pl/, 28.04.2021.

Yan-yan, Li, Long, W. (2013). The integration model of supply chain resource allocation: LRP, International Asia Conference on Industrial Engineering and Management Innovation (IEMI2012) Proceedings, China, 1741–1666.

Yongle, W., JunZhang, Ch. (2013). Hijacking spoofing attack and defense strategy based on Internet TCP sessions, 2nd International Symposium on Instrumentation and Measurement, Sensor Network and Automation (IMSNA), Toronto, Canada, doi.org/10.1109/IMSNA.2013.6743326.

Zaawansowane Informacje o Ładunku (ACI - Advanced Cargo Information). (2020). Available at: http://www.sgs.pl, 02.08.2020.

Zarządzanie opakowaniami zwrotnymi (RTI management), Logistyka opakowań czyli zarządzanie obiegiem opakowań zwrotnych (rotom.pl) (2021). Available at: www.2return.pl/usligi/Zarządzanie-opakowaniami-zwrotnymi

Zarządzanie ryzykiem. (2020). Available at: https://wiedza.pkn.pl/web/wiedza-normalizacyjna/zarzadzanie-ryzykiem, 20.11.2020.

Zaskórski, P. (2015). Informacja ciągłości działania determinantą bezpieczeństwa organizacji, [w:] *Nie-bezpieczny świat Systemy Informacja Bezpieczeństwo*, AON, Warszawa.

Zaworski, J. (2021). Systemy biometryczne. Available at: www.monitorlocalnews .com/2002_01_10_systemy_biometryczne, 02.12.2015

Zelek, A. (2003). *Zarządzanie kryzysem w przedsiębiorstwie: perspektywa strategiczna*, Instytut Organizacji i *Zarządzania* w Przemyśle ORGMASZ, Warszawa.

Zhang, H., Hu, D. (2010). A palm vein recognition system, International Conference on Intelligent Computation Technology and Automation (ICICTA), 1, doi.org/10 .3807/JOSK.2015.19.5.467.

Zhu, X., Yao, Li Q., Chen, Y. (2011). Challenges and models in supporting logistics system design for dedicated-biomass-based bioenergy industry, *Bioresource Technology*, 102(2), doi.org/10.1016/j.biortech.2010.08.122.

Zieliński, L. (2015). *BHP w magazynie*, Wiedza i Praktyka, Warszawa.

Živanić, D., Ilanković, N., Zelić, A. (2019). Fire safety measures in warehouses, 16th International Conference of Occupational Health and Safety, Ohrid, North Macedonia.

Złoch, M. (2021). *6 razy Pick – automatyka magazynowa*. Available at: http://nm .pl/systemy- skladowania/1524/6_razy_pick_8211_automatyka_magazynowa/, 25.02.2021.

List of Basic Legal Acts Concerning Rail Transport

Polish and European Regulations

Ustawa z dnia 28 marca 2003 r. o transporcie kolejowym (Dz.U. z 2007 r. Nr 16, poz. 94 ze zm.).

Rozporządzenie Ministra Infrastruktury z dnia 18 lipca 2005 r. w sprawie ogólnych warunków prowadzenia ruchu kolejowego i sygnalizacji (Dz.U. Nr 172, poz. 1444 ze zm.).

Rozporządzenie Ministra Transportu z dnia 19 marca 2007 r. w sprawie systemu zarządzania bezpieczeństwem w transporcie kolejowym (Dz.U. Nr 60, poz. 407 ze zm.).

Rozporządzenie Ministra Infrastruktury z dnia 20 lipca 2010 r. w sprawie wspólnych wskaźników bezpieczeństwa CSI (Dz.U. Nr 142, poz. 952).

Rozporządzenie Ministra Transportu z dnia 5 grudnia 2006 r. w sprawie sposobu uzyskania certyfikatu bezpieczeństwa (Dz.U. Nr 230, poz. 1682).

Rozporządzenie Ministra Transportu z dnia 12 marca 2007 r. w sprawie warunków oraz trybu wydawania, przedłużania, zmiany i cofania autoryzacji bezpieczeństwa, certyfikatów bezpieczeństwa i świadectw bezpieczeństwa (Dz.U. Nr 57, poz. 389).

Rozporządzenie Ministra Infrastruktury z dnia 18 lutego 2011 r. w sprawie licencji maszynisty
(Dz.U. Nr 66, poz. 346 ze zm.).

Rozporządzenie Ministra Infrastruktury z dnia 18 lutego 2011 r. w sprawie świadectwa maszynisty (Dz.U. Nr 66, poz. 347).

Rozporządzenie Ministra Infrastruktury z dnia 15 marca 2011 r. w sprawie wpisu na listę podmiotów uprawnionych do przeprowadzania badań w celu sprawdzenia spełniania wymagań zdrowotnych, fizycznych i psychicznych, niezbędnych do uzyskania licencji oraz świadectwa maszynisty (Dz.U. Nr 66, poz. 348).

Rozporządzenie Ministra Infrastruktury z dnia 18 lutego 2011 r. w sprawie pracowników zatrudnionych na stanowiskach bezpośrednio związanych z prowadzeniem i bezpieczeństwem ruchu kolejowego, prowadzeniem określonych rodzajów pojazdów kolejowych oraz pojazdów kolejowych metra (Dz.U. Nr 59, poz. 301 ze zm.).

Rozporządzenie Ministra Infrastruktury z dnia 12 października 2005 r. w sprawie ogólnych warunków technicznych eksploatacji pojazdów kolejowych (Dz.U. Nr 212, poz. 1771 ze zm.).

Rozporządzenie Ministra Infrastruktury z dnia 26 września 2003 r. w sprawie wykazu typów budowli i urządzeń przeznaczonych do prowadzenia ruchu kolejowego oraz typów pojazdów kolejowych, na które wydawane są świadectwa dopuszczenia do eksploatacji (Dz.U. Nr 175, poz. 1706).

Rozporządzenie Ministra Infrastruktury z dnia 15 lutego 2005 r. w sprawie świadectw prawności technicznej pojazdów kolejowych (Dz.U. Nr 37, poz. 330).

Rozporządzenie Ministra Transportu z dnia 2 listopada 2006 r. w sprawie dokumentów, które powinny znajdować się w pojeździe kolejowym (Dz.U. z 2007 r. Nr 9, poz.63).

Rozporządzenie Ministra Transportu z dnia 19 lutego 2007 r. w sprawie zawartości raportu z postępowania w sprawie poważnego wypadku, wypadku lub incydentu kolejowego (Dz.U. Nr 41, poz. 268).

Rozporządzenie Ministra Transportu z dnia 30 kwietnia 2007 r. w sprawie poważnych wypadków, wypadków i incydentów na liniach kolejowych (Dz.U. Nr 89, poz. 593).

Rozporządzenie Ministra Infrastruktury z dnia 22 października 2009 r. w sprawie opłaty za udzielenie licencji i licencji tymczasowej na prowadzenie działalności gospodarczej w zakresie transportu kolejowego (Dz.U. Nr 196, poz. 1515).

Rozporządzenie Ministra Transportu z dnia 12 marca 2007 r. w sprawie trybu wykonywania kontroli przez Prezesa Urzędu Transportu Kolejowego (Dz.U. Nr 57, poz. 388 ze zm.).

Dyrektywa Parlamentu Europejskiego i Rady 2004/49/WE z dnia 29 kwietnia 2004 roku. w sprawie bezpieczeństwa kolei wspólnotowych oraz zmieniająca dyrektywę Rady 95/18/WE w sprawie przyznawania licencji przedsiębiorstwom kolejowym, oraz dyrektywę 2001/14/WE w sprawie

alokacji zdolności przepustowej infrastruktury kolejowej i pobiera-
nia opłat za użytkowanie infrastruktury kolejowej oraz certyfikację w
zakresie bezpieczeństwa (Dz.U. UE. L. 2004. 164. 44 ze zm.).

Dyrektywa Parlamentu Europejskiego i Rady 2008/110/WE z dnia 16
grudnia 2008 roku zmieniająca dyrektywę w sprawie bezpieczeństwa
kolei wspólnotowych (Dz.U. UE. L. 2008.345. 62).

Dyrektywa Parlamentu Europejskiego i Rady 2008/57/WE z dnia 17 czerwca 2008 r. w sprawie interoperacyjności systemu kolei we Wspólnocie
(Dz.U. UE. L. 2008. 191. 1 ze zm.).

Zarządzenie Nr 5/2011 Zarządu PKP PLK S.A. z dnia 8 lutego 2011 r. w
sprawie wprowadzenia do stosowania regulaminu przydzielania tras
pociągów i korzystania z przydzielonych tras pociągów przez licenc-
jonowanych przewoźników kolejowych w ramach rozkładu jazdy
2011/2012 – niepublikowane.

Instrukcja o prowadzeniu ruchu pociągów Ir-1 (tekst ujednolicony
przyjęty uchwałą PKP PLK SA, Nr 176/2008 z dnia 2 kwietnia 2008 r.)
– niepublikowana.

Instrukcja o postępowaniu w sprawach poważnych wypadków, wypadków, incydentów oraz trudności eksploatacyjnych na liniach kolejowych
Ir-8 – niepublikowana.

Instrukcja o organizacji i użytkowaniu sieci radiotelefonicznych Ir-14
– niepublikowana.

Zarządzenie Nr 14 Zarządu PKP PLK SA w sprawie wprowadzenia
Warunków technicznych utrzymania nawierzchni na liniach kolejowych" Id-1 (D-1) – niepublikowane.

Zarządzenie Nr 14 Zarządu PKP PLK SA w sprawie wprowadzenia
Warunków technicznych utrzymania nawierzchni na liniach kolejowych" Id-1 (D-1) – niepublikowane.

Zarządzenie Nr 16/2007 Zarządu PKP PLK SA z dnia 21 czerwca 2007 r.
wprowadzające Instrukcję sygnalizacji Ie-1 (E-1) – niepublikowane.

Normative and Legal Regulations of the European Union

Directive 2001/12/EC of the European Parliament and of the Council
of February 26, 2001 amending Council Directive 91/440/EEC on the
development of the Community's railways (L. 2001.75.1.).

Directive 2001/13/EC of the European Parliament and of the Council of
February 26, 2001 amending Council Directive 95/18/EC on the licens-
ing of railway undertakings (L. 2001.75.26.).

Directive 2008/68/EC of the European Parliament and of the Council of September 24, 2008 on the inland transport of dangerous goods (L 260/13.).

REGULATION (EEC) No 1191/69 of the Council of June 26, 1969 on action by Member States concerning the obligations inherent in the concept of a public service in transport by rail, road and inland waterway (Dz.U.UE.L.1969.156.1) together with Council Regulation (EEC) No. 1893/91 of June 20, 1991 amending Council Regulation (EEC) No. 1191/69 on the action of the Member States on the obligations related to the concept of public service in rail, road and inland waterway transport (L.1991.169.1).

Directive (EU) 2016/798 of the European Parliament and of the Council of May 11, 2016 on railway safety (L 138/102)

Directive 2004/50/EC of the European Parliament and of the Council of April 29, 2004 amending Council Directive 96/48/EC on the interoperability of the trans-European high-speed rail system and Directive 2001/16/EC of the European Parliament and of the Council on the interoperability of the trans-European conventional rail system (L 164/114).

Opinion of the European Economic and Social Committee on the Proposal for a Directive of the European Parliament and of the Council amending Council Directive 91/440/EEC on the development of the Community's railways. (L.2004.164.164).

Regulation (EC) No 881/2004 of the European Parliament and of the Council of April 29, 2004 establishing a European Railway Agency (L.2004.164.1)

Directive 2007/58 / EC of the European Parliament and of the Council of October 23, 2007 (amending Council Directive 91/440 / EEC on the development of the Community's railways and Directive 2001/14 / EC on the allocation of railway infrastructure capacity and the levying of charges) for the use of railway infrastructure (L. 2007.315.44)

Regulation (EC) No 1371/2007 of the European Parliament and of the Council of October 23, 2007 on rail passengers' rights and obligations (L 2007.315.14)

Directive 2007/59 / EC of the European Parliament and of the Council of October 23, 2007 on the certification of train drivers operating locomotives and trains on the railway system in the Community (L. 2007.315.51)

European Communities' Directives and Polish Acts on Hygiene and Food Safety

Regulation (EC) No 2232/96 of The European Parliament and of the Council of October 28, 1996 laying down a Community procedure for flavoring substances used or intended for use in or on foodstuffs.

Regulation (EC) No 258/97 of the European Parliament and of the Council of January 27, 1991 concerning novel foods and novel food ingredients.

Regulation (EC) No 178/2002 of the European Parliament and of the Council of January 28, 2002 laying down the general principles and requirements of food law, establishing the European Food Safety Authority and laying down procedures in matters of food safety.

Regulation (EC) No 1829/2003 of the European Parliament and of the Council of September 22, 2003 on genetically modified food and feed.

Regulation (EC) No 1830/2003 of the European Parliament and of the Council of September 22, 2003 concerning the traceability and labelling of genetically modified organisms and the traceability of food and feed products produced from genetically modified organisms and amending Directive 2001/18/EC.

Regulation (EC) No 1946/2003 of the European Parliament and of the Council of July 15, 2003 on transboundary movements of genetically modified organisms.

Regulation (EC) No 2065/2003 of the European Parliament and of the Council of November 10, 2003 on smoke flavorings used or intended for use in or on foods.

Regulation (EC) No 852/2004 of the European Parliament and of the Council of April 29, 2004 on the hygiene of foodstuffs.

Regulation (EC) No 882/2004 of the European Parliament and of the Council of April 29, 2004 on official controls performed to ensure the verification of compliance with feed and food law, animal health and animal welfare rules.

Regulation (EC) No 1935/2004 of the European Parliament and of the Council of October 27, 2004 on materials and articles intended to come into contact with food and repealing Directives 80/590/EEC and 89/109/EEC.

Regulation (EC) no 396/2005 of the European Parliament and of the Council of February 23, 2005 on maximum residue levels of pesticides in or on food and feed of plant and animal origin and amending Council Directive 91/414/EEC.

Regulation (EC) No 1924/2006 of the European Parliament and of the Council of December 20, 2006 on nutrition and health claims made on foods.

Regulation (EC) No 1925/2006 of the European Parliament and of the Council of December 20, 2006 on the addition of vitamins and minerals and of certain other substances to foods.

Regulations Regulation (EC) No 1331/2008 of the European Parliament and of the Council of December 16, 2008 establishing a common authorization procedure for food additives, food enzymes and food flavorings.

Regulation (EC) No 1332/2008 of the European Parliament and of the Council of December 16, 2008 on food enzymes and amending Council Directive 83/417/EEC, Council Regulation (EC) No 1493/1999, Directive 2000/13/EC, Council Directive 2001/112/EC and Regulation (EC) No 258/97.

Regulation (EC) No 1333/2008 of the European Parliament and of the Council of December 16, 2008 on food additives.

Regulation (EU) no 1169/2011 of the European Parliament and of the Council of October 25, 2011 on the provision of food information to consumers, amending Regulations (EC) No 1924/2006 and (EC) No 1925/2006 of the European Parliament and of the Council, and repealing Commission Directive 87/250/EEC, Council Directive 90/496/EEC, Commission Directive 1999/10/EC, Directive 2000/13/EC of the European Parliament and of the Council, Commission Directives 2002/67/EC and 2008/5/EC and Commission Regulation (EC) No 608/2004.

Regulation (EC) No 882/2004 of the European Parliament and of the Council of April 29, 2004 on official controls performed to ensure the verification of compliance with feed and food law, animal health and animal welfare rules.

Directive 2002/46 / EC of the European Parliament and of the Council of June 10, 2002 on the approximation of the laws of the Member States relating to food supplements.

Rozporządzenie Ministra Pracy i Polityki Socjalnej z 26 września 1997 r. w sprawie ogólnych przepisów bezpieczeństwa i higieny pracy (Dz.U. z 2003 r. Nr 169, poz. 1650 ze zm.).

Rozporządzenie Rady Ministrów z 29 maja 2012 r. w sprawie środków bezpieczeństwa fizycznego stosowanych do zabezpieczania informacji niejawnych.

Commission Directive of July 8, 1980 laying down the Community method of analysis for the official control of the vinyl chloride monomer level in materials and articles which are intended to come into contact with foodstuffs.

Commission Directive 81/432 / EEC of April 29, 1981 establishing a Community method of analysis for the official control of vinyl chloride released into foodstuffs from materials and articles.

Commission Directive 81/712 / EEC of July 28, 1981 establishing Community methods of analysis for checking compliance with purity criteria of certain additives used in foodstuffs.

Council Directive 82/711 / EEC of October 18, 1982 laying down the basic principles necessary for testing the migration of components of plastic materials and articles intended to come into contact with foodstuffs.

Council Directive 84/500 / EEC of October 15, 1984 on the approximation of the laws of the Member States relating to ceramic articles intended to come into contact with foodstuffs.

Council Directive 85/572 / EEC of December 19, 1985 establishing a list of simulants for use in migration tests of the constituents of plastic materials and articles intended to come into contact with foodstuffs.

Council regulation (EURATOM) No 3954/87 of December 22, 1987 laying down maximum permitted levels of radioactive contamination of foodstuffs and of feeding stuffs following a nuclear accident or any other case of radiological emergency.

Council Directive of December 21, 1988 on the approximation of the laws of the Member States relating to quick-frozen foodstuffs for human consumption.

Commission Regulation (Euratom) No 944/89 of April 12, 1989 laying down maximum permitted levels of radioactive contamination in minor foodstuffs following a nuclear accident or any other case of radiological emergency.

Council Directive 89/369 / EEC of June 14, 1989 on indications or marks identifying the lot to which a foodstuff belongs.

Council Directive 92/52 / EEC of June 18, 1992 on infant formulas and formulas intended for export to third countries.

Council Regulation (EEC) No 315/93 of February 8, 1993 laying down Community procedures for contaminants in food.

Council Directive 93/5 / EEC of February 25, 1993 on assistance to the Commission and cooperation by the Member States in the scientific study of questions relating to food.

Commission Directive 93/11 / EEC of March 15, 1993 concerning the release of N-nitrosamines and N-nitrosatable substances from baby nipples and soothers made of natural rubber or synthetic elastomers.

Commission Directive 96/3 / EC of January 26, 1996 granting a derogation from certain provisions of Council Directive 93/43 / EEC on the hygiene of foodstuffs as regards the transport by sea of liquid oils and fats in bulk.

Commission Directive 96/8 / EC of February 26, 1996 on foods intended for use in energy-reduced diets.

Commission Directive 98/28 / EC of April 29, 1998 derogating from certain provisions of Directive 93/43 / EEC on the hygiene of foodstuffs as regards the transport by sea of unrefined sugar in bulk.

Directive 1999/2 / EC of the European Parliament and of the Council of February 22, 1999 on the approximation of the laws of the Member States relating to foods and food ingredients treated with ionizing radiation.

Commission Regulation (EC) No 1565/2000 of July 18, 2000 laying down the measures necessary for the adoption of an evaluation program in application of Regulation (EC) No 2232/96 of the European Parliament and of the Council.

Commission Directive 2001/15 / EC of February 15, 2001 on substances that may be added for particular nutritional purposes to foods for particular nutritional uses.

Commission Regulation (EC) No 2073/2005 of November 15, 2005 on microbiological criteria for foodstuffs.

Commission Regulation (EC) No 1895/2005 of November 18, 2005 on the restriction of use of certain epoxy derivatives in materials and articles intended to come into contact with food.

Commission Regulation (EC) No 401/2006 of February 23, 2006 laying down the methods of sampling and analysis for the official control of the levels of mycotoxins in foodstuffs.

Council Regulation (EC) No 509/2006 of March 20, 2006 on agricultural products and foodstuffs as traditional specialties guaranteed.

Commission Regulation (EC) No 627/2006 of April 21, 2006 implementing Regulation (EC) No 2065/2003 of the European Parliament and of the Council as regards quality criteria for validated analytical methods for sampling, identification and characterization of primary smoke products.

Commission Directive 2006/125 / EC of December 5, 2006 on processed cereal-based foods and baby foods for infants and young children.

Commission Regulation (EC) No 1881/2006 of December 19, 2006 setting maximum levels for certain contaminants in foodstuffs.

Commission Regulation (EC) No 1882/2006 of December 19, 2006 laying down methods of sampling and analysis for the official control of the levels of nitrates in certain foodstuffs.

Commission Regulation (EC) No 1883/2006 of December 19, 2006 laying down methods of sampling and analysis for the official control of levels of dioxins and dioxin-like PCBs in certain foodstuffs.

Commission Regulation (EC) No 1981/2006 of December 22, 2006 on detailed rules for the implementation of Article 32 of Regulation (EC) No 1829/2003 of the European Parliament and of the Council as regards the Community reference laboratory for genetically modified organisms.

Commission Regulation (EC) No 2023/2006 of December 22, 2006 on good manufacturing practice for materials and articles intended to come into contact with food.

Commission Regulation (EC) No 333/2007 of March 28, 2007 laying down the methods of sampling and analysis for the official control of the levels of lead, cadmium, mercury, inorganic tin, 3-MCPD and benzo(a) pyrene in foodstuffs.

Regulations Council Regulation (EC) No 834/2007 of June 28, 2007 on organic production and labelling of organic products and repealing Regulation (EEC) No 2092/91.

Commission Directive 2007/42 / EC of June 29, 2007 relating to materials and products made of regenerated cellulose film intended to come into contact with foodstuffs.

Commission Regulation (EC) No 282/2008 of March 27, 2008 on recycled plastic materials and articles intended to come into contact with foods and amending Regulation (EC) No 2023/2006.

Commission Regulation (EC) No 353/2008 of April 18, 2008 establishing implementing rules for applications for authorization of health claims as provided for in Article 15 of Regulation (EC) No 1924/2006 of the European Parliament and of the Council.

Commission Directive 2008/60 / EC of June 17, 2008 establishing specific purity criteria for sweeteners for use in foodstuffs.

Regulations Council Regulation (EC) No 733/2008 of July 15, 2008 on the conditions governing imports of agricultural products originating in third countries following the accident at the Chernobyl nuclear power station.

Commission Regulation (EC) No 1235/2008 of December 8, 2008 laying down detailed rules for implementation of Council Regulation (EC) No 834/2007 as regards the arrangements for imports of organic products from third countries.

Commission Regulation (EC) No 41/2009 of January 20, 2009 concerning the composition and labelling of foodstuffs suitable for people intolerant to gluten.

Commission Regulation (EC) No 124/2009 of February 10, 2009 setting maximum levels for the presence of coccidiostats or histomonostats in food resulting from the unavoidable carry-over of these substances in non-target feed.

Commission Regulation (EC) No 450/2009 of May 29, 2009 on active and intelligent materials and articles intended to come into contact with food Regulation (EC) No 470/2009 of the European Parliament and of the Council of May 6, 2009 laying down Community procedures for the establishment of residue limits of pharmacologically active substances in foodstuffs of animal origin, repealing Council Regulation (EEC) No 2377/90 and amending Directive 2001/82/EC of the European Parliament and of the Council and Regulation (EC) No 726/2004 of the European Parliament and of the Council.

Commission Regulation (EC) No 669/2009 of July 24, 2009 implementing Regulation (EC) No 882/2004 of the European Parliament and of the Council as regards the increased level of official controls on imports of certain feed and food of non-animal origin and amending Decision 2006/504/EC.

Commission Regulation (EC) No 953/2009 of October 13, 2009 on substances that may be added for specific nutritional purposes in foods for particular nutritional uses.

Commission Regulation (EC) No 983/2009 of October 21, 2009 on the authorization and refusal of authorization of certain health claims made on food and referring to the reduction of disease risk and to children's development and health.

Commission Regulation (EC) No 984/2009 of October 21, 2009 refusing to authorize certain health claims made on food, other than those referring to the reduction of disease risk and to children's development and health.

Regulations Commission Regulation (EC) No 889/2008 of September 5, 2008 laying down detailed rules for the implementation of Council Regulation (EC) No 834/2007 on organic production and labelling of organic products with regard to organic production, labelling and control.

Appendix

Appendix 1
Characteristics of Participants (Enterprises) in the Study

1. ***Kuehne+Nagel, Poland*** – a company founded in 1992. With nearly 1,600 employees, it offers logistics services to domestic companies and international corporations.
2. ***Faurecia Automotive Poland*** – a manufacturer of car fittings and metal seat structures. It belongs to the French Faurecia group, employing 84,000 people in 270 factories in 33 countries. In Poland, the total revenue of Faurecia amounted to over PLN 3,657 million in 2012, while sales revenues amounted to over PLN 3,613 million.
3. ***DACHSER, Poland*** – currently, the company employs 332 people in the processes of goods and information flow. DACHSER is one of the leading logistics service providers in Europe.
4. ***DTW Sp. z o.o.*** – a company operating in the electronics, electro-technical and electricity industries. It was founded in 1991 as a private enterprise. In 2011, it became part of SMA Solar Technology, a leading manufacturer of inverters for photovoltaics. The feature that distinguishes the company from the competition is its unique technology, the use of state-of-the-art production management tools and a dedicated research and development team that, in cooperation with the customer, develops optimal, individualized solutions. The company sells a significant portion of its products in foreign markets, mainly in Germany, but also in the United States and Canada.
5. ***Frigo Logistics Sp. z o.o.*** – a modern logistics center for frozen products based in Żnin near Bydgoszcz, Poland. It is one of the leading domestic logistics operators for these products. It has its own high-bay warehouses operating at −23/−24°C in Żnin and Radomsko. The

company was founded in 2001. Three years later, it was acquired by Nichirei Holding Holland B.V. based in Rotterdam, which is part of the Japanese Nichirei group based in Tokyo. Nichirei is the leading organization in Japan specializing in services for the food industry and one of the world leaders in the field of logistics of products requiring controlled temperatures.

6. **Wamtechnik** – a global supplier of intelligent power sources that guarantee the highest quality, reliability and safety. A rich background of experience, 20 years of tradition, a production plant specializing in the design and production of battery and storage battery packs and technologies based on the latest solutions have allowed Wamtechnik to achieve a leading position in its industry.

7. ***Przedsiębiorstwo Naprawy Taboru PKS Sp. z o.o.*** – has been operating on the Polish market since January 1, 1957. Initially, as the Repair Department of the Provincial PKS Enterprise, then as the Repair Department of the National Motor Transport. Since January 7, 1990 an independent state enterprise, and since January 1, 2001 it has been known as Przedsiębiorstwo Naprawy Taboru Przedsiębiorstw Komunikacji Samochodowej Sp. z o.o.

8. ***Panalpina Polska Sp. z o.o.*** – offers products and solutions in the field of sea and air transport. Sea freight includes global groupage (LCL) and full container load (FCL) services. In addition, air transport (export/import) is largely organized based on the network of connections through the largest European ports: Frankfurt and Luxembourg. The company is a leading provider of logistics services in Poland, helping its clients with planning, consulting and implementation of solutions in air and sea freight.

9. ***CENZIN sp. z o. o.*** – a leading Polish trading company operating on the international arms, special equipment and logistics market. As part of its export operations, the company provides specialized supplies of equipment and services for the armed forces, police, uniformed services and special units of many countries around the world. As part of its import operations, the company offers equipment, tools and services to secure the needs of units and services subordinate to the Ministry of National Defense and the Ministry of the Interior, including the police and special units as well as other licensed institutional recipients and civil customers.

10. **WSK "PZL-KALISZ" S.A.** – communication equipment manufacturing plant; it has operated in the Polish aviation industry since 1952. It is the

only manufacturer of the ASz-62 IR piston engine. In the field of aviation production, it cooperates with the most important world producers.

11. ***Morska Stocznia Remontowa Gryfia S.A***. – belongs to the group of
the most famous repair shipyards in Poland and abroad. It has the technical equipment necessary for the correct diagnosis and provision of
high-quality services in the construction of steel and offshore structures.
It owns quays with a total length of over 2.5 km, which allow for the
loading of large-size structures, and production halls with a total area of
over 26 thousand square meters.

Appendix 2
Abbreviations and Explanations

1. **4G** a mobile telephony system – a technology based on a radio network with fast transmission and multifunctional transmitting and receiving points. The main feature that distinguishes 4G from its predecessor
(3G) is the speed of transfer between devices.
2. **5G** – the latest standard in the cellular network – the fifth generation of
mobile technology, replacing 4G.
3. **7 Rs** – *right product, right quantity, right condition, right place, right
time, right customer, right price.*
4. **ADC** – is entering data into computer information systems by means of
special devices (direct data input without the use of a keyboard).
5. **ADN** – European regulations concerning the international carriage of
dangerous goods by inland waterways.
6. **ADR** – international convention concerning the carriage of dangerous
goods by road, signed in Geneva on September 30, 1957.
7. **Adware** – unwanted software used to display advertisements on a
computer screen, most often in a web browser window. Some security
experts consider them as PUPs (potentially unwanted programs) that
are common these days. Typically, these programs use various methods of impersonating desired applications or attaching to them to trick
the user into installing them on his or her computer, tablet or mobile
device.
8. **An active attack** – a direct breach of the security of a computer system by exploiting vulnerabilities in the operating system or a running
program. The mechanism for sharing files and folders can serve as an
example. It is often the case that the user does not use any password,
which is an incentive for the hacker and sheer carelessness. This type of

attack is also used by Trojan horses which, when entering unnoticed a victim's computer, have virtually unlimited access to it.

9. **ARTR** – a technology used to identify and locate motor vehicles based on registration numbers. The system records the vehicle, along with time and its whereabouts, and automatically recognizes and assigns vehicle registration numbers to the numbers entered in the system search engine.

10. **Automation** – the introduction of automatic devices to transport, warehouse processes, order processing and customer services, packaging services, office work etc.

11. **Security in the supply chain** – is a state that gives a sense of confidence and guarantees: the flow of material goods and services and, consequently, meeting the material needs of the participants in the supply chain in accordance with the 7 Rs rule and the flow of information for the purposes of planning and managing logistics processes; protection and continued existence in a period of dangerous situations (threats); adapting to new conditions (vulnerability to unplanned situations).

12. **Big data** – data sets that are characterized by a large volume, variety, real-time stream inflow, variability, complexity, as well as require the use of innovative technologies, tools and information methods for extracting new and useful knowledge from them.

13. **Blockchain** – a distributed database, based on blockchains, used for storage and transmission of information about transactions concluded on the Internet. One block contains information about a certain number of transactions; after it is saturated with information, another block of data is created, followed by subsequent blocks, creating a kind of chain.

14. **BRC (*British Retail Consortium*)** – a global food safety standard that has been developed to define operational and quality criteria that should be applied in production plants to ensure compliance with user/ customer needs and legal requirements.

15. **Car sharing (shared ownership)** – a system that is currently working mainly in Germany and is being experimentally introduced in other countries, including in the Czech Republic. It consists of several users owning one car and sharing the costs of its maintenance, fuel and repairs. The monthly fee also depends on the time the car is used and the number of kilometers traveled. The keys are placed in special safes at car-sharing stations.

16. **CCTV** – closed-circuit television. Generally, a CCTV system is understood as a set of cooperating devices for receiving, processing,

transmitting, archiving and displaying video and sound in monitored facilities. A CCTV system includes industrial cameras, lenses, image recording devices, monitors, power supplies, transmission cables or wireless systems.

17. **SCF-PP (*System/component failure or malfunction (power-plant)*)** – failure or malfunction of the system/its component related to the drive unit.

18. **CGI (*Common Gateway Interface*)** – a standardized interface that allows communication between the web server software and other programs on the server.

19. **Chatbot** – innovative, intelligent software for companies that increases the efficiency of helpline consultants and online sellers, simulates and reflects human conversation, thus providing services through a chat. The technology behind chatbots is AI – artificial intelligence – a technology that recognizes the intentions and questions of customers and immediately answers their inquiries, received through social media (e.g. Facebook) or websites. Chatbot, also known as Virtual Advisor or Virtual Assistant, enables machines (websites, online stores, IoT devices) to understand and answer the user's question asked in a natural language during a chat.

20. **Cloud computing** – in Polish also known as IT cloud, cloud computing. This concept refers to computing services (support) offered by external entities, available on request at any time and regulated as needed.

21. **CRM** – Consumer Relationship Management.

22. **Cybersecurity** – methods used by an organization to reduce the risk of cyber-attacks, their potential impact on operations and to protect its devices and services.

23. **DAB** – Digital Audio Broadcasting – a system designed for terrestrial and satellite broadcasting – for both stationary and mobile receivers. DAB's tasks include: receiving programs with the use of stationary, transportable and portable receivers (rod antenna) in an environment causing reflections and signal loss, and transmitting additional information (apart from programs), including the use of the existing RDS (Radio Data System), TMC (Traffic Message Channel) and EWS (Early Warning System) systems.

24. **DDoS (*Distributed Denial of Service*)** – a distributed attack on computer systems or a network service that prevents proper operation by seizing all free resources (a characteristic feature of DDoS is that the

attack occurs not from one but from many sources at the same time, which makes it very difficult to prevent).

25. **DNS (*Domain Name System*)** – a protocol whose main function is to translate easy-to-remember domain names into computer-understandable numerical data (the DNS server searches for the IP address of a given website based on the phrase entered by the user in the address field of the search engine).

26. **DoS (*Denial of Service*)** – an attack on an email server, Internet server or even a telephone system, consisting of overloading the system with mock queries to such an extent that it is not able to properly handle the right ones.

27. **EAM (*Enterprise Asset Management*)** – a system for the management of fixed assets.

28. **eCall** – a pan-European system of rapid notification of road accidents. eCall is linked to the eSafety initiative, which is part of the European Commission's comprehensive strategy to keep roads safe and improve transport efficiency in Europe.

29. **ECR (*Efficient Consumer Response*)** – a system for effective consumer service.

30. **EDGE (*Enhanced Data rates for GSM Evolution*)** – a technology used in GSM networks for data transmission.

31. **The effectiveness of supply chain security** – the relationship between specific participants (links) and the possibilities (potential) of their security. Effectiveness can be expressed in terms of indicators (structural, productivity and qualitative indicators).

32. **Reverse logistics** – all the processes of waste flow management (including complete and damaged products considered by their disposers as waste), as well as the management of the information (related to these flows), from the places where they are generated (appear in the logistics system) to their destination for the purpose of their re-use, recovery of value (through repair, recycling or processing) or their proper disposal and long-term storage so as to render these flows economically effective and minimize the negative impact on the natural environment.

33. **Entropy** – the smallest average amount of information needed to encode the fact of the occurrence of an event from a set of events with given probabilities (or the average amount of information per sign symbolizing the occurrence of an event from a certain set – events in this set are assigned probabilities of occurrence).

34. **EPC – Electronic Product Code** (synonyms are used interchange-ably: RFID (Radio Frequency IDentification) code, RFID tag, RFID transponder).
35. **ERA** – European Union Agency for Railways.
36. **ERTMS** – European Railway Traffic Management System.
37. **FOD** – foreign object damage.
38. **GDSN** – Global Data Synchronization Network.
39. **GIAI** – Global Individual Asset Identifier.
40. **GIS (*Geographical Information System*)** – a term used to describe a computerized system enabling the collection, storage, analysis and imaging of data related to a specific location in a geographical environment.
41. **GNSS** – Global Navigation Satellite System.
42. **Circular economy** – an economic concept in which products, materi-als and raw materials should remain in the economy as long as pos-sible, and the generation of waste should be minimized as much as possible.
43. **Raster graphics** – presentation of an image using a vertical-horizon-tal grid of appropriately colored pixels on a color monitor, printer or another output device.
44. **GRAI** – Global Returnable Asset Identifier.
45. **GS1 eCom** – a set of standard electronic messages that allow compa-nies to quickly, efficiently and accurately transfer business data between trading partners electronically, in the form of classic Electronic Data Interchange (EDI) messages or XML documents.
46. **GSCF** – Global Supply Chain Forum.
47. **GUI** – graphical user interface, often also referred to as graphical envi-ronment – a general definition of the way information is presented by the computer and interaction with the user, consisting in drawing and handling basic elements, e.g. a window, an edit box, a slider, a button.
48. **HTML (*HyperText Markup Language*)** – the language used to cre-ate web pages. It is also a markup language, which means that in addi-tion to the main text, a document contains information that describes it.
49. **HTTP (*Hypertext Transfer Protocol*)** – a protocol that defines the rules for transferring resources and the rules of communication between the client and the server (the HTTP protocol defines the standardized way in which information is shared, processed and read by the server and what the response to requests looks like).
50. **ICAO** – International Civil Aviation Organization.

51. **IFS** – the International Food Safety Standard, required by the majority of Western European retail chains (except Great Britain, where the BRC standard is required).

52. **Smart Factory** – put simply, a modern type of production plant, based on cyber-physical systems, their integration with advanced production technologies and innovative methods of production management and organization.

53. **Internet of Things (IoT)** – a network that connects wired or wireless devices characterized by autonomous (not requiring human involvement) activity in the field of acquiring, sharing, processing data or interacting with the environment under the influence of these data. It is a concept of building telecommunications networks and highly dispersed IT systems that can be used, among others, to create intelligent control and measurement systems, analytical or control systems, practically in every field.

54. **Interoperability (in the context of railways)** – the ability of the trans-European rail system to run trains safely and uninterruptedly while delivering the performance levels required. In practice, this means that interoperable rolling stock can move using interoperable railway infrastructure and move between the railway networks of individual countries without having to stop at the borders, replace locomotives and train drivers. These features are to ensure a high level of security and quality of services.

55. **IoP** – Institute of Packaging.

56. **ITS (*Intelligent Transport Systems*)** – solutions using various technologies – IT, telecommunications, automation of mobile objects in the field of road transport, including infrastructure, vehicles and their users.

57. **Quality** – the degree to which a set of inherent properties meets the requirements according to PN-EN 9000: 2001.

58. **Data collectors** – portable pocket computers, PDAs (Personal Digital Assistants), palmtop computers equipped with an integrated barcode reader, keyboard, LCD display and memory. They are designed to collect, store and transmit data.

59. **KPBwLC** – the National Program of Safety in Civil Aviation (Pol. Krajowy Program Bezpieczeństwa w Lotnictwie Cywilnym).

60. **LRP (*Logistics Requirements Planning*)** – a system for planning logistic needs.

61. **Supply chain** – a network of manufacturers and service providers that work together to process and move goods – from the raw material

phase to the end-user level. All these entities, such as enterprises (production and service companies) and institutions are connected by the flows of physical goods, information flows and cash flows, constituting a logistic system (consisting of companies and relations between them and the environment).

62. **Trial and error method** – a method of solving tasks and problems in the absence of information on how to achieve a positive effect; usually a series of randomly performed actions, lasting until the right solution is found; it generates new information that is analyzed and thus the number of redundant actions may be reduced; one of the most important methods of animal and human learning.

63. **Modal (most probable) points** of the logistics network are defined as all places where products stop, i.e. warehouses, transport points and nodes as well as factories, distribution networks etc.

64. **MRP** – Material Requirements Planning.

65. **MRP II** – Manufacturing Resource Planning.

66. **ERP** – Enterprise Resource Planning.

67. **Reliability of the functioning of a supply chain** – a set of properties that describe the readiness of a supply chain to constantly maintain resilience during the performance of logistics processes at a certain level.

68. **Food defense** – efforts focused on protecting food resources from deliberate contamination with various chemical, biological or other harmful substances by those who seek to harm a plant or population. Deliberately introduced contaminants may contain compounds that are not naturally present in food or are not tested for food contact. An attacker may aim to harm a food producer, damage a country's economy or kill people. The intended actions are usually not rational and difficult to predict.

69. **Observation and measurement (in the context of logistics)** – concerns the basic and relevant logistics indicators and measures that assess: the efficiency of logistics activities, own and external delivery services, time of logistics activities, costs according to various criteria etc.

70. **OEM (*Original Equipment Manufacturer*)** – a company that sells its own brand products manufactured by other companies. The term is misleading because an OEM is not always the manufacturer, not even a producer, but sometimes only a seller of end-user equipment, although it also happens to be its designer.

71. **OLAP (*Online Analytical Processing*)** – a tool that allows for multi-dimensional analysis of business data collected in a data warehouse and for personalized access to analysis results using selected communication media. It enables data analysis at the lowest level of detail, as well as allows for various generalizations and summaries of data. If the data in the database is pre-processed, calculated and prepared for presentation, then the search efficiency and the speed of response to the user's query are the highest. OLAP allows for multidimensional data analysis initiated by the end-user from his or her workstation while using a computer; it also includes the ability to manipulate dimensions and complex mechanisms for reporting and data visualization.

72. **Patch cord** – a term for a network cable with connectors at both ends (it can be RJ45, RJ11 or even optical fiber).

73. **Phishing** – a form of fraud in which a hacker pretends to be another person or institution in order to steal confidential information (e.g. login details, credit card details), infect the computer or persuade the victim to take specific actions.

74. **Block letters** – a type of handwriting between regular and technical writing; it has no inter-letter joining.

75. **Magnetic writing** – written with a special type of ink, containing powdered magnetic substances, used to manually fill out forms which are read with special character readers.

76. **Independent demand** – or primary demand, is the demand resulting from the market situation (external demand, sales forecasts).

77. **Dependent demand** – demand resulting from the demand for products of higher complexity. It should be calculated in detail based on the relations recorded in the description of the product structure.

78. **Supply chain security potential** – a reasonable amount of possessed resources (human, physical, financial, organizational, information resources) to use stocks, reserves in emergency (crisis) situations, to return to normal, previously planned conditions.

79. **Ransomware** – malware that blocks access to a computer until the appropriate ransom is paid to the criminal's account.

80. **RBC** – Radio Block Center.

81. **RID** – regulations for the international carriage of dangerous goods by rail.

82. **RIS** – River Information Services.

83. **Robot** – a device that replaces a human in performing certain activities.

84. **Robotization** – replacing human work with robots.

85. **Risk (for the purposes of the supply chain)** – conditions in which mining, production, trade and service companies operating in various areas and their customers, between which there is a flow of products and information, know the probability of obtaining the result of their activity.

86. **SaaS** – software that enables users to connect to and use cloud-based applications over the Internet. Common examples include email, calendar and office tools (such as Microsoft Office 365).

87. **SCF – PP (*System/component failure or malfunction (power-plant)*)** – failure or malfunction of a system/its component related to the drive unit.

88. **SCM** – Supply Chain Management.

89. **SCOR** – Supply Chain Operation Reference-Model – the reference model of the supply chain

90. **Service level** – a measure corresponding to the required conditions in which customer orders can be fulfilled, with normal – accepted by the market – delivery conditions.

91. **SGLN** – Serialized Global Location Number.

92. **SGTIN** – Serialized Global Trade Item Number.

93. **SMS** – Safety Management System.

94. **Sniffer** – a computer program or device whose task is to capture and possibly analyze data flowing in the network.

95. **SSCC** – Serial Shipping Container Code.

96. **Stalkerware** – a type of malware that records data entered into a device and sends it to a third party that is delivered to the program upon installation. Stalkerware works without the victim knowing that information is being collected; as such, it is a breach of privacy and is considered an unwanted program.

97. **Business strategy** – identifying the company's target customers and specifying the time frame for implementation and performance goals.

98. **Supply chain strategy** – identifying a network of producers and service providers who cooperate to process, move goods and define the time frame for implementation and the sequence of events that increase the value of the product.

99. **Switch** – also referred to as a network switch, is a device responsible for connecting all devices in an internal network. It can connect computers, routers, printers, scanners and other accessories that require connectivity.

100. **EDI (*Electronic Data Interchange*)** – a developed data exchange technique based on the principles of email operation, the characteristic

feature of which is independence from the characteristics of the hardware and software used.

101. **4G mobile communication system** – a technology based on a radio network with fast transmission and multifunctional transmitting and receiving points. The main feature that distinguishes 4G from its predecessor (3G) is the speed of transfer between devices.

102. **Weighted Average Cost** – a calculation of the company's total cost that assigns each category a proportionate weighting.

103. **Terminal** – a device that allows a person to work with a computer or computer system.

104. **Voice terminal** – a solution enabling dialogue between warehouse employees and the warehouse management system. The device combines fast and precise recognition of voice commands with the resistance and reliability required in harsh industrial conditions.

105. **TMS** – Transport Management System.

106. **TNT-T (*Trans-European Transport Networks*)** – an EU program for road, rail, water and air networks.

107. **Traceability** – the ability to trace (recreate the history of) the flow of goods in supply chains and networks, along with the registration of parameters identifying these goods and all locations covered by the flow. Ensuring the safety of products delivered to the market involves registering and collecting data about them at every stage of the supply chain.

108. **VTMS** – Vessel Traffic Monitoring and Information System.

109. **VTS** – Vessel Traffic Services.

110. **Validation** – the confirmation by providing objective evidence that the requirements for a specific use or application have been met (PN-EN ISO 9000: 2001). Validation is generally assumed to be obtaining evidence that the control measures adopted under a particular plan are effective.

111. **Boundary conditions** – may be defined by parameters such as: readiness to provide logistics services, order fulfillment time, waiting time between the message of completion of work processes and the commencement of transport, the degree of implementation of the components: goal-effect, outlay-effect, purpose-outlay etc.

112. **Wi-Fi** – wireless networks based on 802.11 standards, range up to 10 m.

113. **WLAN** – wireless network (Wireless LAN) implemented without the use of wires, range up to 100 m.

114. **WMS (*Warehouse Management System*)** – an IT system supporting the management of warehouse processes, supervising the reasonable distribution of inventories, using ADC techniques.
115. **Major accident** – any accident caused by a collision, derailment or another similar event, having an obvious impact on railway safety regulations or on safety management.
116. **XML (*Extensible Markup Language*)** – a specification for writing data. It is a text format that allows data to be saved in a form that is easy to read by both machines and humans.
117. **Crisis management** – activities that require a response to threats that damage the normal functioning of the supply chain, when repair attempts to date have not been successful. It is a system of events that increases the threat in the implementation of logistics processes or prevents their normal functioning.
118. **Risk management in the supply chain** – a logically ordered set of rules, principles applied in a uniform and constant manner to the activities of the network of organizations involved, by linking with suppliers and customers, in various processes and activities that create value in the form of products and services provided to the final consumers; or the activity or practice of dealing with risks along the entire supply chain.

Index

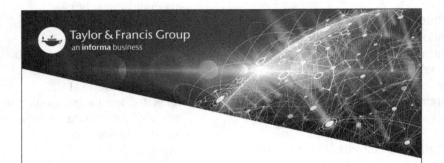

Printed in the United States
by Baker & Taylor Publisher Services